I0902356

BLACK AMERICA SERIES

GEORGETOWN COUNTY
SOUTH CAROLINA

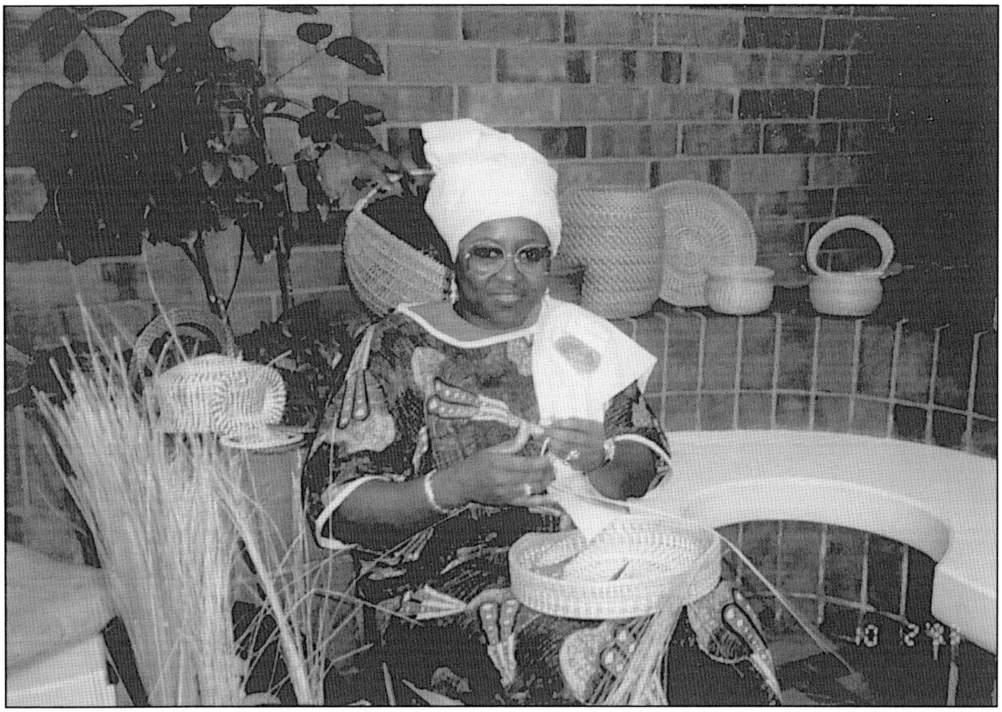

Row upon Row. Mary Graham has been weaving baskets since 1990. A resident of Georgetown, she considers basket sewing a dying art form because most weavers are elderly people, and younger people have no interest in learning the art.

The early history of African-American basketry parallels the rise of rice cultivation on the southeastern coast. African Americans made coiled sea grass fanner and other large agricultural baskets out of black rush, an abundant marsh grass, bound with thin splits of white oak, strips from the stem of the saw palmetto or pine. The fanner was a wide, winnowing tray used to "fan" rice. The threshed and pounded grain was thrown into the air to allow the wind to blow the chaff away. The original Hammock Shop, opened by A.H. "Doc" Lachicotte in 1937, specialized in selling local craftwork such as sea grass baskets, handmade Carolina pottery, rope hammocks, hooked and woven rugs, and hearth brooms. Some of the shop's original bullrush and sweet grass baskets were woven by Welcome Beese, an enslaved African American born on Oatland Plantation. After the days of rice cultivation, the incentive to pursue the craft was mainly economic. Children would be taught the tradition, in order to assist the family in earning. With the coming of the Hammock Shop and further commercial development along Highway 17, local community members were discouraged from selling their products on the highway. Many of the weavers went on to jobs as hammock weavers for the shop. Today, basket vendors can only be observed selling on the Mt. Pleasant section of Highway 17 and in the city of Charleston. The transition of the art has gone from utilitarian to artistic. It is sad to say that traditional bullrush and sweet grass basketry has been relegated to the lost arts. Real estate development has made it increasingly more difficult to attain the materials necessary for the baskets. Grasses have become scarce due to locked gate communities causing inaccessibility to weavers.

BLACK AMERICA SERIES

GEORGETOWN COUNTY

SOUTH CAROLINA

Ramona La Roche

ARCADIA
PUBLISHING

ISBN 978-0-7385-0347-9

Published by Arcadia Publishing
Charleston, South Carolina

Printed in the United States of America

Library of Congress Catalog Card Number: Applied for.

For all general information contact Arcadia Publishing at:
Telephone 843-853-2070
Fax 843-853-0044
E-mail sales@arcadiapublishing.com
For customer service and orders:
Toll-Free 1-888-313-2665

Visit us on the Internet at www.arcadiapublishing.com

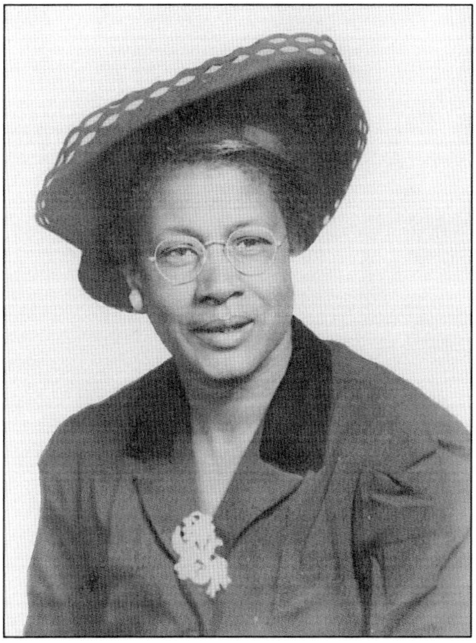

"APPLE." Laura King Armstrong (1910–1984) was the daughter of Jacob and Emmaline Shaw Toomer. At 17, she married Albert King Sr. The couple had nine children and resided in Bettsville Village, east of the Waccamaw River. Despite the difficulties experienced during Albert's tragic death in 1937, Laura rose to the challenges of raising her children alone. Kin and neighbors assisted in taking the family home apart, board by board, placing the parts on a truck and transferring them to the city of Georgetown. The homestead remains on Palm Street to this day. The young widow demanded several things of her children: (1) never tell a lie, use the word or any of its derivatives, as it was recognized as a curse; (2) always recognize God's presence in your life, as demonstrated through church involvement, attendance, and strict recognition of the Sabbath; (3) remain charitable at all times. Laura remained a single homemaker until all of her children were on their own. She made it quite clear that she would never marry another man to "father" her and Albert's children. Years after the children had long gone, Laura married Deacon William Armstrong. She was later employed and retired as a cook at the former Mansfield Plantation. She remained an active member of First Calvary Missionary Baptist Church and the Christian Friendly Aid Society until her death.

Contents

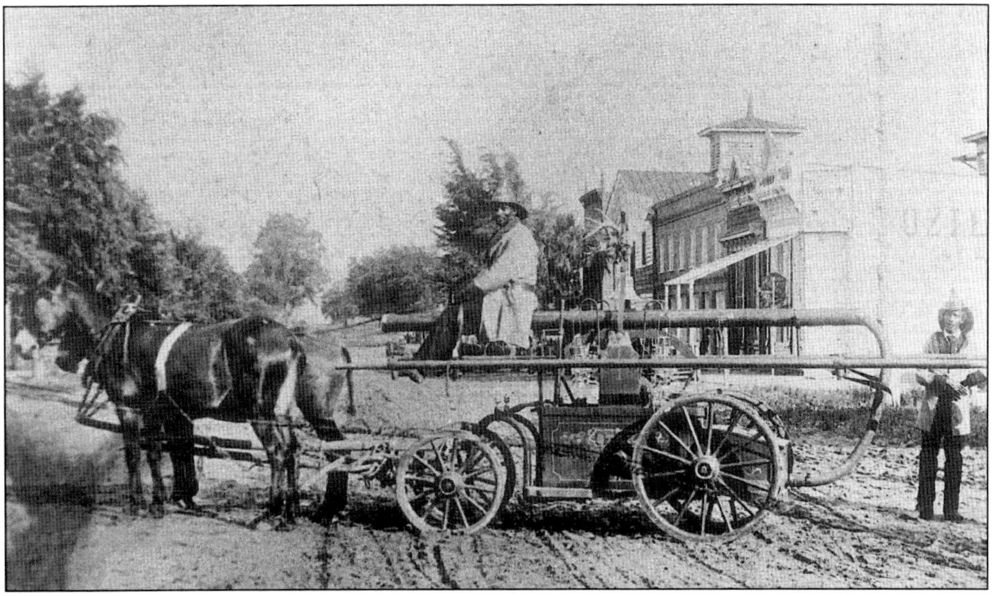

FIREMEN. During 1902, there were four fire engine companies. Two were white, the Winyahs and the Salamanders, and two were black, the Heston and the Star. The latter Star Fire engine is pictured here. The author dedicates this book to grandfather Albert, Uncles Albert Jr., Herman, Ernest King, Cousin Joseph Crump, and sons Ojas and Obsidian of the King family; many of whom were fire signs.

Acknowledgments

The author would like to thank the many individuals who took time to search cardboard boxes, photo albums, dresser drawers, rooms, offices, and memories for their treasured photographs. We reserve special thanks and appreciation of support from the following persons and organizations: Hurriyah Amanuel Asar; Edward Ball; Trudy Bazemore; Richard Balkum; Sam Bonds; Richard Camlin; Katy Close; Rosemary Cooper; Mary Green Covington; Aminah and Yusef Crump; Herbert Dennison; David H. Drayton; Ivan Earle; Evelyn Feagen; Arthur Ford; Veronica Gerald; Marquetta Goodwine; Viola Holmes Green; Vanessa Greene; Kimberly Greene; Alexia Jones Helsley; Isreal Hicks Jr.; Jan Brommell Holmes, Esq.; Barbara Huell; Lamar Iszard; Zelda Jackson Woodson; Lillie Jean Johnson; "Sis" Kelly; Arthur and Agnes King; Herbert and Katherine King; Edna Knox; Ojas La Roche; Obsidian La Roche Balkum; Rhoda McClain; Dan Memminger; Vennie Deas Moore; Vermelle and Andrew Rodrigues; Roslyn Saunders; Susan and Paul Scheno; Louis Simmons; Andrew "Snowie" and Alberta Smalls; Rev. Lorenzo Smalls; Beverly Smith; Bishop John Smith; Craig Stinson; Rev. Dr. William and Cheryl Swinton; Vergie Tennyson; Rev. Phil Thrailkill; Scotty Trotter; Harold Washington; Lee Williams; Leslie Williams; Deborah Wright; Florida Yeldell; Committee for African-American History Observance; Bethel A.M.E. Churches of Georgetown, North Santee; Bethesda Baptist Church; Covenant Missionary Baptist Church; Greater Bibleway Church; First Calvary Missionary Baptist Church; Mt. Olive Baptist Church; First Baptist Church; Duncan United Methodist Church; Prince George Winyah Episcopal Church; Singleton Chapel A.M.E. Church of North Santee; Brookgreen Garden; Cultural Council of Georgetown County; staff of Georgetown County Library; Kaminski House; Mansfield Plantation; Yawkey Wildlife Center; SC African American Heritage Council; Avery Center; Penn Center; South Carolina Arts Commission; and the South Carolina Department of Archives and History.

INTRODUCTION

In 1665, Charles II of England granted territory that included the present state of South Carolina to eight supporters, the Lords Proprietors. The Lords Proprietors had read agriculture reports of crops growing in West Africa—cotton, rice, tobacco, indigo, and other crops—and they believed these same crops could be grown here because of the similarity in climates. This sub-tropical climate continues to draw many to the beauty of the Lowcountry.

The city of Georgetown was founded in 1729 by Elisha Screven. Economic progress was largely made by the introduction of rice, indigo, naval stores, and shipbuilding. Georgetown, in many ways, was quite similar to the Senegambia region of West Africa. Five rivers and the Atlantic Ocean surround Georgetown, creating an abundance of fresh water and wildlife. The tidal flow system of rice cultivation would surely produce results in the new environment. Alligators and snakes, fishing and boating as a way of life based on natural surrounding elements were just some of the similarities between the New World and the western coast of Africa.

Enslaved Africans were brought to Georgetown for the specific use of their knowledge. Many brought the technological expertise necessary for growing cash crops in the New World. It has been stated that the technological skills needed for rice cultivation can be compared to those used to build ancient pyramids in Africa. Skills necessary for rice cultivation were much more complex than cotton. Although indigo, tobacco, cotton, and rice were all grown in South Carolina, it was the cultivation of rice that brought wealth to the Lowcountry, and to Georgetown, in particular. Along with this knowledge, Africans brought a variety of skills and craftsmanship in areas such as ironwork, carpentry, masonry, basketry, netmaking, and tannery. In addition, Africans were experienced with medicinal herbs and plants.

The Committee for African-American History Observance began as an interracial group of Georgetown citizens, representing like-minded businessmen and women and educators. Their initial meetings were held at the county library. The goal was to plan and implement Black History Month activities, and the objectives were to illuminate the contributions of African Americans, to strengthen racial pride, to foster greater appreciation of African-American achievements among whites, and to help fill a void of cultural programming in Georgetown County.

In 1981, the committee declared itself independent of the library, but their close rapport continues today. In 1983, nonprofit status was secured, and an assertive membership drive occurred. The Internal Revenue Service granted the group tax-exempt status in 1987. The committee has made a concerted effort to preserve history and culture by utilizing the Dream Keepers Community Arts Center as a base. The center, established in 1986, was acquired from

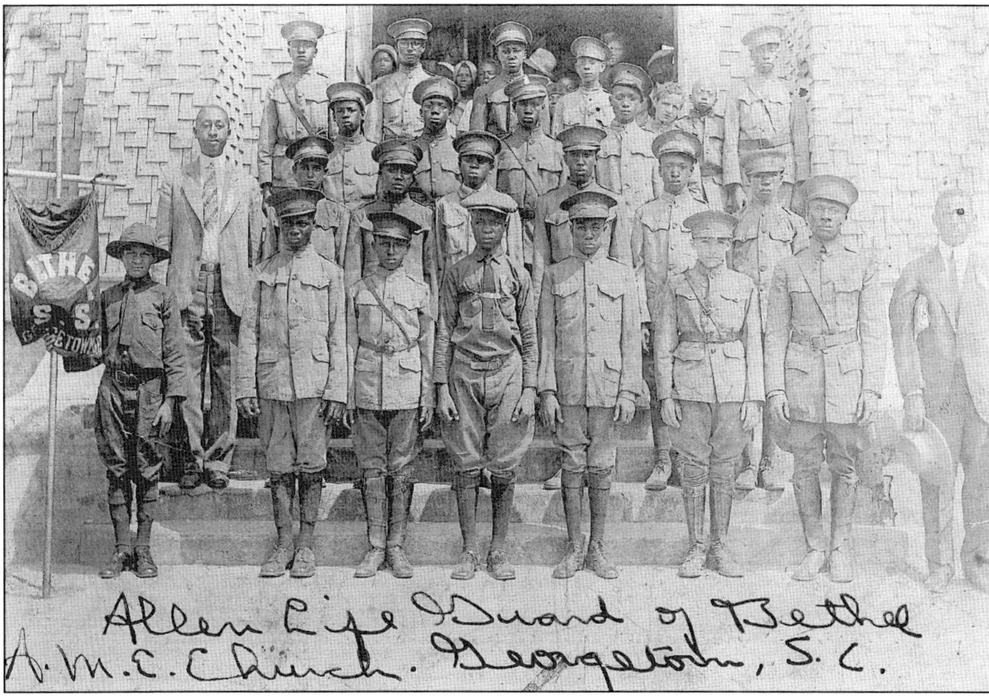

ALLEN LIFE GUARD OF BETHEL A.M.E. CHURCH IN GEORGETOWN. African Americans were not allowed to participate in Boy Scouts, thus the Allen Life Guard was formed. In the second row are Lawrence A. Dunmore Sr. (far left) and Herbert Williams (fifth from left). The latter would later become assistant pastor at the church. (Courtesy of Margretta Knox.)

the Georgetown County Council and was a neglected building on the campus of Howard, the formerly all-black high school. In 1997, the committee was given full ownership of the building. The center provides a base for emerging community artists (visual, performing, storytellers, folk, musicians, etc.), visiting artists, travel exhibitions, literary and visual arts competitions for youth, as well as a meeting place for celebrations and community groups. The committee also organizes an annual parade during Black History Month.

The center has begun to collect and archive much of the cultural history of the African-American community of Georgetown. As time passes, many documents, photographs, and oral histories become fragile from age or loss of memory. Preservation efforts continue to be of utmost importance. Despite a lack of resources and community indifference, we must continue to preserve our past.

Many African Americans know very little about their ancestry, the lands from which they came, and the sources of their traditions, as a result of the enslavement of their ancestors.

It is with the faith of my own ancestors that I pray this pictorial history will inspire the reader to expand his or her consciousness of the significant contributions made by local African Americans. I hope that it will motivate others in our community to research further and share their findings in the ongoing effort to document our own stories. I have made a sincere effort to include a variety of materials, which have added to the contextual tapestry of the African-American community of Georgetown. I am aware that this is only a segment of the rich heritage that exists. There are many areas with stories yet untold. The main focus of this work is the people and their relationships to home, work, church, play, education, and politics. This is not meant to be a comprehensive photo documentary of a people, but the sharing of a community that played a significant role in the history of South Carolina.

One

LABOR

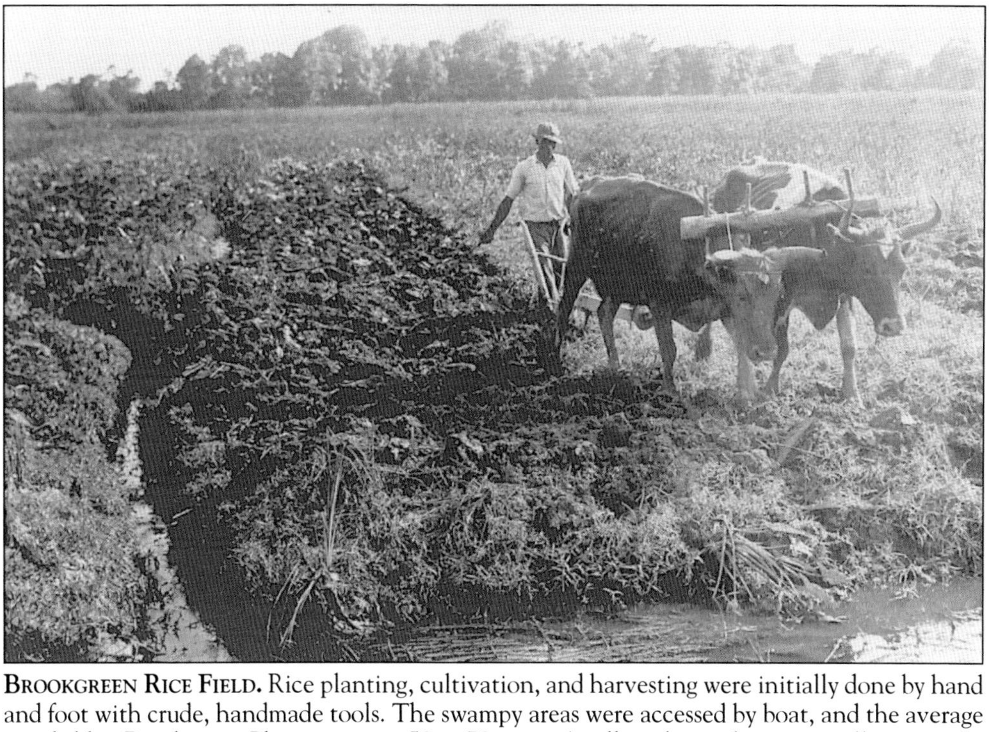

BROOKGREEN RICE FIELD. Rice planting, cultivation, and harvesting were initially done by hand and foot with crude, handmade tools. The swampy areas were accessed by boat, and the average rice field at Brookgreen Plantation was 50 to 70 acres. As all work was done manually, it usually took no less than seven years to clear land, dig canals, and build trunks. The latter were wooden structures used to control the watering of the fields. Bald cypress, tupelo, and pine trees, stumps, and roots were sawed down, removed for lumber, or burned. Most Lowcountry rice fields were usually too wet to accommodate oxen. In later years, oxen were fitted with specially made boots to assist with the plowing on some of the higher fields of land. These boots would prevent the animals from sinking in the earth. This image depicts a man driving an oxen-drawn plow in a rice field during the early 1930s. (Courtesy of the Brookgreen Garden Archives, Murrells Inlet, South Carolina.)

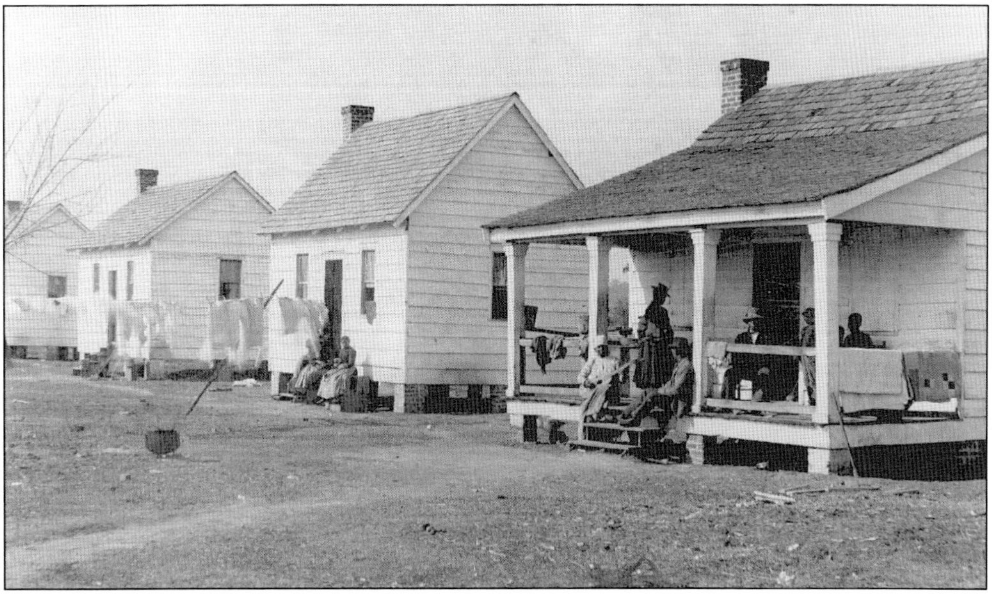

Slave Street on Plantation. A picture of one of many plantation slave streets shows a woman playing guitar, a patch quilt airing on the side of the porch, and a cast-iron pot, probably used to boil water for washing clothes. By 1850, Georgetown County had approximately 175 rice plantations. (Courtesy of the Georgetown County Library Morgan Collection.)

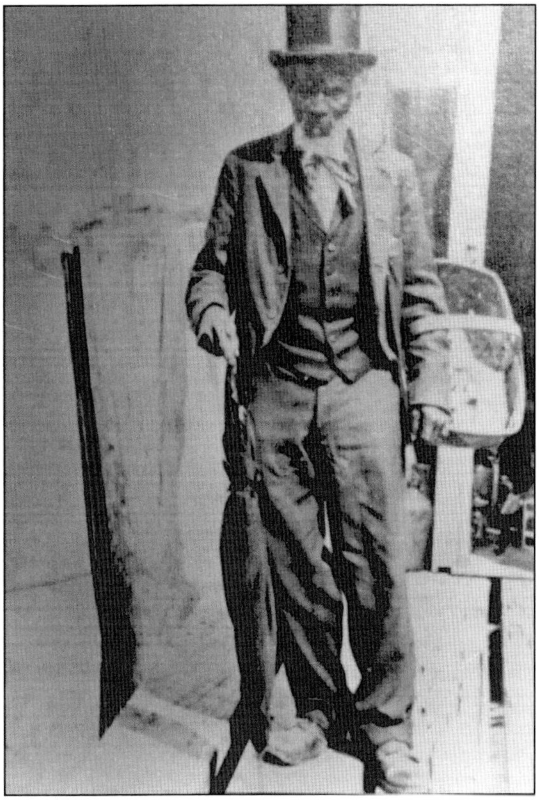

A Taste of Freedom. Edward Herriot, a former enslaved African-American man, is pictured in 1919. (Courtesy of the Committee on African-American History Observance.)

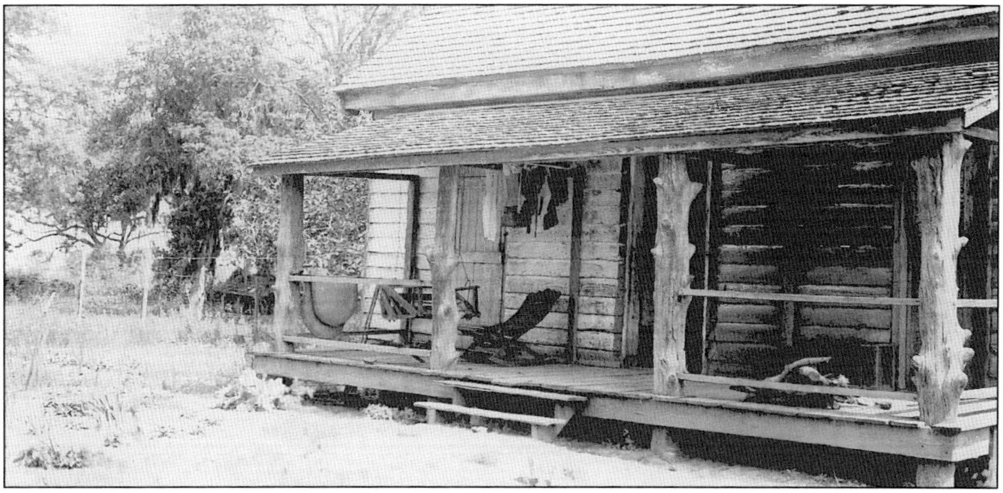

TOM'S CABIN. Tom Duncan served as a companion to Dr. Flagg at Brookgreen. This is a picture of his cabin before repairs were made in 1932. Note the hook rug, chair, swing, and four tree-trunk columns that supported the front porch. (Courtesy of the Brookgreen Gardens Archives, Murrells Inlet, South Carolina.)

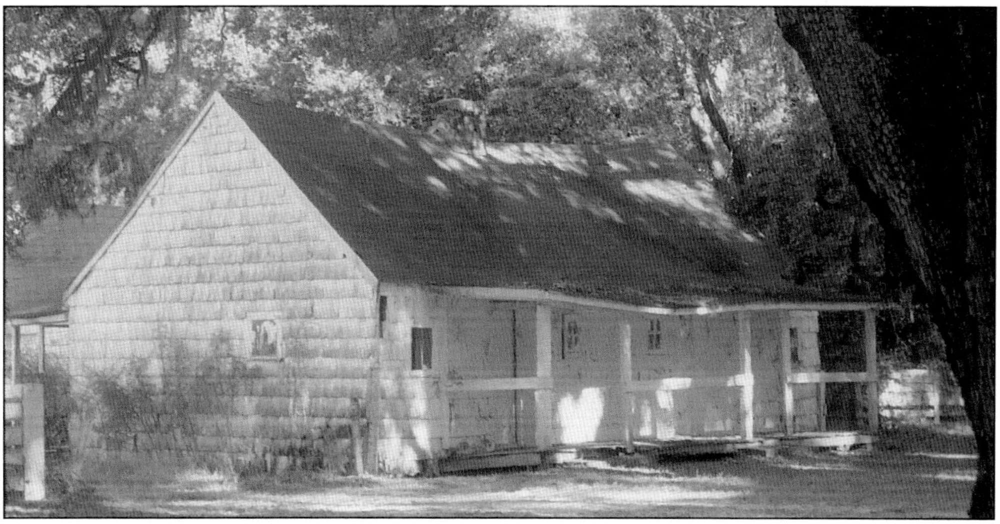

CABIN ON MANSFIELD PLANTATION. Cabins built by enslaved African Americans, although designed to rice planters' British-style specifications, were based on the two-room African floor plan. The larger of the two rooms served several family members for cooking, dining, sewing, and sleeping, while the smaller room served as a bedroom for parents and smaller children. A loft, sometimes in a steep-roofed cabin, also served as a sleeping and storage area. Pictured is a cabin formerly used to house enslaved and, later, freed African Americans and their descendants. Some of the cabins were in use until the 1980s. Similar, but smaller cabins still stand at Friendfield Village. It is the one remaining slave village of the four that once existed on Hobcaw Barony. In 1905, when Bernard M. Baruch purchased Hobcaw, he found the cabins virtually unchanged from 1815, when they were originally built. Cypress- and pine-boarded cabins were somewhat improved for the residents. An additional room was added on the back, wooden shutters were replaced with glass windows, and tin was put over cypress shake wood shingled roofs. A church building remains as well. Although the cabins had no electricity or water, the last residents of the village remained until 1952.

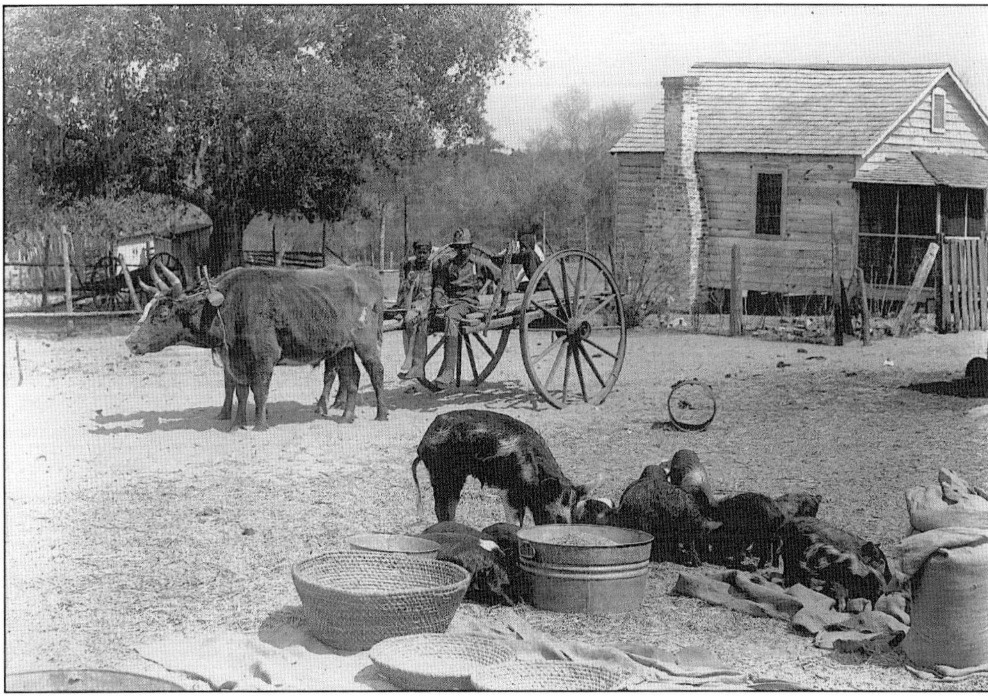

AFTERNOON FEED TIME. The picture depicts an afternoon scene at Brookgreen during the early 1930s. An unidentified boy and man sit on the oxen-drawn cart. A wooden cabin is in the background. Woven sweet grass baskets and galvanized tubs are in the foreground, as pigs take their afternoon feed. (Courtesy of the Brookgreen Gardens Archives, Murrells Inlet, South Carolina.)

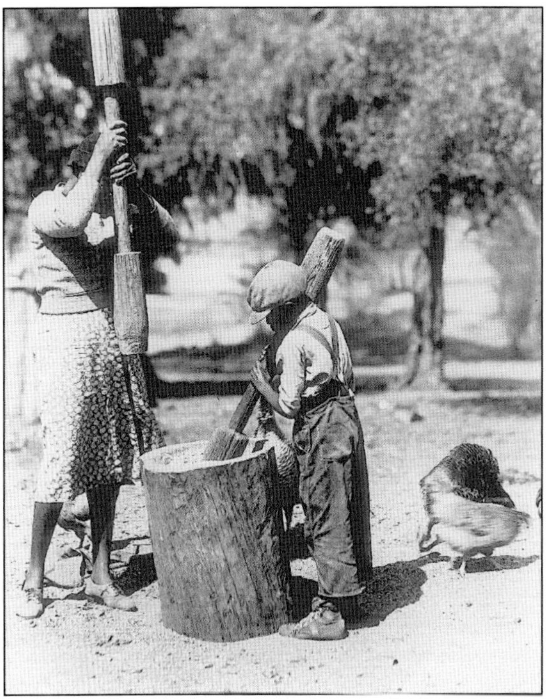

POUNDING THE RICE. Once the rice grains were separated from the plant, they would be placed into a mortar. The receptacle was made from a hollowed tree stump. The rice grains would then be pounded with a wooden pestle to remove the hull. During the period of slavery, it was not unusual for an enslaved person to be given the daily task of pounding seven mortar fills each day. Pictured are a woman and boy pounding rice during the early 1930s at Brookgreen. (Courtesy of the Brookgreen Gardens Archives, Murrells Inlet, South Carolina.)

NOTHING SPARED. Abraham Herriot winnows rice as chickens feed. This picture was taken on Sandy Island in 1930. The winnowing of rice was initially done by hand using large woven sweet grass baskets, known as fanners. This was a tradition brought from West Africa. The rice was tossed in the air, allowing the wind to blow the chaff away. All parts of the rice plants were used; the stalks and stubble were used for animal bedding, and the chaff would be removed and used for animal feed. Although chaff left on the rice allows it to remain brown and produces the healthy substance of bran, it had to be removed to keep the rice from becoming rancid as bushels were exported around the world by ship. (Courtesy of the Brookgreen Gardens Archives, Murrells Inlet, South Carolina.)

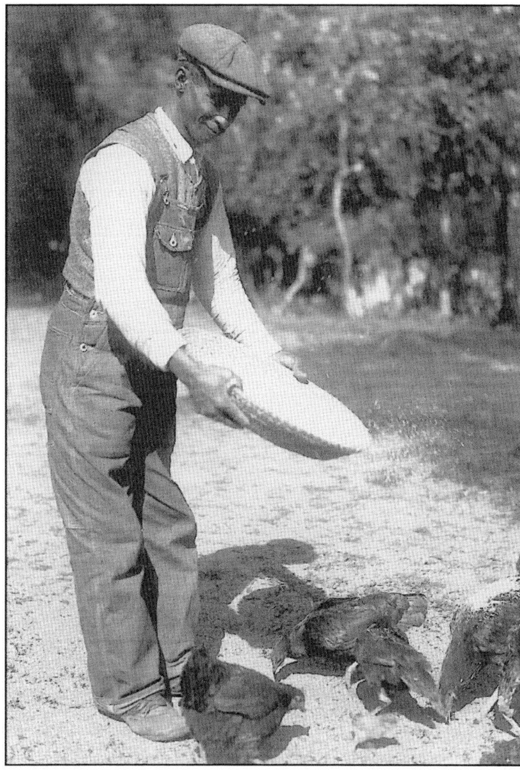

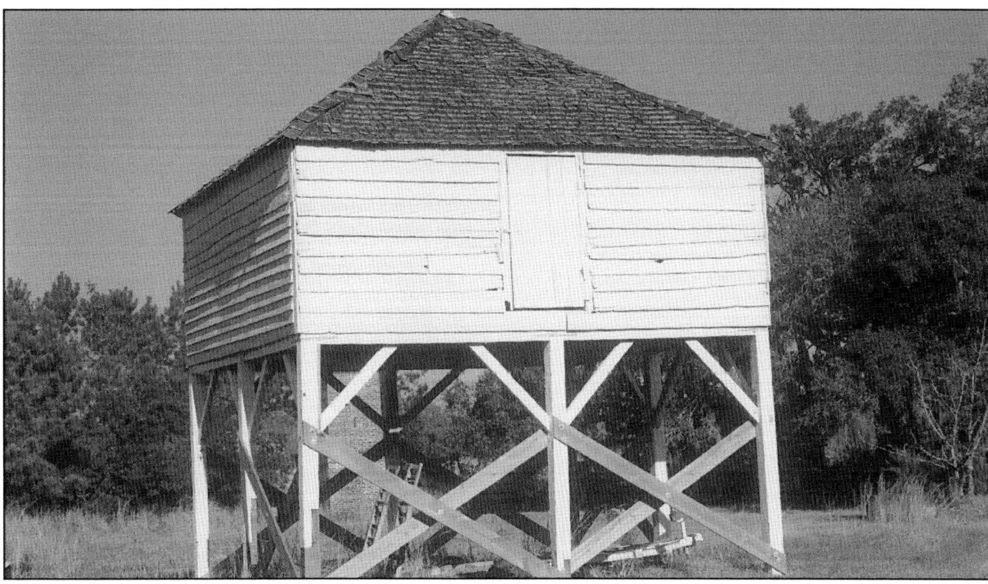

WINNOWING HOUSE ON MANSFIELD PLANTATION. Winnowing houses were built to accommodate larger quantities of rice. The building, which was several feet above ground, was accessed by a wooden staircase. The assigned worker carried sacks of rice up into the building. The grain would be sent through a hole on the floor during high winds; rice was collected on a platform below as the wind blew away the chaff. The structure has been restored and designated a National Historic site.

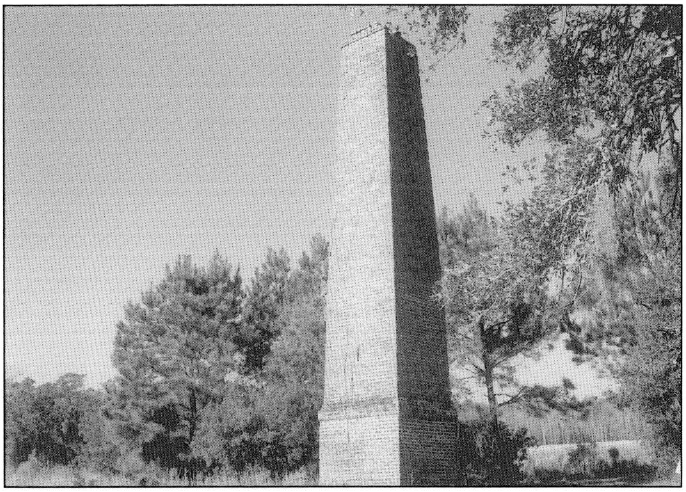

Brick Rice Mill on Mansfield Plantation. This mill was steam driven and indicated the economic status of the planter.

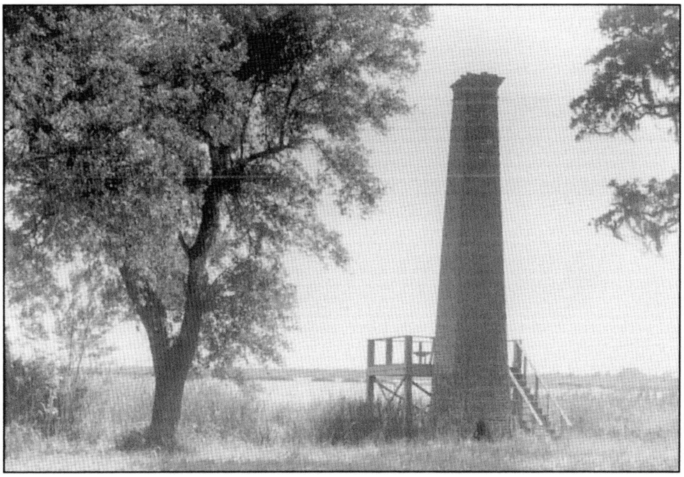

Rice Mill Chimney on Black Out Plantation, South Island. The brick chimney is all that remains of this mill. Williams Phelps owned the former plantation during the 1940s. The structure is the last of its kind standing on the Santee River.

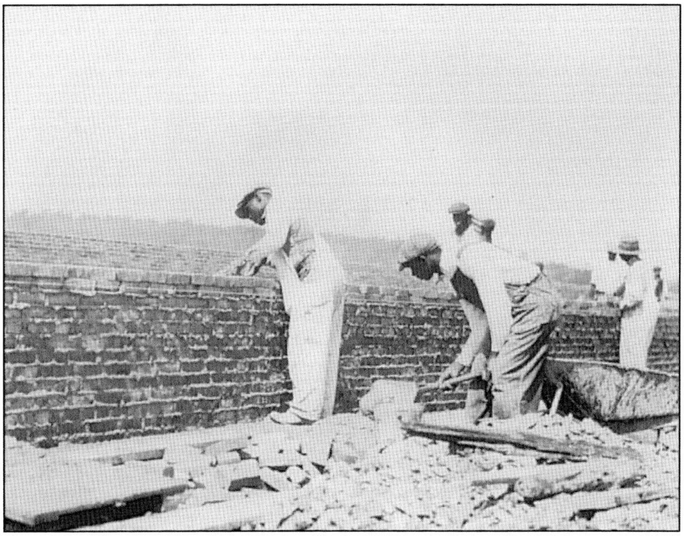

The Art of Masonry. Mr. Beacham served as a masonry teacher to apprentices in the early 1930s at Brookgreen. In 1931, the first floor of the former overseer's house was bricked. Masons were paid $1 per hour for ten hours a day. Pictured here are masons working on the south wing of the Atalaya House at Brookgreen in 1930. (Courtesy of the Brookgreen Gardens Archives, Murrells Inlet, South Carolina.)

JOSEPH EBENEZER (?–1959). Joseph Ebenezer was a farmer in the Plantersville section. Joseph's father, Henry James Ford (1832-1926), served as a Confederate soldier under Captain John Tucker and worked as a cook during the Civil War. The married turpentine farmer and son of George Ford and Kay Furman died at age 94. He is buried at St. Paul African Methodist Episcopal in the Plantersville section of Georgetown. Barbers Arthur and Randy Ford are Joseph's grandsons. (Courtesy of Randolph Ford.)

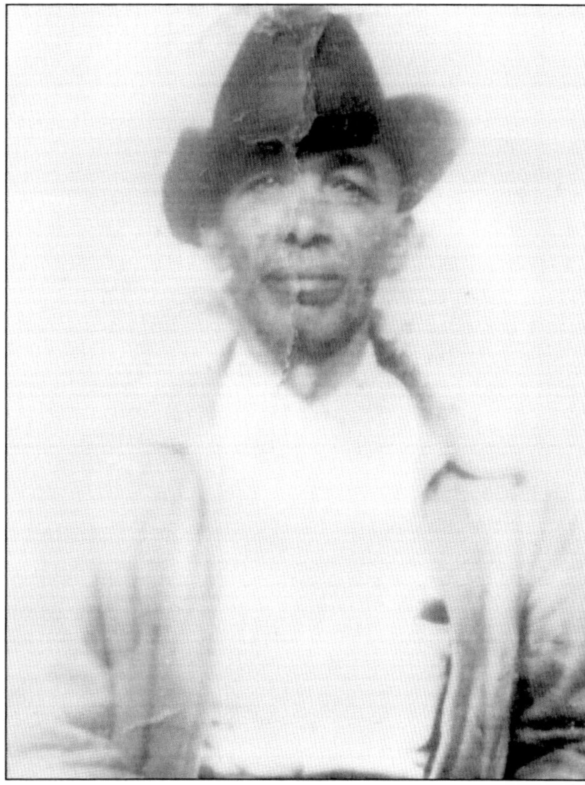

AFRICAN AMERICANS IN THE PALMETTO STATE

In 1860, South Carolina's population included 291,300 whites, 402,206 enslaved, and 9,914 free African Americans. The majority of the state's work force was African American. In fact, South Carolina's agricultural economy had been dependent upon African-American labor since 1720. African Americans were the backbone of the agriculture industry but also worked in masonry, carpentry, and other occupations, such as pilots, stevedores, and boat hands. The signing of the Ordinance of Secession and the firing of the shot on Fort Sumter drove South Carolina to war in 1862. The state needed labor to support combat troops, to build and maintain fortifications, to man essential industries, and to produce food to supply military and domestic needs.

During the winter of 1862, the Executive Council named Governor Pickens as the state executive authority. In March 1862, Colonel A.M. Manigault was impressing slaves in the Georgetown area to obstruct the mouth of the Winyah Bay. Similarly, Gen. R.S. Ripley was impressing African Americans to complete fortifications around Charleston.

On April 27, 1862, Ripley wrote Governor Pickens the following: "If you want me to go on with the works in the harbor as the necessity of the time requires, you must send labor as fast as you can. I want a thousand Negroes." Enslaved individuals between the ages of 16 and 50 were eligible for impressment, but only one-fourth of an individual's work force could be taken at one time. Some owners procrastinated or avoided compliance, while others saw their workers impressed and retained beyond their terms of service. In August, the council extended the call for African-American labor from the countryside to include incorporated municipalities. At least 1,800 men were called at a time and served for usually a month. It should be noted that coastal African Americans were often held beyond their terms.

African Americans were generally employed in limited capacities by the Confederate forces. Many served as cooks, servants, and teamsters, although the state also drew large numbers to build coastal fortifications and man essential industries.

1866—South Carolina provides short-lived disability compensation.
1887—Pension relief for regular Confederate soldiers was approved.
1923—South Carolina recognizes African Americans' Confederate service.

On March 16, 1923, the legislature approved "An Act to Provide Pensions for certain faithful Negroes who were engaged in the service of the State in the War Between the States." Act 63 stated that African Americans who served the Confederacy as servants, cooks, or attendants were eligible for a pension. Later amendments required state residency and at least six months of service. This provision eliminated laborers and teamsters, as well as those who served from other states and laborers impressed for work on fortifications. Pensions did not exceed $25 annually.

The following pension applicants are excerpted African-American Confederate Pensioners from Georgetown County. These applications constitute one of the few sources on the Confederate service of South Carolina's African Americans.

Cooper, Amos (Oceda, Georgetown Co.)
Cook [Jan 1864–April 1865]; applied 21 April 1923
App. # 4050; 4/21/23–d. 6/7/1925
Buried 6/8/1925 St. Mary's
Son of Cecelia Wright and Henry Cooper

Ford, Edwin P. (Georgetown, Georgetown Co.)
Cook & Drummer [1861–65 served]
App. # 4061

Ford, Henry James (Plantersville, Georgetown Co.)
Cook—Captain John Tucker [1862–65 served]
App. # 4063 [a married turpentine farmer]
94 years old, died 8/1926
Son of George Ford & Kay Furman, born 8/10/1832
Buried at St. Paul. Informant, Nasa Ford, Plantersville.

Gaillard, Philip (Campfield, Georgetown Co.)
Wagon Driver—Capt. Manigault, 104th Regt. [2/1861–2/1865]
App. # 4064; 4/30/1923

Gasque, John (Sampit, Georgetown Co.)
Cook—James Williams, Co. A, Capt. Albert Thomas, Gen. Mart Gary. [4/18/63—Appomattox 1865]
App. # 4065; [widowed farmer]
80 years old, died 8/3/1924
Son of Joe and Katie Gasque.
Buried St. Paul, Sampit. Informant—Ella Alston.

Hardy, Derry (Georgetown, Georgetown Co.)
Servant—Capt. Calvin Mills (North Carolina) [entered 1861]
App. # 4070; 5/15/1923 [Derry Hardee, widower, laborer]
85 years old, died 11/21/1927
Buried McDonnell. Informant—W.J. Wilson, undertaken, Georgetown, SC

Moultrie, Sheddrick (Georgetown, Georgetown Co.)
Orderly—Capt. James Trapier [1861–65]
App. # 4086; 5/9/1923

Small, Elisha (Murrells Inlet, Horry Co.)
Cook—Capt. Joshua Ward, Ward's Art [1861]
App. # 6428

Vereen, Wesley (Rhems, Georgetown Co.)
Servant [8/3/1861–7/1862]
App. # 4108

Two

Industry and Business

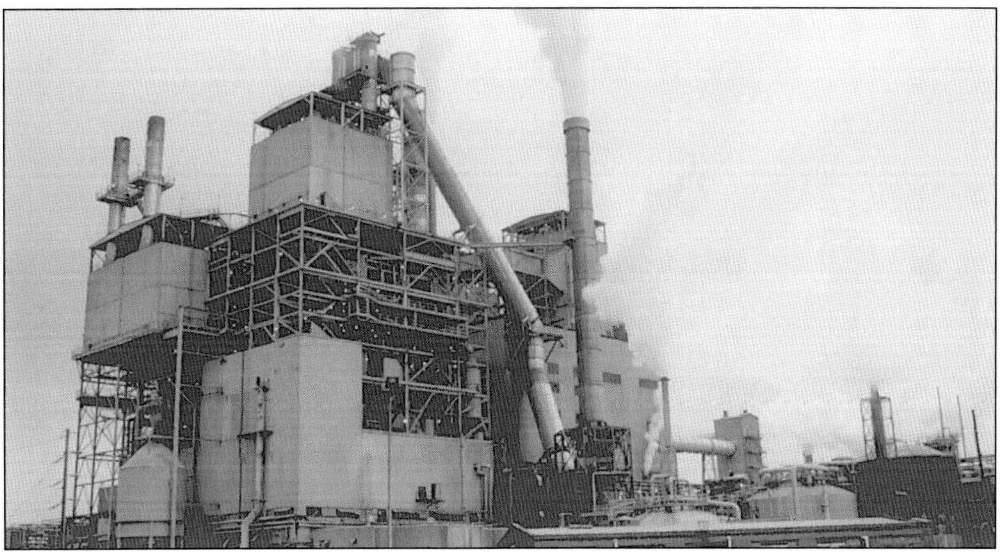

International Paper Company. The construction of the mill began on a 525-acre site in 1936, and the first pulp was made in June 1937. By 1942, the Southern Kraft Division of the International Paper Company had become the largest Kraft paper mill in the world. In July 1962, it employed 1,700 persons in the mill, 400 in the Container Plant, and 250 in its Woodlands Division, totaling 2,350 employees. The county census for 1960 was 34,798. Higher wages and fringe benefits from the company have served as a model for other employers. The Georgetown Steel Mill and International Paper Company are among the highly sought after employment opportunities in the county.

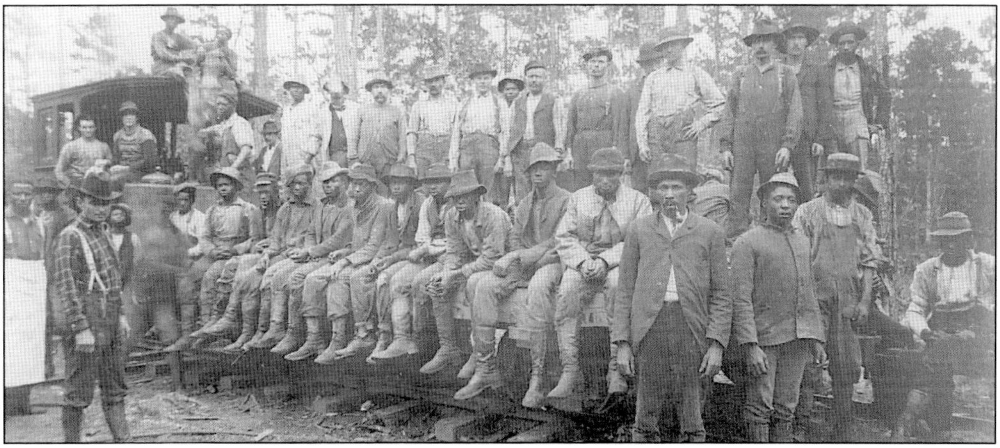

All Aboard on the Log Train. The Atlantic Coast Lumber Company (ACL) opened in 1899 in the West End section of Georgetown and incorporated in 1903. By 1916, the company controlled the timber rights on 250,000 acres in eight South Carolina counties, bearing about 2 billion feet of lumber. The plant covered 56 acres in the bend of the Sampit River. The company appointed foremen to run six camps, and there were 40 mule and horse teams in scattered areas. Logs were shipped by rail or river raft. In 1900, 4,585 blacks and whites were employed in the lumber and timber products industry. ACL provided numerous jobs for hundreds of African-American laborers in Georgetown left without work by the decline of rice planting. Some worked in the mills in the city, while others stayed in the country to cut timber for the company or for sale to ACL. Housing was provided for black and white employees of the Atlantic Coast Lumber Company. A small rental fee included scrap wood for cooking and heating. As this section of town experienced growth as new families moved into the neighborhood near the mill, the Georgetown Methodist Church felt the area needed its own church. Thus, the West End Methodist Episcopal Church was organized. The church was first housed in a tiny wooden structure, but the congregation soon grew to 200 members and a new brick sanctuary was built with financial assistance from the Methodist conference and Atlantic Coast Lumber. With the Depression came the closure of the lumber mill in 1932. The church finally closed its doors and merged with Duncan Methodist Episcopal Church in 1933. James Bank Washington and Jerry Blake (lumber graders), Sam Monroe and Cornelius Rhodes (foremen), Frank "Rooster" Wragg (assistant foreman), Ben Cooper, Henry Smith, and others worked ten-hour days for $1 to $3 a day. Pictured here are Atlantic Coast Lumber Company employees sitting on a log train. (Courtesy of the Georgetown County Library Morgan Collection.)

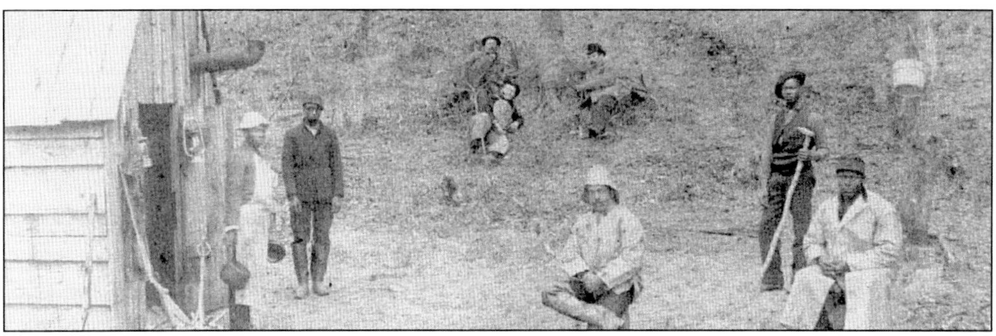

Atlantic Coast Lumber Company Rural Workers. The picture depicts workers at one of the company's timber sites in a rural area of the county. (Courtesy of the Georgetown County Library Morgan Collection.)

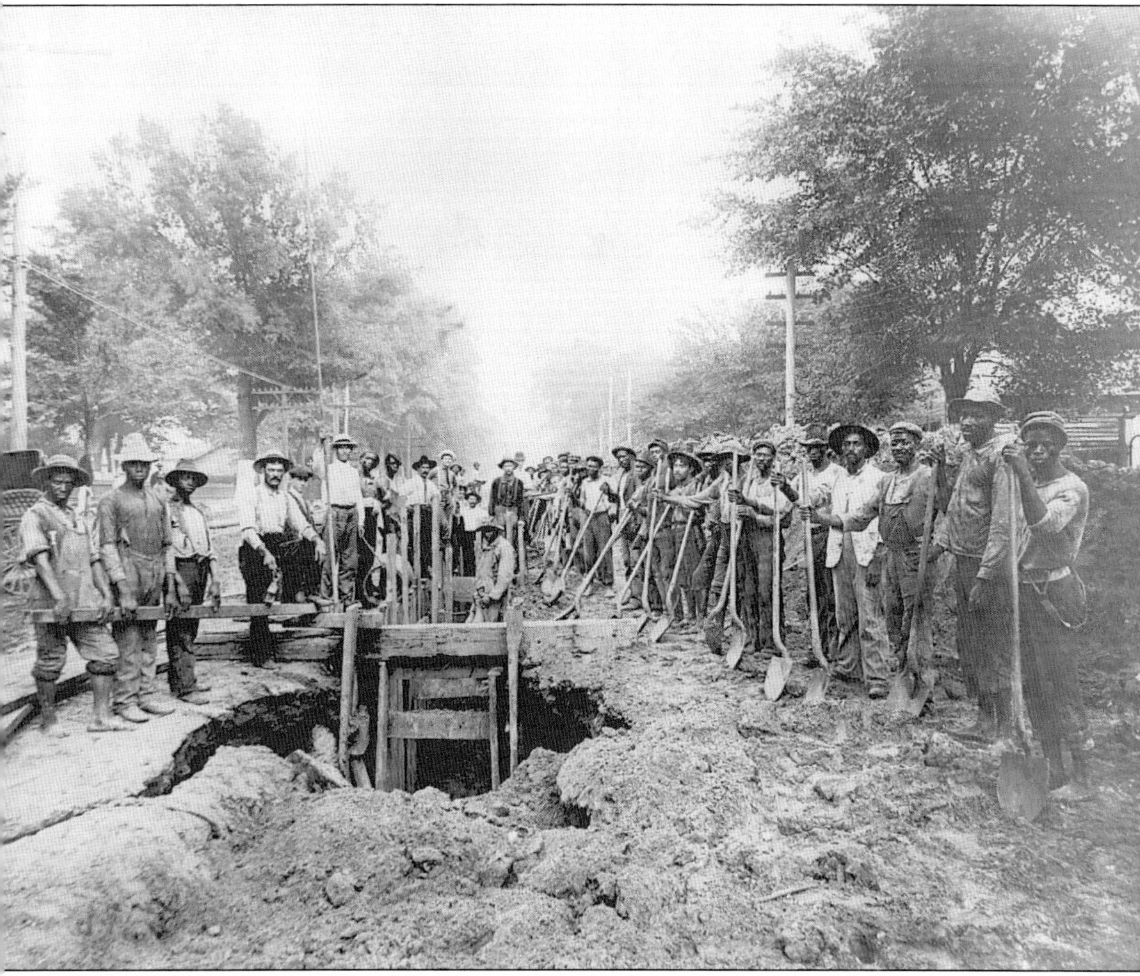

A Magnificent Engineering Feat. A labor crew dug the ditch to install the city of Georgetown's first water sewer system at Front and Wood Streets, the highest ground in town. To function, pipe had to be laid 22 feet deep. The city floated a bond issued for $75,000 for the project, and the system served the city from 1904 until 1992. (Courtesy of the Georgetown County Library Morgan Collection.)

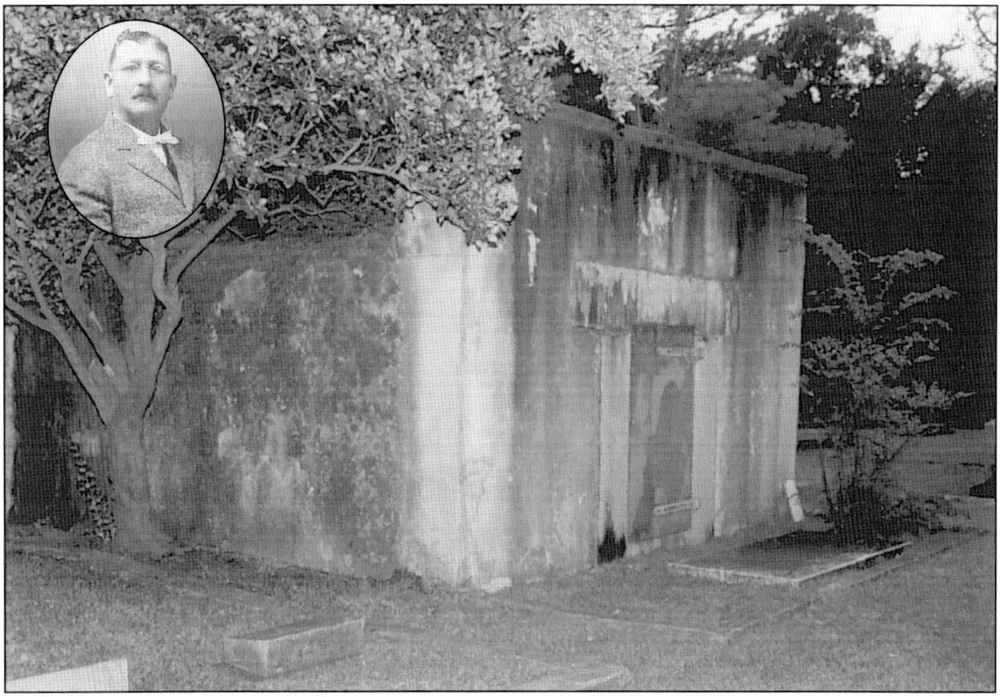

William Christopher Atkinson Sr. (1857–1920). W.C. Atkinson, seen in the inset, was a successful merchant serving the entire community of Georgetown. W.C. Atkinson and Sons was the first African-American family business along Front Street during the late 1800s. (Courtesy of Margretta Knox.) The vault, seen here, is located in the Prince George Winyah Episcopal Church cemetery. The only inscription is "W.C. Atkinson."

An Article from the *Georgetown Times*, April 21, 1920

"Pay Tribute of Respect: Prominent Families of George-Town Attend Negro's Funeral" Georgetown, SC A demonstration considered remarkable occurred here Sunday at the funeral of William C. Atkinson, in the African Methodist Church, when a large section of the spacious interior set aside for the purpose was filled to overflowing with white men and women of the most prominent families of the city, met to pay tribute of respect to a worthy member of the colored race. The floral offerings covering the casket and banked around the pulpit, were largely tributes from the white friends of the deceased.

Born in 1856 in Georgetown County, William Atkinson grew up on a rice plantation, there learning from the gentlefolk of the manor good manners, which couple with native judgment, honesty and devotion to duty, in whatever sphere it came to him, had brought him not only business success and the respect and high esteem of all who knew him, both white and black. The Negroes from all the county literally swarmed in to attend the funeral.

A fitting and impressive service was carried out by the various pastors of the city and the selected choir. The Reverend Perrin, pastor of the deceased, delivered a panegyric.

"Bill" Atkinson died last Thursday, April 15, having been in failing health for some months. For the past twenty years, he has conducted a very successful green grocery here and general store. His patronage included nearly everybody to a greater or less extent and his standard of doing business was such that everyone had implicit faith in him.

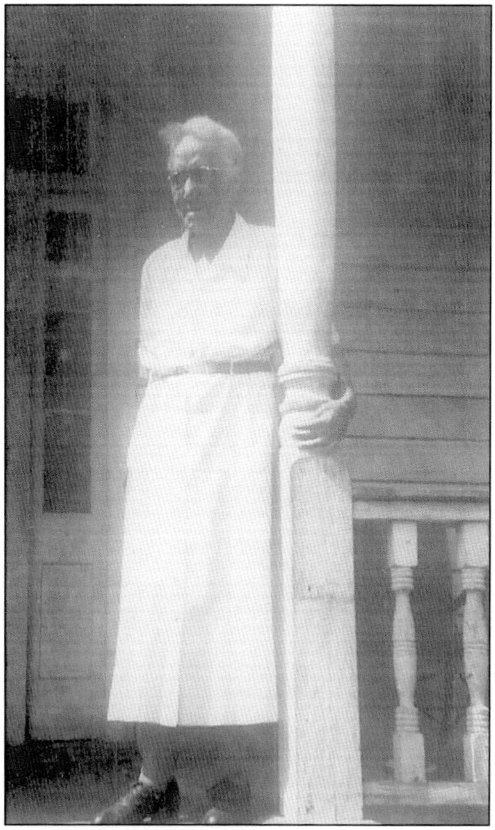

MAUDEST KELLY ATKINSON. Mrs. Maudest Atkinson, the wife of W.C., was born on Cat Island. The couple had nine children: William Jr., Ernest W., Huger, Theodore, Lena, Florence, Amelia, Orilla, and Janie. They resided at the present 819 Duke Street homestead. Maudest left Cat Island after an 1893 hurricane for the city of Georgetown. (Courtesy of Clementine Atkinson Kelly.)

W.C. ATKINSON AND SONS GROCERY AND MEAT MARKET. The family business was first located on the street in front of 709 Front at Screven Street, where the Rice Museum is today. The business later moved to 822 Front Street. William Christopher Atkinson Jr. was a trustee of Bethel A.M.E., and he is buried at Bethesda Baptist Church cemetery. Pictured, from left to right, are William Christopher Atkinson Jr., Vernon Vanderhorst, Theodore Atkinson (son), Huger Atkinson (son), and Ernest Atkinson (son). (Courtesy of the Committee on African-American History Observance.)

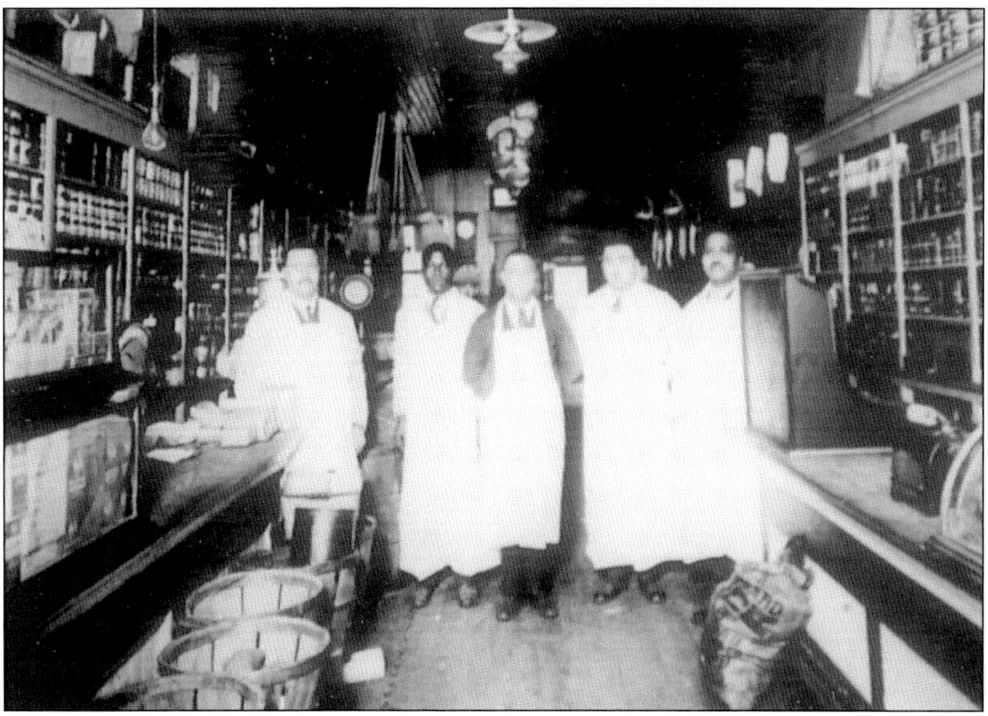

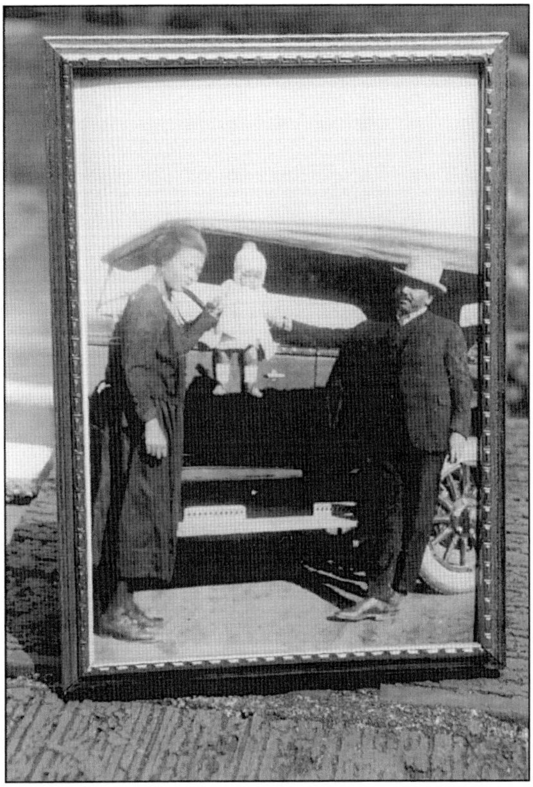

SUNDAY AFTERNOON DRIVE. Leola Ellen Reeder and Ernest Williard Atkinson prepare for a Sunday afternoon drive with baby Clementine, their first-born daughter. The family poses in front of a classic 1923 Buick. A drive around town after church was a pleasurable family treat for those who were fortunate enough to have access to an automobile. The children of this union were Clementine, Cynthia, Ernest Jr., Maudest, and William Reeder Atkinson. (Courtesy of Clementine Atkinson Kelly.)

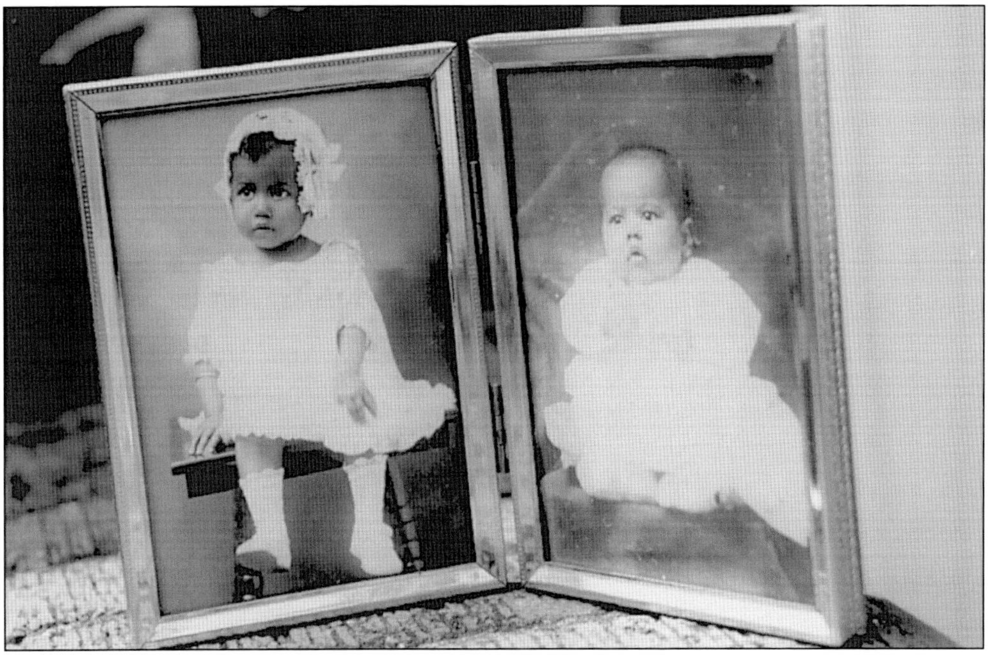

LITTLE AND BABY CLEM. Clementine Atkinson is seen here as a child in 1926 and as a baby in 1922. (Courtesy of Clementine Atkinson Kelly.)

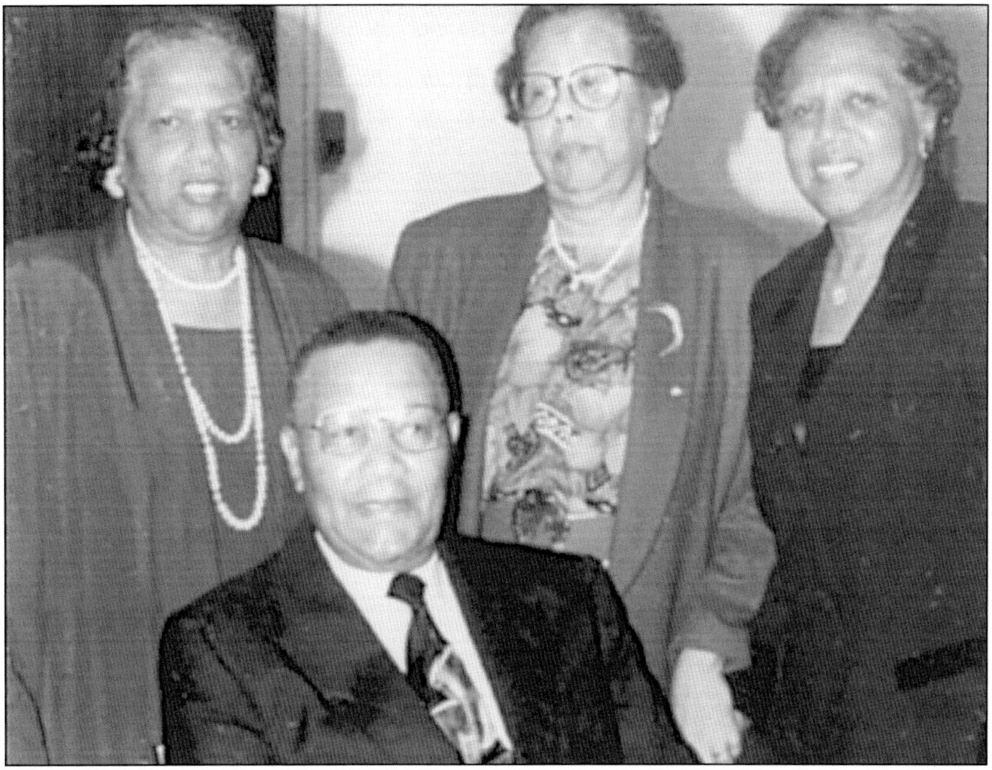

A Sibling Portrait. The Atkinson siblings are seen here during the funeral of their mother, Leola Ellen Reeder Atkinson, in January 1994. Pictured, from left to right, are Cynthia A. Smith, Clementine A. Kelly, Maudest A. Coleman, and Ernest Willard Atkinson Jr. Ernest died in 1995. (Courtesy of Clementine Atkinson Kelly.)

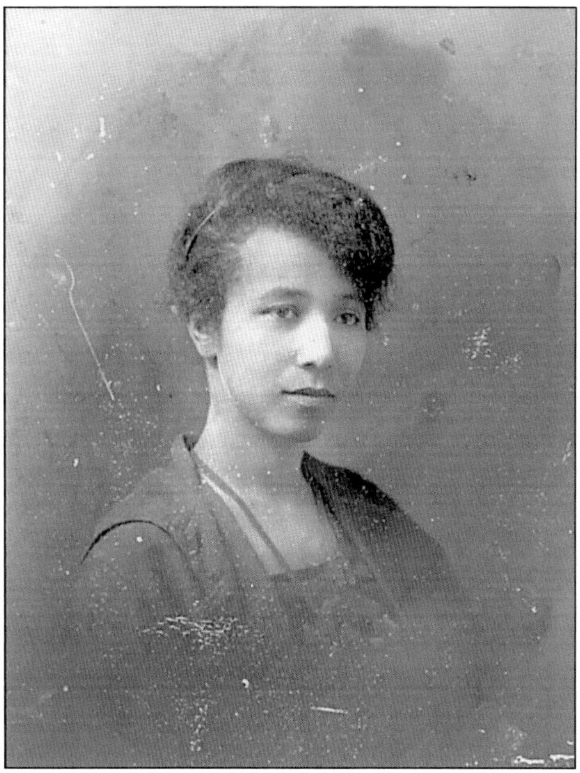

Florence Atkinson Dunmore (1900–1988). Florence was the daughter of W.C. and Maudest Atkinson. She married Lawrence A. Dunmore *c.* 1921. The couple had four children: James, Lawrence Jr., Laura, and Margretta. (Courtesy of Margretta Knox.)

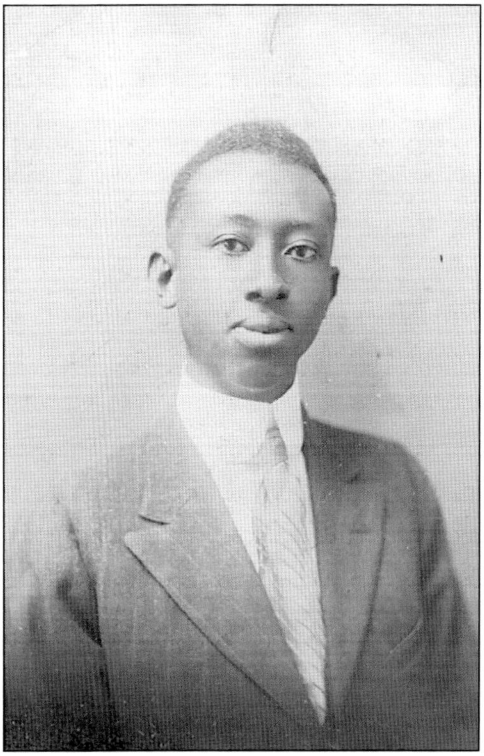

Lawrence Alfred Dunmore Sr. (1900–1991). Lawrence published his first book of poetry, *Musings of a Teenager (15 years old)*, in 1915. Excerpts from The Howard High School Band read,

> *Oh, look at the crowd, I wonder what's the matter, Looks like fire to me, But where is the ladder? Now I'm right in the crowd that's kicking up so, But if I ever get out of here, I'll never come back anymore. Look out there fellow, What's the matter with you? You step on it again then, You'll see what I will do. Bet you wouldn't be fitten, When I get thru with you. It's the Howard High School Band; Aren't those boys a stepping, Kicking up the sand. Watch those girl a dancing. Such music will tempt you tho, But I have promised my Saviour, That I won't dance anymore.*

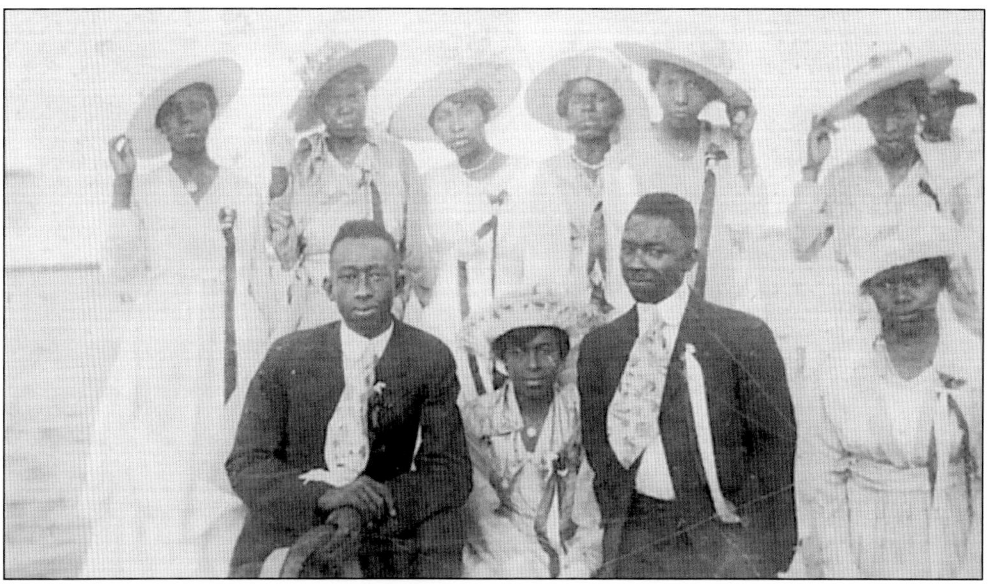

Howard High School Class of 1918. Pictured on first row is Lawrence A. Dunmore Sr. (far left), and on the back row is Florence Atkinson (fifth from left). (Courtesy of Margretta Knox.)

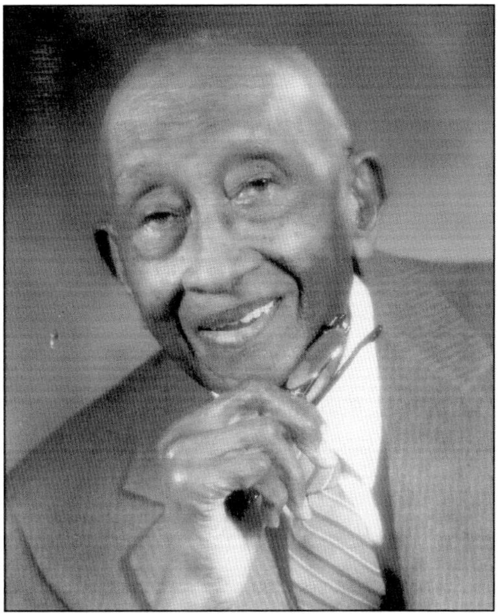

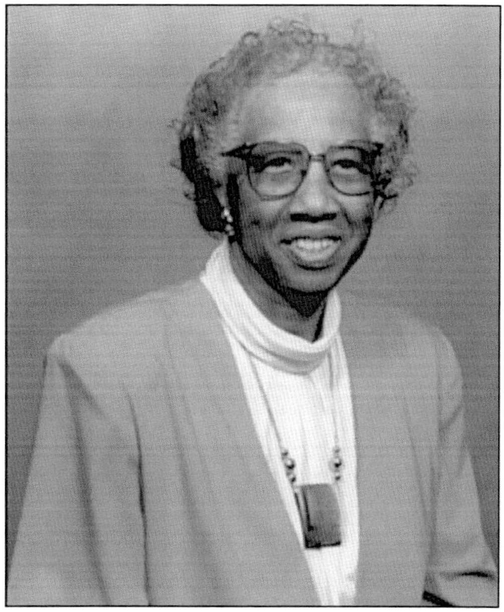

Left: **LAWRENCE DUNMORE SR.** An insurance agent for North Carolina Mutual Life for over 34 years, Dunmore was the first African American to serve in government on the city council (1970–1974) since Reconstruction. He also operated the Apex Barber Shop on Front Street. *Right:* **MARGRETTA DUNMORE KNOX.** Mrs. Knox is an active member of Bethel African Methodist Episcopal Church in Georgetown. Among her many callings are church trustee, treasurer, and historian. She is a retired educator. (Courtesy of Margretta Knox.)

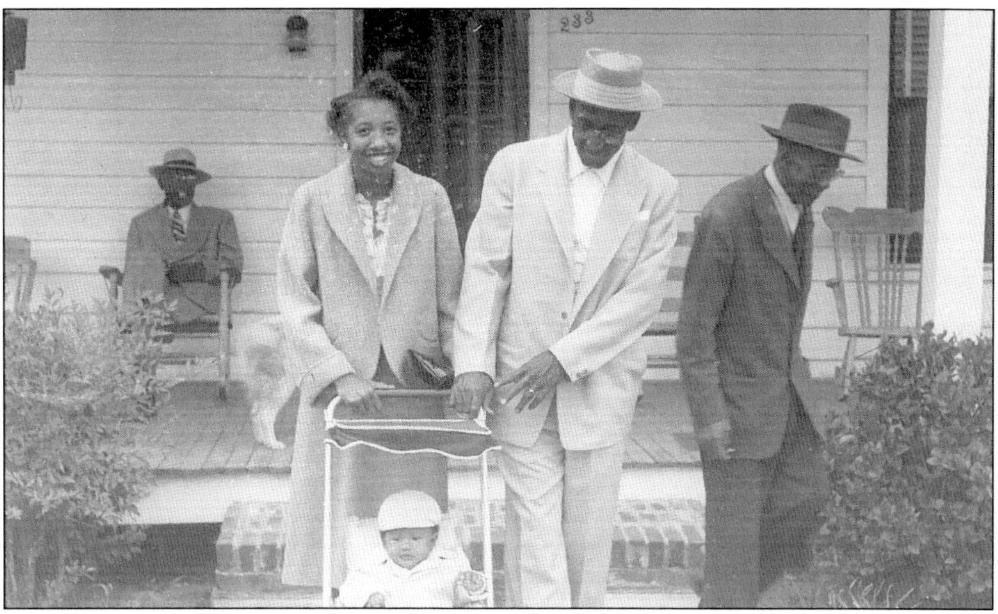

MARGRETTA'S FAMILY. Pictured are Margretta and Clifton Knox Sr. pushing Clifton Jr. in a stroller (at left), Margretta's father, Lawrence (on the porch), and her grandfather, Sampson Dunmore (at right), in front of 233 St. James Street in 1955. (Courtesy of Margretta Knox.)

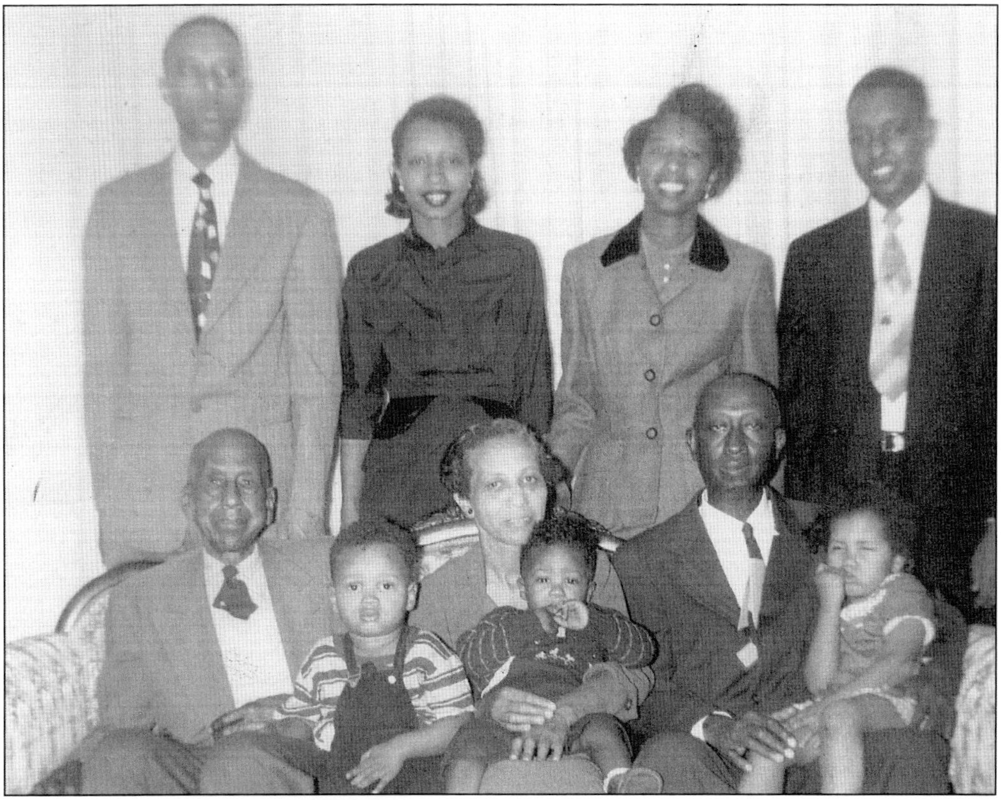

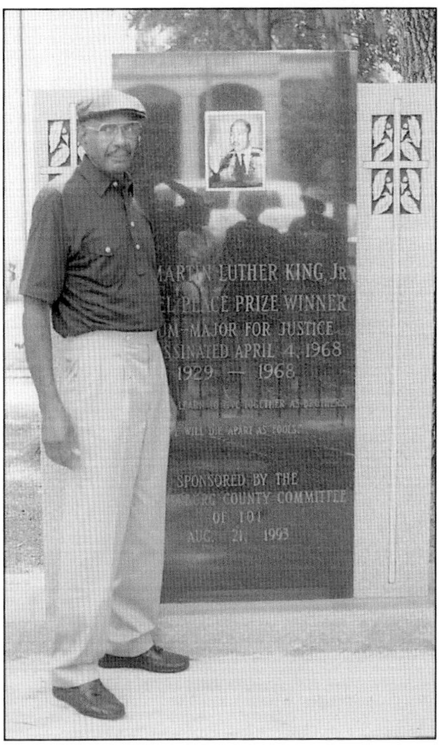

Four Generations of the Dunmore Family. Pictured, from left to right, are (front row) Floyd, John, and Brenda Woody; (second row) Sampson Dunmore, Florence Atkinson Dunmore, and Lawrence Alfred Dunmore Sr.; (back row) Lawrence Jr., M.D., Laura Dunmore Woody, Margretta Dunmore Knox, and James W. Dunmore, D.D.S., in 1952. (Courtesy of Margretta Knox.)

Moody Stafford (1927–1995). Moody Stafford founded Sampit Monument in 1978 after retiring from the Georgetown Steel Mill. Prior to his establishment of the business, the nearest memorial stones had to be ordered from the Brown Memorial Co. in Florence, South Carolina. Stafford is pictured here standing in front of one of several memorial stones he created in honor of Dr. Martin Luther King Jr. He was commissioned by the Williamsburg County Committee in Kingstree, South Carolina, in August 1993 to create a memorial statue. The business is now operated by Lorenza and Angela Cox Stafford, Moody's son and daughter-in-law. (Courtesy of Sampit Monument.)

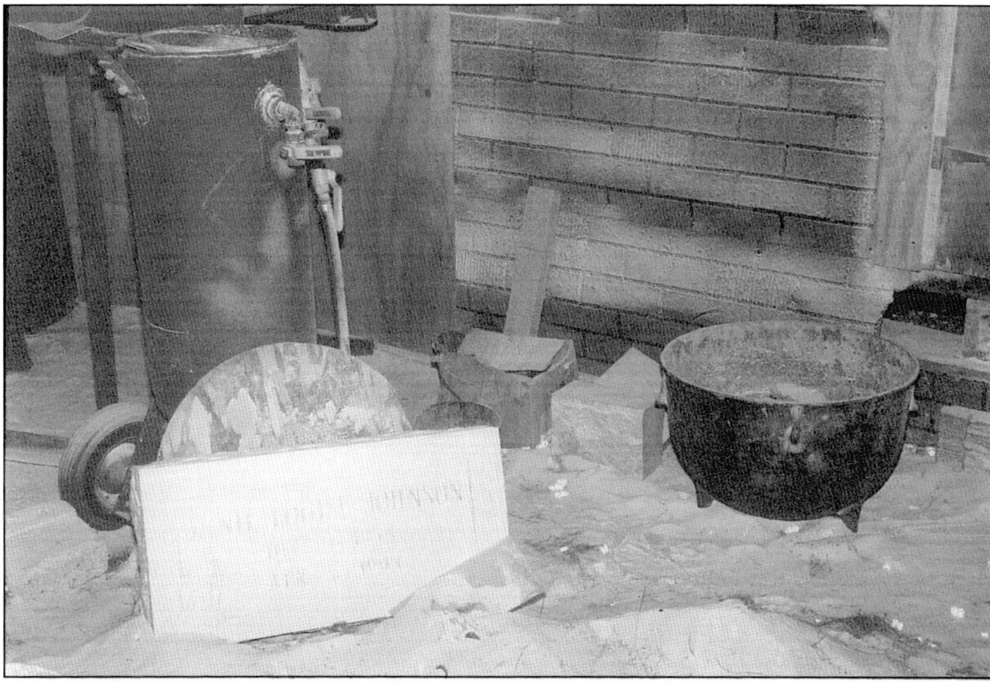

GRAVESTONE SHOP. Interior views of the Sampit Monument shop shows the tools, materials, and machinery used to create gravestones, markers, stone works, and monuments—granite, marble, compressors, sandblasters, and cast-iron pots.

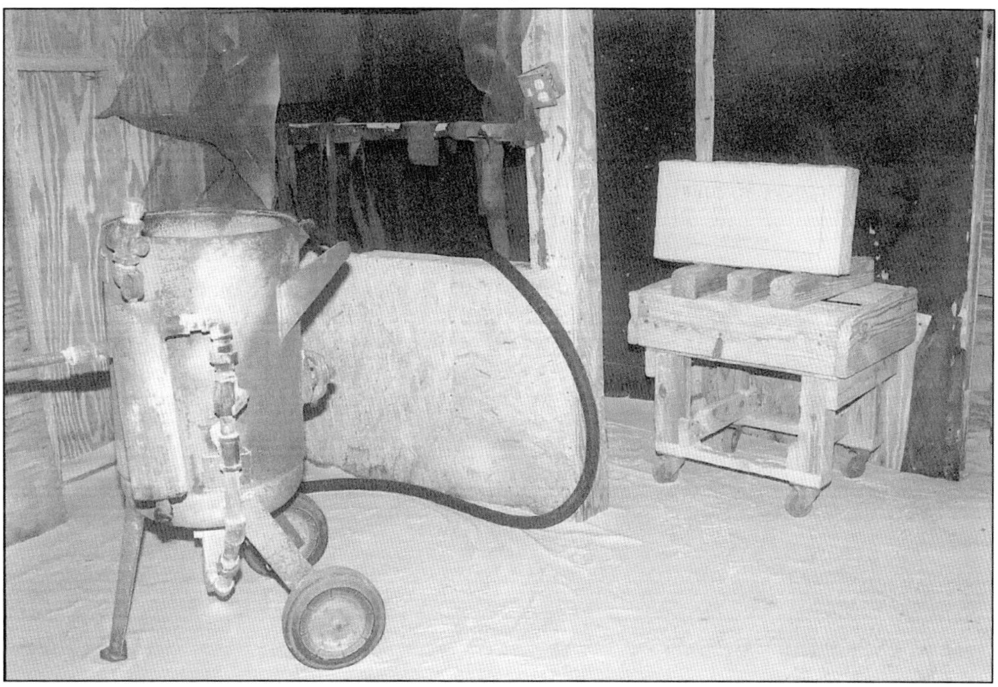

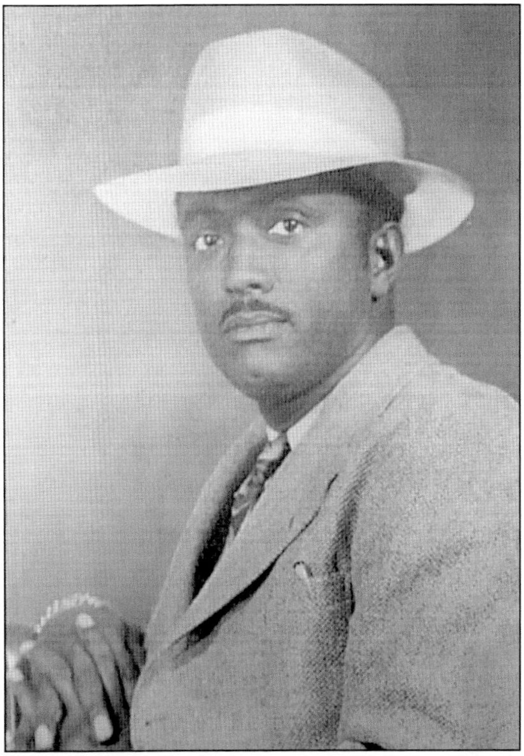

Walter W. Manigault Sr. Manigault was a 1930 graduate of the Renouard Training School for Embalmers in New York City. In 1937, he established Manigault & Sons Funeral Home, Inc. located at 2917 High Market Street. He is pictured to the left during that same year, and, below, he is in the second row on the far left. (Courtesy of Walter Manigault Jr.)

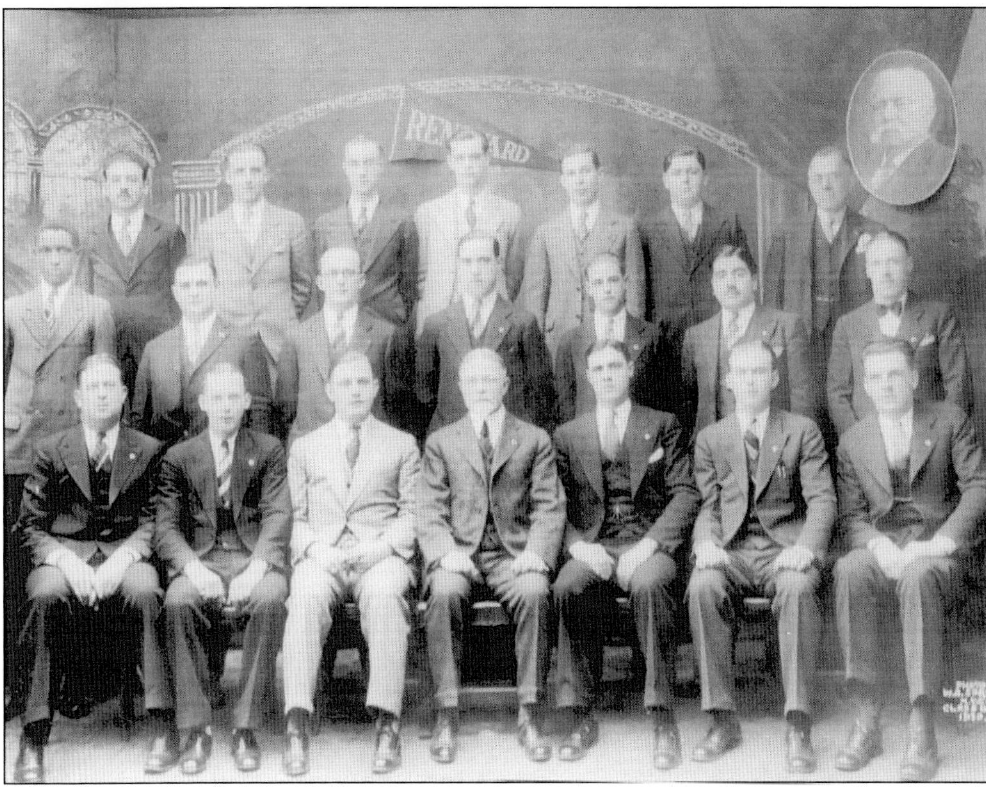

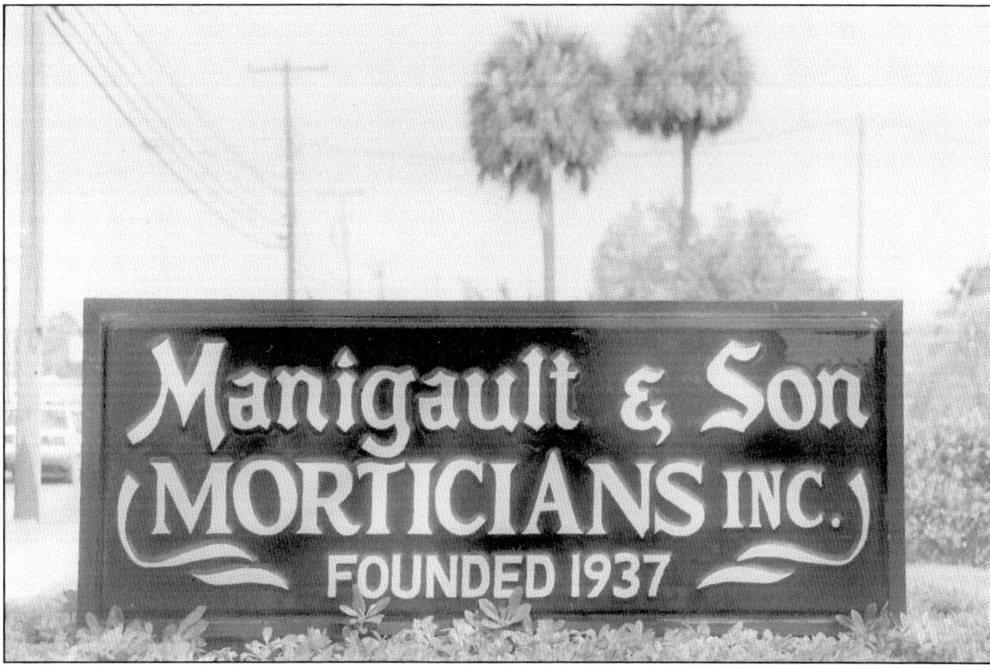

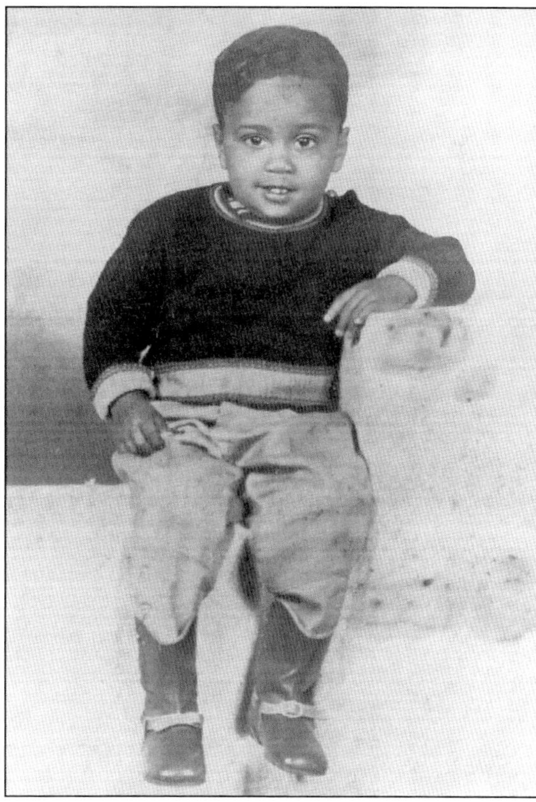

YOU'LL BE GLAD YOU CALLED US. Walter Manigault Sr. used little Walter Jr. for the Walter Manigault Funeral Home Calendar in 1941. He was three years old. This was the first advertisement of its kind in the Georgetown area. Walter Manigault Jr., a 1961 graduate of Eckels College of Mortuary Science, is a licensed embalmer, funeral director, and present owner of the business. (Courtesy of Walter Manigault Jr.)

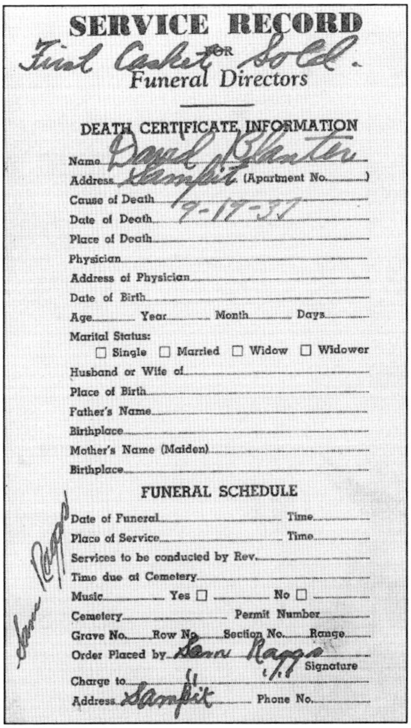
SERVICE RECORD
FOR
Funeral Directors
First Casket Sold.

DEATH CERTIFICATE INFORMATION

Name David Blanter
Address Sampit (Apartment No.)
Cause of Death
Date of Death 9-17-37
Place of Death
Physician
Address of Physician
Date of Birth
Age Year Month Days
Marital Status:
☐ Single ☐ Married ☐ Widow ☐ Widower
Husband or Wife of
Place of Birth
Father's Name
Birthplace
Mother's Name (Maiden)
Birthplace

FUNERAL SCHEDULE

Date of Funeral Time
Place of Service Time
Services to be conducted by Rev.
Time due at Cemetery
Music Yes ☐ No ☐
Cemetery Permit Number
Grave No. Row No. Section No. Range
Order Placed by Sam Raggs Signature
Charge to
Address Sampit Phone No.

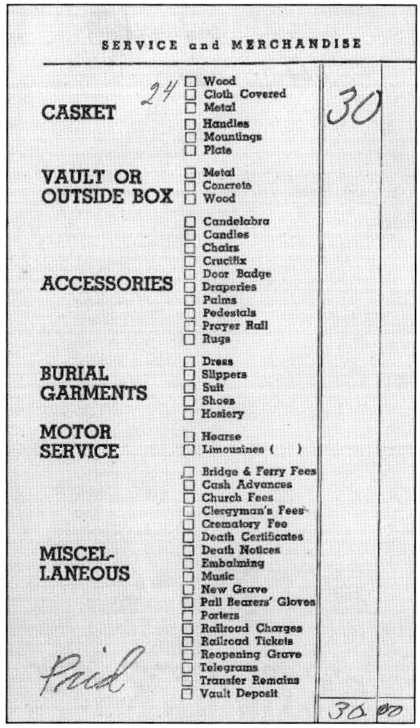
SERVICE and MERCHANDISE

CASKET	24 ☐ Wood ☐ Cloth Covered ☐ Metal ☐ Handles ☐ Mountings ☐ Plate	30
VAULT OR OUTSIDE BOX	☐ Metal ☐ Concrete ☐ Wood	
ACCESSORIES	☐ Candelabra ☐ Candles ☐ Chairs ☐ Crucifix ☐ Door Badge ☐ Draperies ☐ Palms ☐ Pedestals ☐ Prayer Rail ☐ Rugs	
BURIAL GARMENTS	☐ Dress ☐ Slippers ☐ Suit ☐ Shoes ☐ Hosiery	
MOTOR SERVICE	☐ Hearse ☐ Limousines ( )	
MISCEL-LANEOUS	☐ Bridge & Ferry Fees ☐ Cash Advances ☐ Church Fees ☐ Clergyman's Fees ☐ Crematory Fee ☐ Death Certificates ☐ Death Notices ☐ Embalming ☐ Music ☐ New Grave ☐ Pall Bearers' Gloves ☐ Porters ☐ Railroad Charges ☐ Railroad Tickets ☐ Reopening Grave ☐ Telegrams ☐ Transfer Remains ☐ Vault Deposit	
Paid		30 00

Service Records for Funeral Directors. The service sheets above price the business' first casket sold for $30 in the fall of 1937. The second record (at bottom of page) indicates the $60 charge for a casket and the $7.50 charge for motor service. (Courtesy of Walter Manigault Jr.)

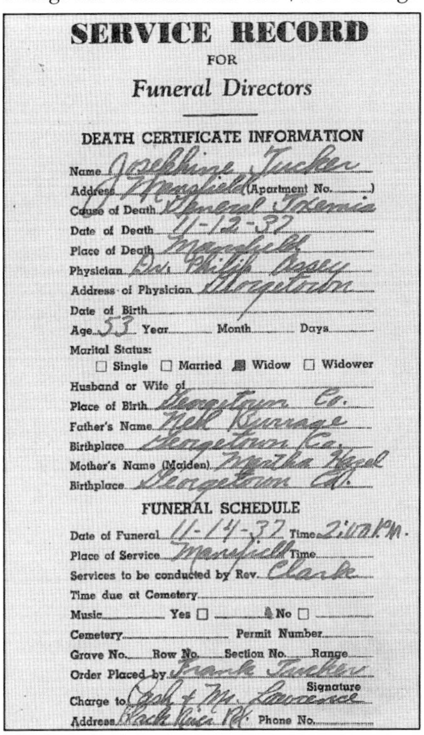
SERVICE RECORD
FOR
Funeral Directors

DEATH CERTIFICATE INFORMATION

Name Josephine Tucker
Address Mansfield (Apartment No.)
Cause of Death General Toxemia
Date of Death 11-12-37
Place of Death Mansfield
Physician Dr. Philip Bosey
Address of Physician Georgetown
Date of Birth
Age 53 Year Month Days
Marital Status:
☐ Single ☐ Married ■ Widow ☐ Widower
Husband or Wife of
Place of Birth Georgetown Co.
Father's Name Nell Burrage
Birthplace Georgetown Co.
Mother's Name (Maiden) Martha Hazel
Birthplace Georgetown Co.

FUNERAL SCHEDULE

Date of Funeral 11-14-37 Time 2:00 P.M.
Place of Service Mansfield Time
Services to be conducted by Rev. Clarke
Time due at Cemetery
Music Yes ☐ No ☐
Cemetery Permit Number
Grave No. Row No. Section No. Range
Order Placed by Frank Tucker Signature
Charge to Cash & Mr. Lawrence
Address Black River Rd. Phone No.

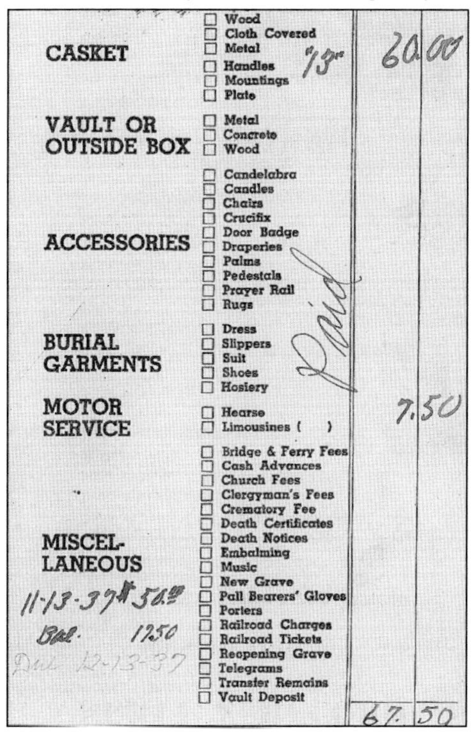
CASKET	☐ Wood ☐ Cloth Covered ☐ Metal ☐ Handles ☐ Mountings ☐ Plate 73"	60.00
VAULT OR OUTSIDE BOX	☐ Metal ☐ Concrete ☐ Wood	
ACCESSORIES	☐ Candelabra ☐ Candles ☐ Chairs ☐ Crucifix ☐ Door Badge ☐ Draperies ☐ Palms ☐ Pedestals ☐ Prayer Rail ☐ Rugs	
BURIAL GARMENTS	☐ Dress ☐ Slippers ☐ Suit ☐ Shoes ☐ Hosiery	Paid
MOTOR SERVICE	☐ Hearse ☐ Limousines ( )	7.50
MISCEL-LANEOUS	☐ Bridge & Ferry Fees ☐ Cash Advances ☐ Church Fees ☐ Clergyman's Fees ☐ Crematory Fee ☐ Death Certificates ☐ Death Notices ☐ Embalming ☐ Music ☐ New Grave ☐ Pall Bearers' Gloves ☐ Porters ☐ Railroad Charges ☐ Railroad Tickets ☐ Reopening Grave ☐ Telegrams ☐ Transfer Remains ☐ Vault Deposit	
11-13-37 # 50.00 Bal. 1250 Due 12-13-37		67.50

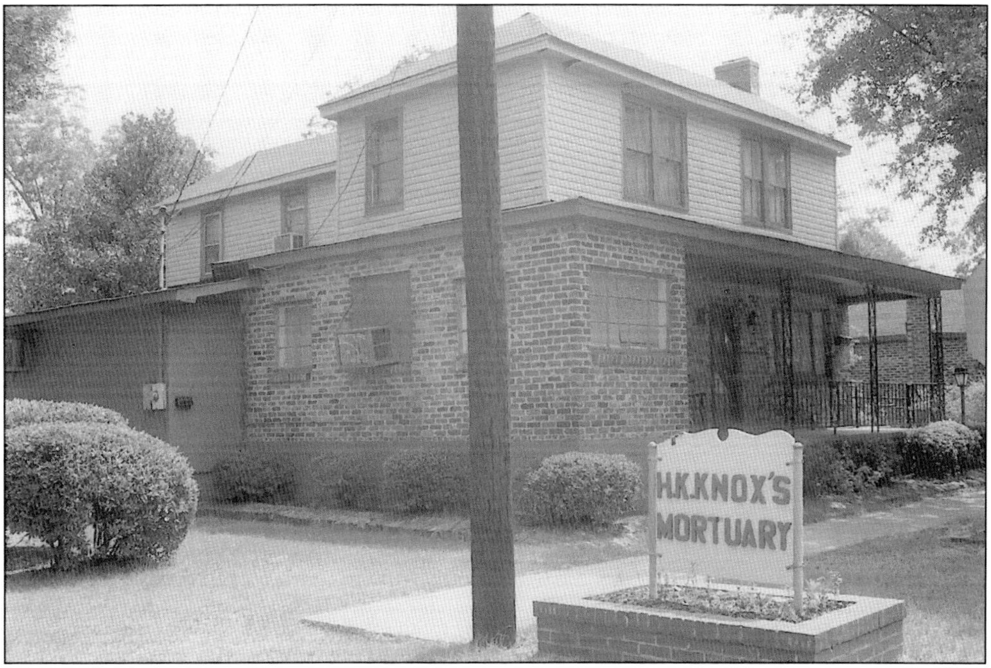

H.K. KNOX'S MORTUARY. Herbert Knox is a retired teacher. He established the mortuary business in 1977. An avid community activist, Mr. Knox has served on city council, as magistrate, and on the Board of Directors of the Waccamaw Regional Planning Council. He has a long history of being involved with civil rights and politics. The business was established in 1977.

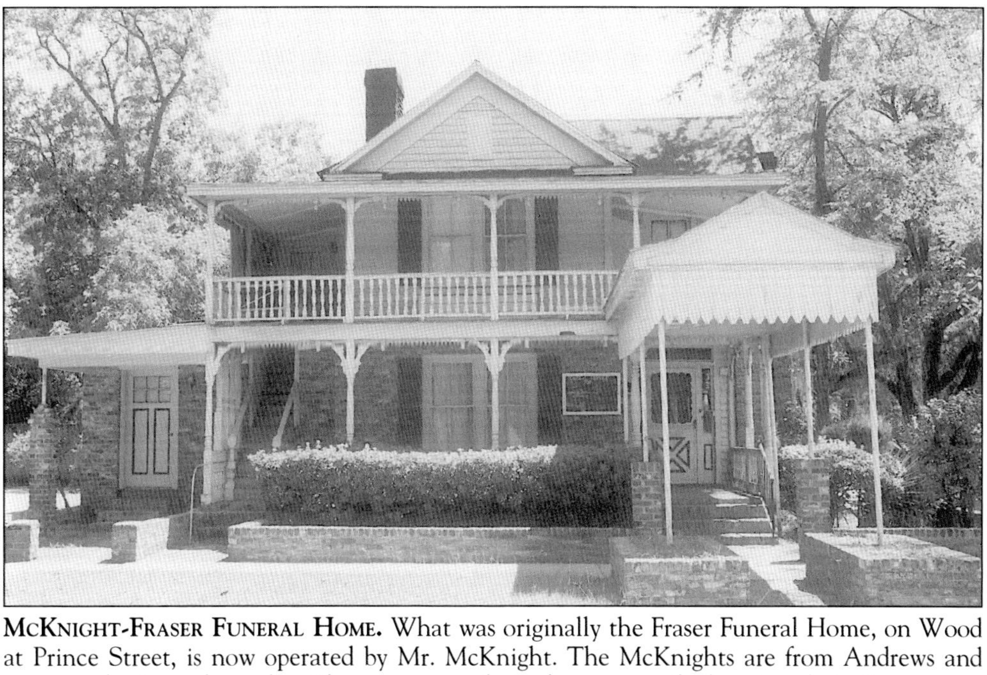

MCKNIGHT-FRASER FUNERAL HOME. What was originally the Fraser Funeral Home, on Wood at Prince Street, is now operated by Mr. McKnight. The McKnights are from Andrews and operate a business there also. They are presently in the process of relocating their Georgetown business to Front Street.

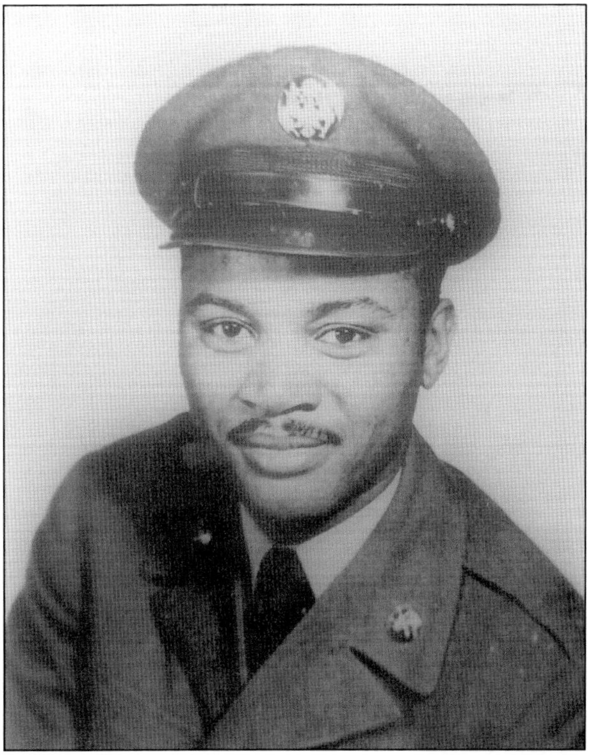

Herman Elliot King (1928–1968). Herman graduated from Howard High School and went into the military; he served in Germany during World War II. He later attended and graduated from the American Academy of Embalming and Mortuary Research, Inc. in New York City after his military discharge in 1948. Returning to Georgetown, King served as an intern to W.J. Wilds, Undertaker. In 1955, Herman married Rosana Duke of Kingstree, South Carolina, and the couple relocated to Dillon, South Carolina. King became an employee of the Mutual Funeral Home, with the understanding that he would acquire an interest in the establishment later. The couple purchased the business in 1960.

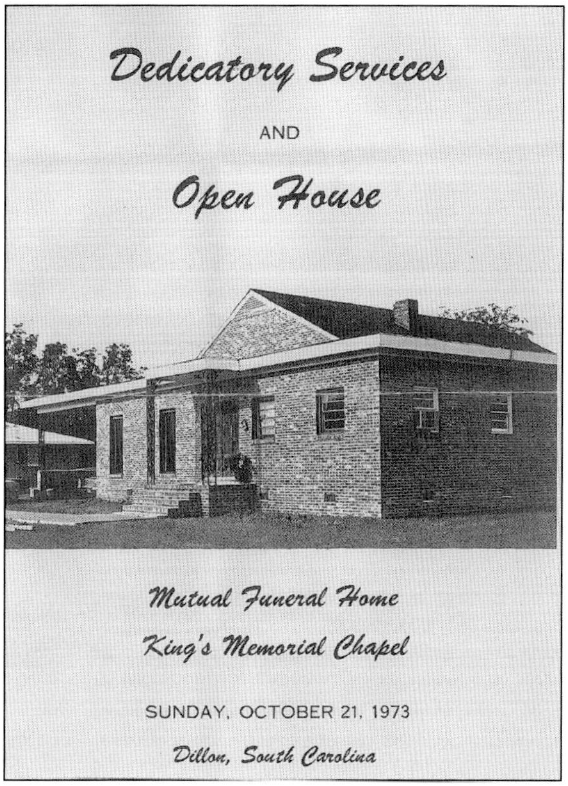

Mutual Funeral Home: King's Memorial Chapel Dedicatory Services and Open House Program. Mrs. Rosana King became the sole proprietor of the establishment upon her husband's death in 1968. The business was remodeled to include a memorial chapel to Mr. King in 1973.

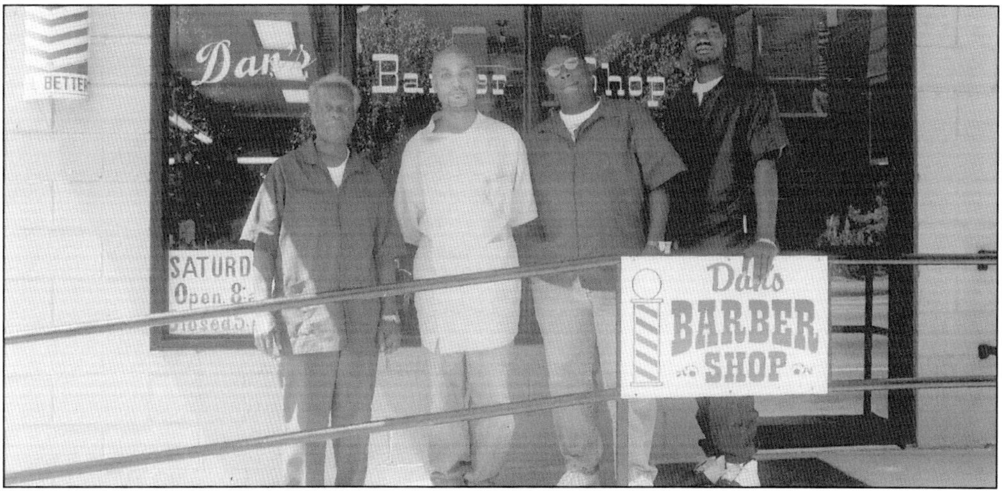

Eight Decades of Service. In 1918, Dan Memminger Sr. was injured at the Atlantic Coast Lumber Mill. Since this was a time prior to workmen's compensation, disability benefits were not yet available. Memminger opted for self-employment and opened his first small business, Dan's Barber Shop, on G and Emmanuel Streets. The second location of Dan's Barber Shop was on Front Street, and later, he relocated to the Hub Building on King Street. The back part of the Hub Building, owned by Manigault of Manigault Funeral Services and Dr. Thompson, a dentist, served as a recreation center. Formerly located behind the present Apex Barber Shop, the Hub Building was torn down several years ago. Howard High School hosted basketball games and proms at the site. Dan Memminger Jr. has operated the barbering business since 1968. In December 1997, he purchased property and relocated his shop to Fraser Street, just opposite the Georgetown Steel Mill. The business has been in operation for 81 years. Dan Memminger Jr. is married to Vera Memminger, and the couple has two sons, Dan Larry and Kayvin. The latter works with his father. Pictured, from left to right, are Kayvin J. Memminger, Dan Memminger Jr., Kevin T. Bessellieu, and Tevis Burroughs.

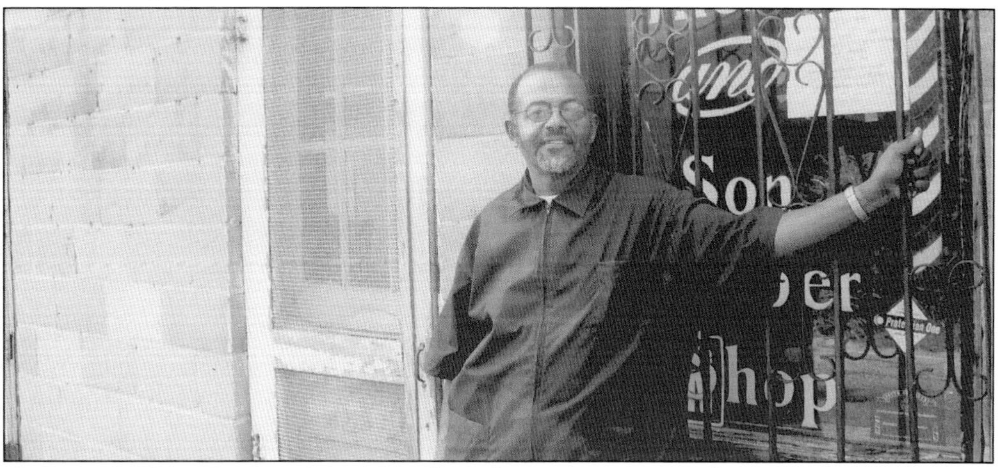

Hicks and Son Barber Shop. Isreal Hicks Jr., proprietor of a barbering business, is pictured in front of his shop. Hicks and Son has operated for 56 years on G Street, recently renamed Alex Alford Avenue, on the west end of the city. The business patriarchy includes Willie Alfred (great-grandfather), Isreal Sr. (grandfather), Isreal Jr. (father), and Terrence J. Hicks (son). Isreal Hicks Jr. is a member of Mt. Olive Baptist Church, the Odd Fellows, and the Masons.

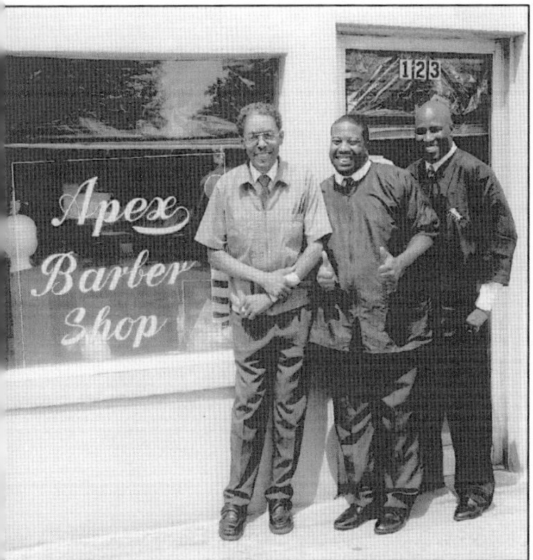

Apex Barber Shop. Arthur Ford began his barbering career at the Apex Barber Shop on King Street with Lawrence Dunmore, Elias Sumter, and Rev. John McQueen in 1962. By 1966, Ford became the proprietor. A 1961 Howard High School graduate, he found working at Myrtle Beach not supportive of his health challenges relating to sickle cell anemia. Ford feels strongly that all families affected by sickle cell disease should not let the illness control their lives. He urges that parents not impede the growth of a child facing the sickness and, above all, should refrain from being overly concerned or sometimes even over protective. The son of Robert Henry Ford of the Plantersville section and Missouria McBride of Williamsburg County, Ford married Modestine White Ford of Andrews, and the couple has one daughter, Arthelia, and a granddaughter. He is a member of St. Stephens A.M.E. Church, Mason Lodge #426, and volunteers for the American Red Cross and the Inmate Fellowship Program. Pictured, from left to right, are Arthur Ford, Jason Collins, and Wardell Eaddy Jr.

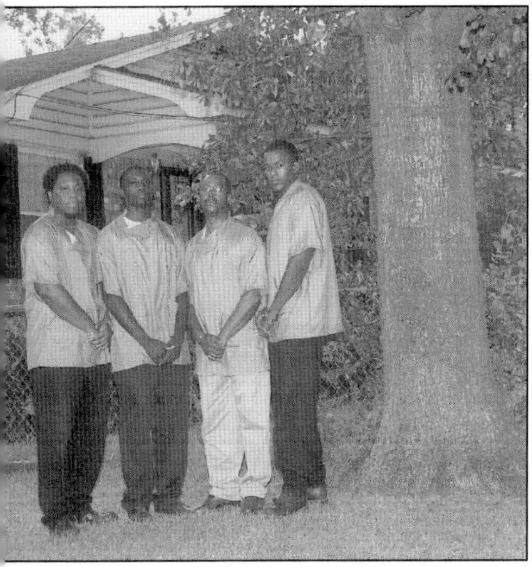

Randy's Barber Shop. Randolph Ford of the Plantersville section operates Randy's Barber Shop. Established in 1985, the shop is located on Church Street. Mr. Ford established the Choppee High School Mentor Program for male youth in 1994. Pictured, from left to right, are William R. Greene III, Jefferson Simmons, Randolph Ford (proprietor), and Kevin J. Alston. Arthur Ford (previous picture) and Randolph are cousins.

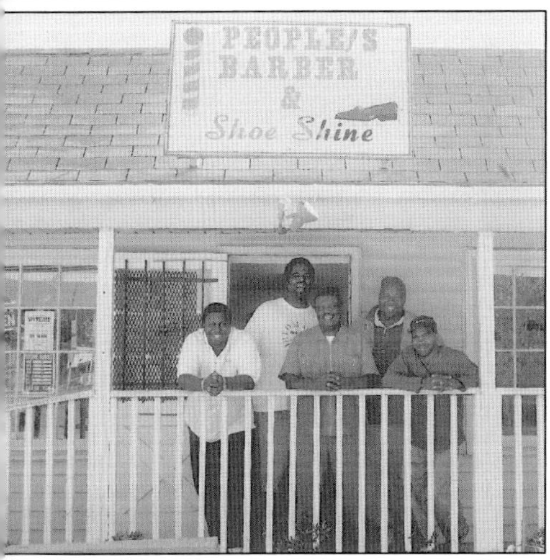

Peoples Barber. Louis Simmons is the proprietor of Peoples Barber Shop and Shoe Shine, located in Iszard's Square on Merriman Road. A retired officer of the Washington, D.C. Police Department and a 1956 graduate of Howard High School, Simmons is an ordained deacon and a member of Bethel A.M.E. Church in Georgetown. Pictured, from left to right, are the following: (front row) Boris Gibson, patron; Louis Simmons; and Quinton Harris, patron; (back row) Kenny Jones, barber, and Ernie Brown, patron.

Three

People, Gatekeepers, and Organizations

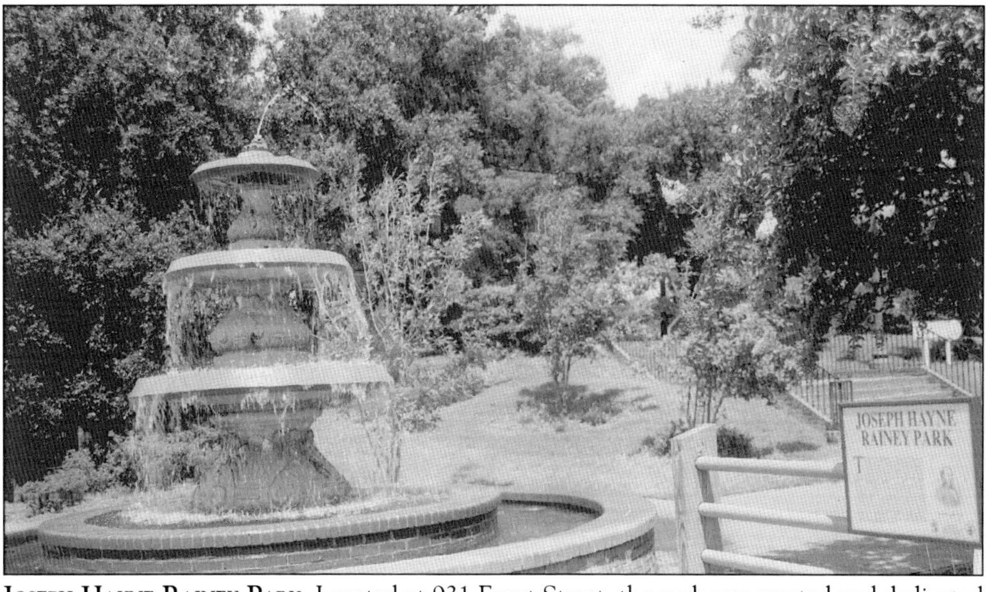

Joseph Hayne Rainey Park. Located at 931 Front Street, the park was created and dedicated in 1993 to honor the country's first African-American member of Congress. The following is an excerpt from the address to the white inhabitants of the state of South Carolina at the South Carolina Colored People's Convention in Charleston in November 1865:

"We simply ask that we shall be recognized as men: that there be no obstructions placed in our way; that the same laws which govern white men shall govern black men, that we have the right of trial by jury of our peers; that schools be established for the education of colored children as well as white; and that the advantages of both colors shall, in this respect, be equal; that no impediments be put in the way of our acquiring homesteads for ourselves and our people; that, in short, we be dealt with the way others are—in equity and justice."

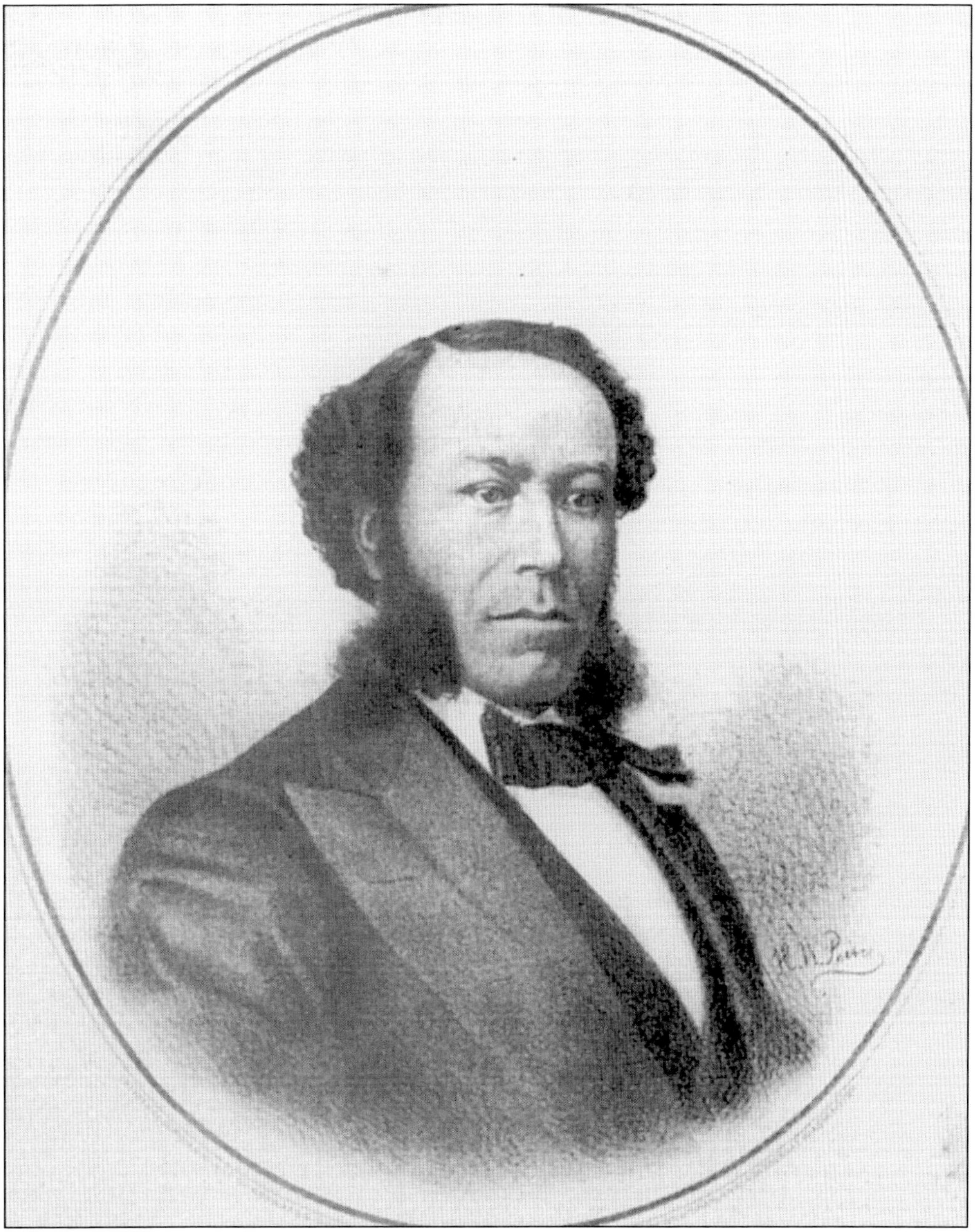

Honorable Joseph Hayne Rainey (1832–1887). Joseph Rainey served in the United States House of Representatives from 1870 to 1879. His political career began in 1867, when he was appointed to the South Carolina Republican Party Executive Committee. In 1868, he was elected to the South Carolina State Senate. His father, Edward L. Rainey, a barber, was also a slave but was able to purchase freedom for himself, his wife, Gracia, and his children. Educated through private instruction, Rainey became a barber like his father, and the two ran a prosperous business. Joseph married Susan in 1859. He is buried "in the Baptist Cemetery," though the exact location of the grave is unknown.

JOSEPH HAYNE RAINEY HOUSE (c. 1760) AND HISTORIC MARKER. Located at 909 Prince Street, this two-and-a-half story clapboard house contains many of the original windows and doors. The interior features original woodwork, wide plank heart pine flooring, and two original firebacks. The marker reads, "This National Historic Landmark was the family home of Joseph H. Rainey, the first African American elected to the U.S. House of Representatives, 1870–1879. Born in Georgetown County in 1852. Rainey, it is said, made blockage-running trips during the Civil War. He was a delegate to the Constitutional Convention of 1868, served two years in the SC Senate, and two years as internal revenue agent of SC. He died in Georgetown, SC in 1887." Erected by Georgetown Chapter Delta Sigma Theta 1994.

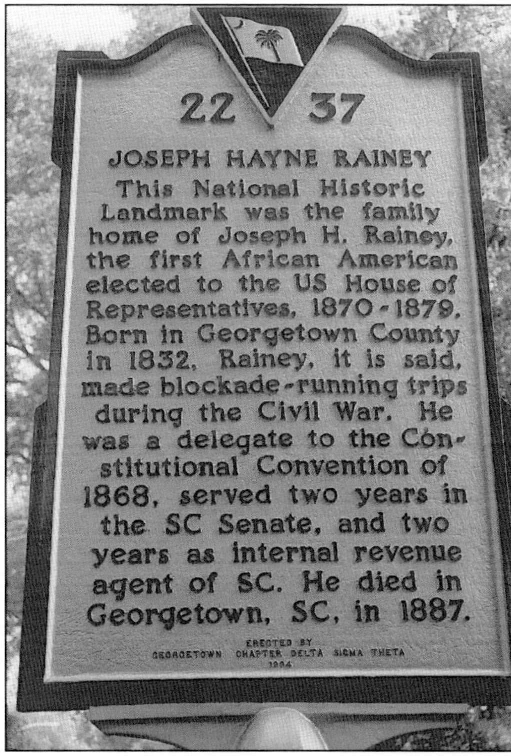

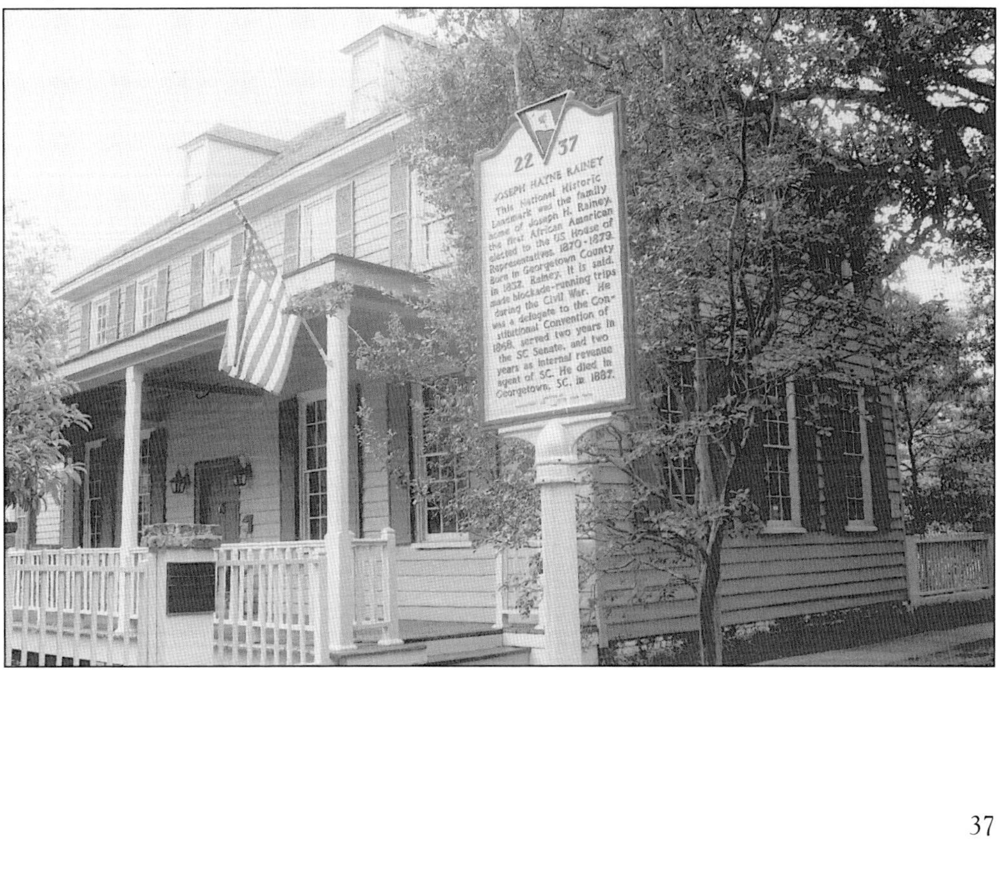

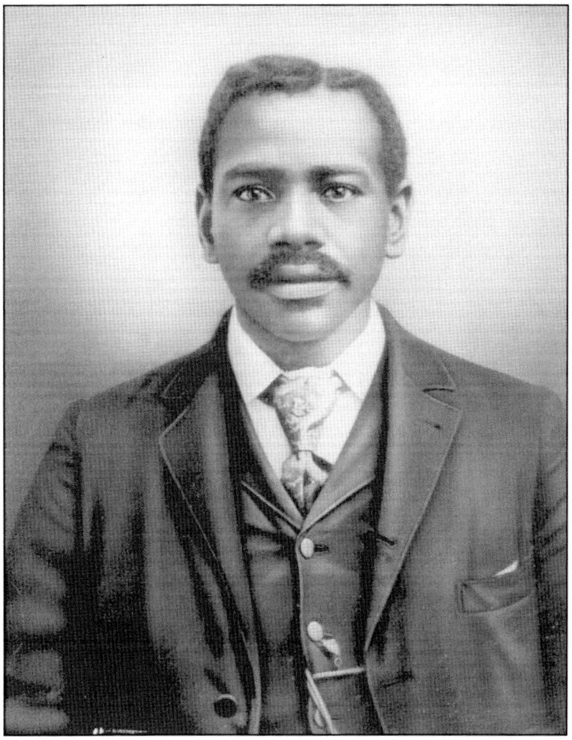

John William Bolts (1861–1921). Bolts, elected in 1898 and 1900 on a fusion ticket from Georgetown, was the last African American to serve in the South Carolina House of Representatives. It would be 70 years before African Americans were again represented in the state legislature. Bolts received a private education in the Plantersville section of the county, and later, he attended Benedict College in Columbia, South Carolina, and began teaching. During this period, schools were only in session for four months each year. Bolts divided his annual duties at Plantersville, Laurel Hill, and Sandy Island Schools. He was married to Gertrude Ford, and the couple had four children: John Samuel, Robert Dewey, Alethea, and Mary Jane. Their home was located on the southwest corner of Merriman Road and Gilbert Street.

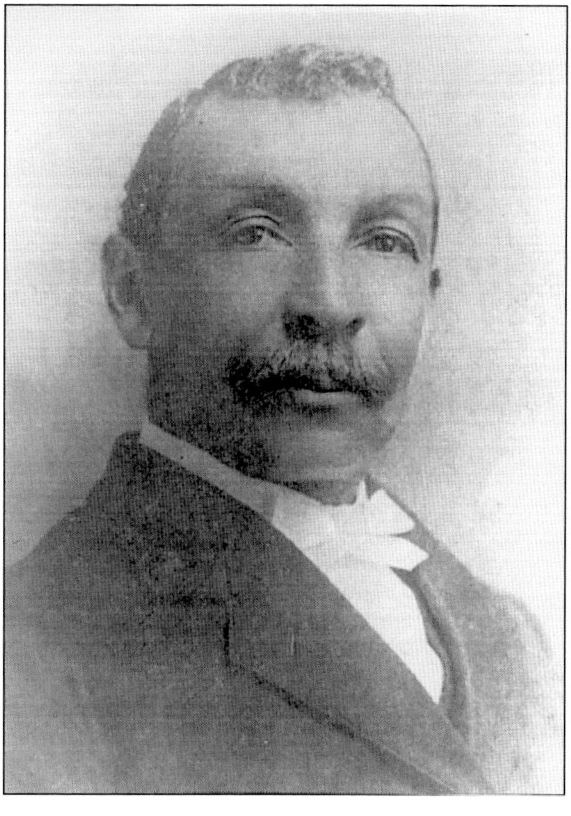

Jonathan Alexander Baxter (1854–1927). Baxter, elected with Bruce H. Williams, was born a free man in Charleston before the Civil War. He learned the shoemaker's trade from his father and pursued it for some years. Educated in the public schools of Georgetown, he became a teacher. In 1878, he served as a commissioner of election in Georgetown. During 1884, he served one of three terms in the South Carolina House of Representatives.

ROBERT BANNEKA ANDERSON SR. (?–1914). Anderson was born in Georgetown. Educated in the public schools, he became a schoolteacher and, later, the town warden of Georgetown. He went on to serve four consecutive terms in the state legislature (1890–1896) and was a delegate to the Constitutional Convention in 1895. He later became the postmaster at Georgetown. He was married to Judith Dunmore. Robert J. Jackson and Anderson were the first two African-American letter carriers to serve the city of Georgetown. Jackson is pictured on the page with the Bethesda Baptist Church Trustees on page 119. Peter C. Kelly, the first rural carrier in the county, scored a rating of 96 for the rural carrier exam, as is depicted on his examination report letter of May 1911. William J. Moultrie served as postmaster (1886), Willie Beamer served as a sub-carrier, and Sam Wilson was the special delivery carrier.

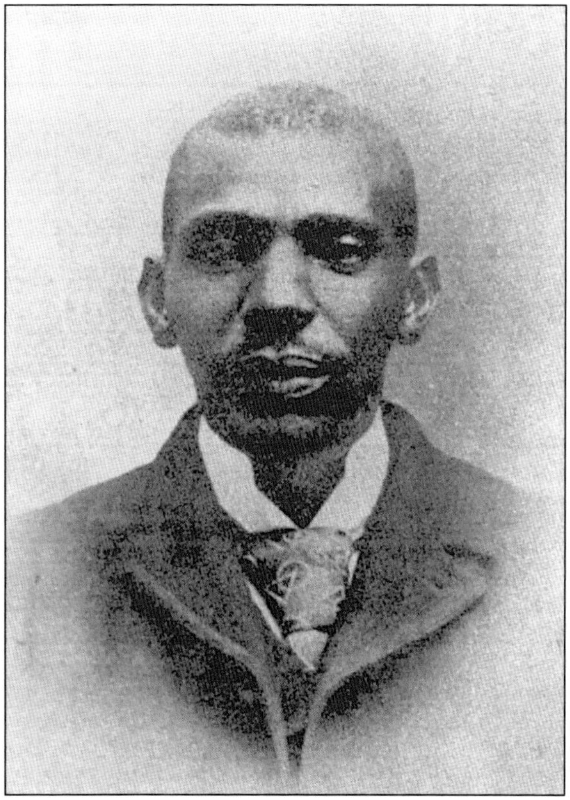

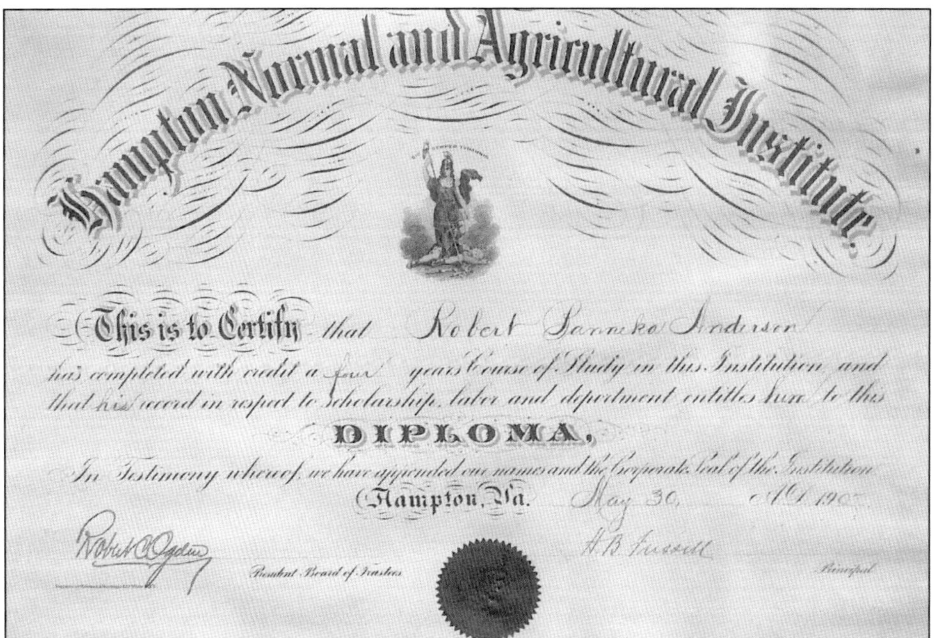

Hampton Normal and Agricultural Institute.

This is to Certify that Robert Banneka Anderson has completed with credit a four years Course of Study in this Institution and that his record in respect to scholarship, labor and department entitles him to this

DIPLOMA.

In Testimony whereof, we have appended our names and the Corporate Seal of the Institution

Hampton, Va. May 30, A.D. 190[illegible]

Robert C. Ogden, President Board of Trustees

H. B. Frissell, Principal

HAMPTON UNIVERSITY DEGREE. Robert Banneka Anderson Jr. graduated from Hampton University in 1907. He returned to Georgetown and served as a mail carrier for the city of Georgetown from 1908 until 1953, a total of 45 years.

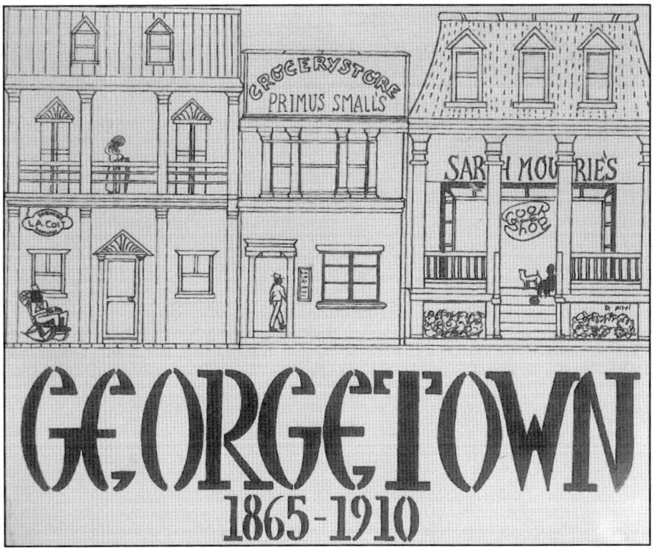

FRONT STREET—AN UNTOLD STORY. The Front Street exhibit project depicted the economic life of African Americans in Georgetown County during the years of 1865 to 1910. The project was sponsored by the Committee on African-American History Observances, and was supported by the South Carolina State Arts Council, the Humanities Council, the State Museum, the McKissick Museum, and others in 1994. Listed are many of those business owners during this period.

Brown, Munchy 900 block, Front Street Grocer/Butcher
Brunson, Phillip Front Street Tailor
Clark, Tommy Furniture Maker
Coit, L.A. Front Street shoemaker business (1896)
Dennison, W.E. Front & Orange Streets barber shop (1896)
Dunmore, Eton
Dunmore, D.J.
Eaton, Dr. B.H. 800 block Front Street Drug Store
Flowers, Elizabeth Front Street Retail Drugstore
Furgeson, Andrew Front Street Blacksmith
Gadson, Emma Front Street General Merchant
Gill, A.J. Front Street Tailor
Golding, C. Carpenter
Gourdine, Pinky Front Street Blacksmith
Green, Fred Businessman, born 1893
Harlot, P.M. Front Street Retail Merchant
Harrell, James Front Street Blacksmith
Harrison, Van Buren Front Street General Merchant
Hughes, James Front Street Retail Merchant
Hughes, John Front Street barbershop
James, Ben and Fraser Front Street Tailor/Dry Cleaner
Knox, Mr. Barber shop
Lawrence, O.B. Contractor and builder
McCoy, Ladson Shoe store
Moultrie, Sarah Restaurant
Jackson, J.A. Broad Street feed and livery stable (1896)
Primus Smalls 800 block, Front & Orange Street Grocery store (1896)
Rainey, Edward L. Retail Merchant (brother of Joseph Rainey)
Richardson, Marcus 1100 block, Front Street Shoe Shop
Robinson, Willie and George 900 block, Front Street Merchants
Sinclair, William Writer, turn of the century
Singleton, John 300 block Front Street Grocery Store
Washington, John W. Barber shop Front Street, 900 block
Williams, Benjie Front Street Tailor
Wilson, Robert Front Street Huckster
Wineglass, Ladson 800 block, Front Street barber shop (1896)

Invincible Building & Loan Association
Front Street Brokerage & Banking Firm
I. J. McCottrie, President
W. H. Robinson, Vice president
R.J. Jackson, Secretary and Treasurer

Newspapers established by African Americans
Georgetown Planet weekly, Republican, black publication, 1873-1875. James A. Bowley (editor), R.G. Bush (associate editor), Planet Publishing Company.

Georgetown Advocate weekly, black publication, 1902–1905. R.B. Salters, G.E. Herriot, W.P. Carolina (editors), Georgetown Advocate Company. Motto: "God bless all our people, both white and black."

Pilots
Prince Colt, Cuffee Gardner, Thomas Fraser, Edward K. Morse, J.W. Rumley, Anton A. Smith, J.E. Uptegrove, W.J.L. Uptegrove, George Vincent, Henry and William Watson, G.H. Watts, Addison Wilson, Frank Woodbury, Peter Woodbury.

SAMUEL BENJAMIN WILLIAMS. Samuel B. Williams, a riverboat engineer, transported passengers throughout the county on his riverboat. This photo was taken c. 1920.

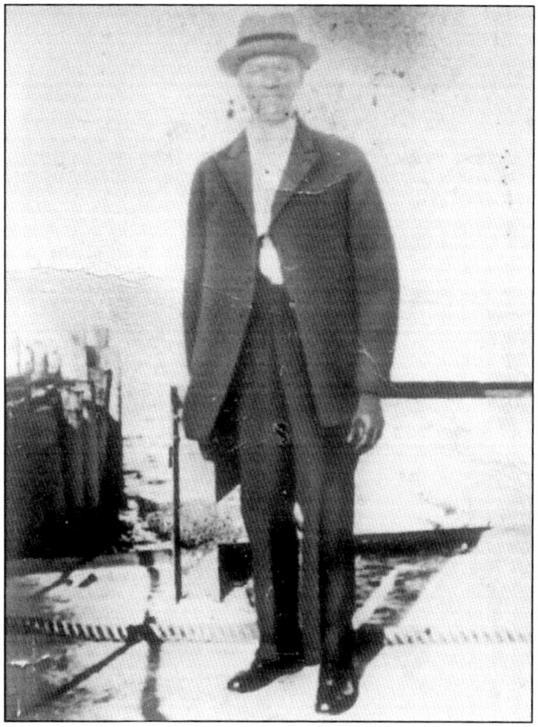

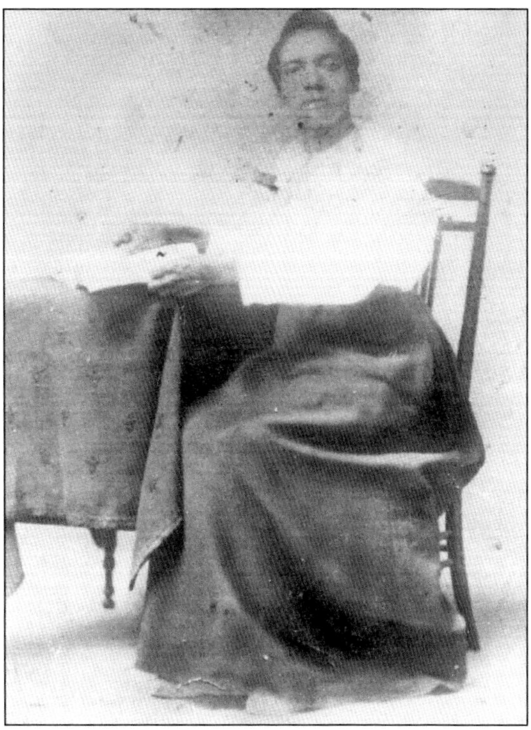

ELLEN JONES WILLIAMS, C. 1918. Ellen Jones, the wife of riverboat engineer Samuel Benjamin Williams, was a seamstress. They were the parents of Rev. Herbert Williams.

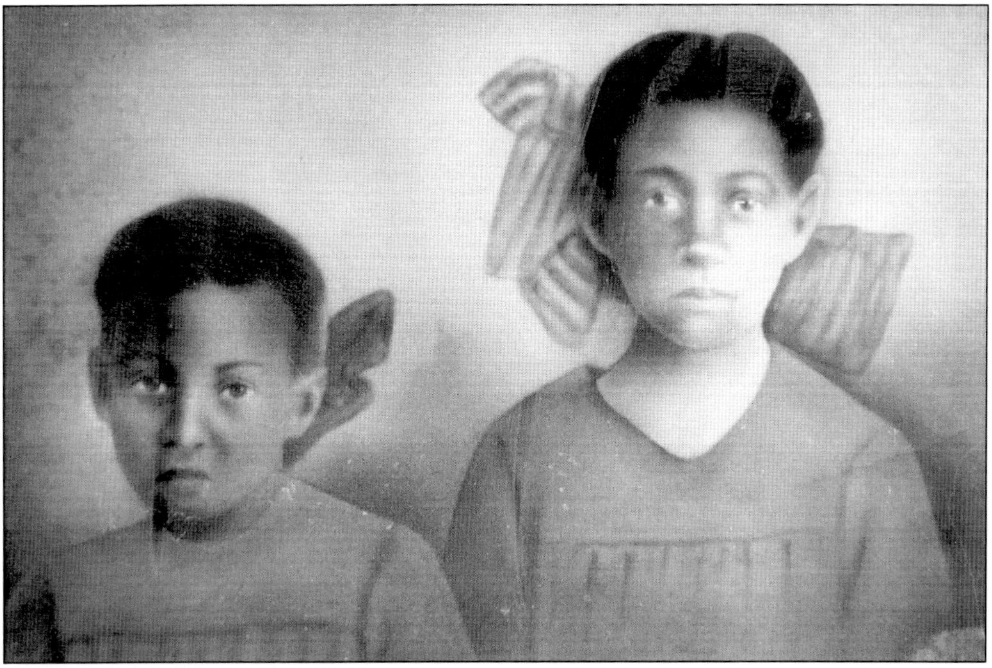

SISTERS, 1910. Evelyn Washington Nesbitt and Mildred Washington Clemons were the daughters of Jonathan Washington, a sea pilot. (Courtesy of Evelyn Washington Nesbitt.)

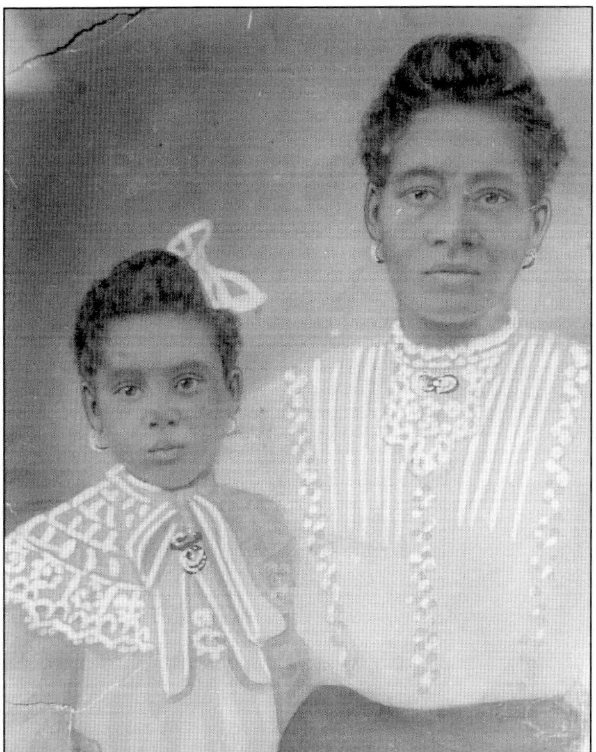

MIDWIFE ANNIE MCCANTS JONES (1875–1955). Hundreds of babies in Georgetown came into the world with the help of Mrs. Jones, the wife of Edward Jones. The couple raised three of Annie's sister's children, as well as four of their own. They worshipped at Mt. Zion Baptist Church on Emanuel Street in the west end of the city. Mrs. Jones is pictured with Jones Holmes, her six-year-old daughter. (Courtesy of Viola Holmes Green.)

MIDWIFE LUCINDA WRIGHT HUGHIE. ('Huger' is a spelling variation of her surname.) Lucinda poses for a picture during an excursion to Atlantic Beach. The beach, once designated for "colored only," is north of Myrtle Beach. Lucinda was the daughter of Rev. Abraham W. Wright, a Baptist minister. (Courtesy of Thelma H. Weathers.)

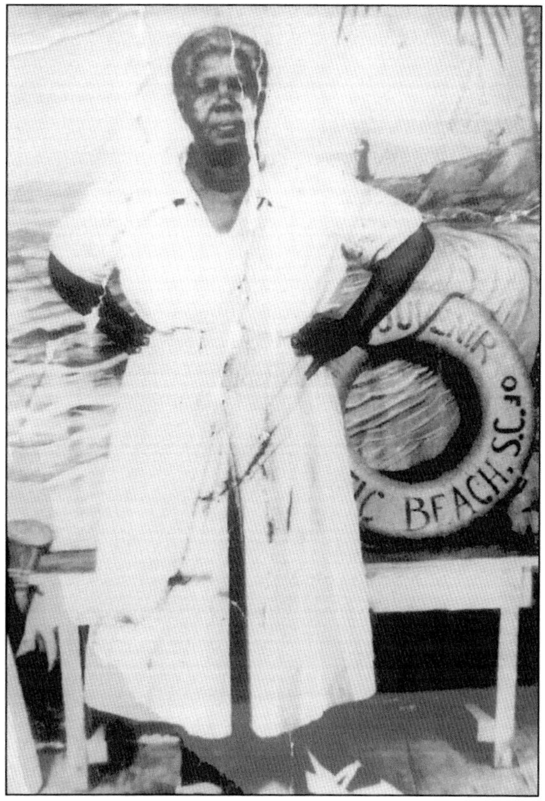

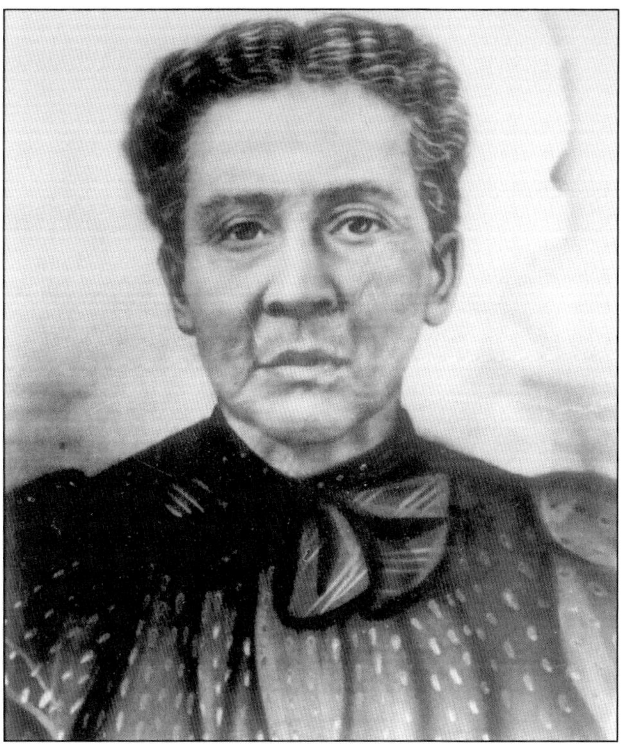

MIDWIFE JULIA WYATT, c. 1920. (Courtesy of Evelyn Washington Nesbitt.)

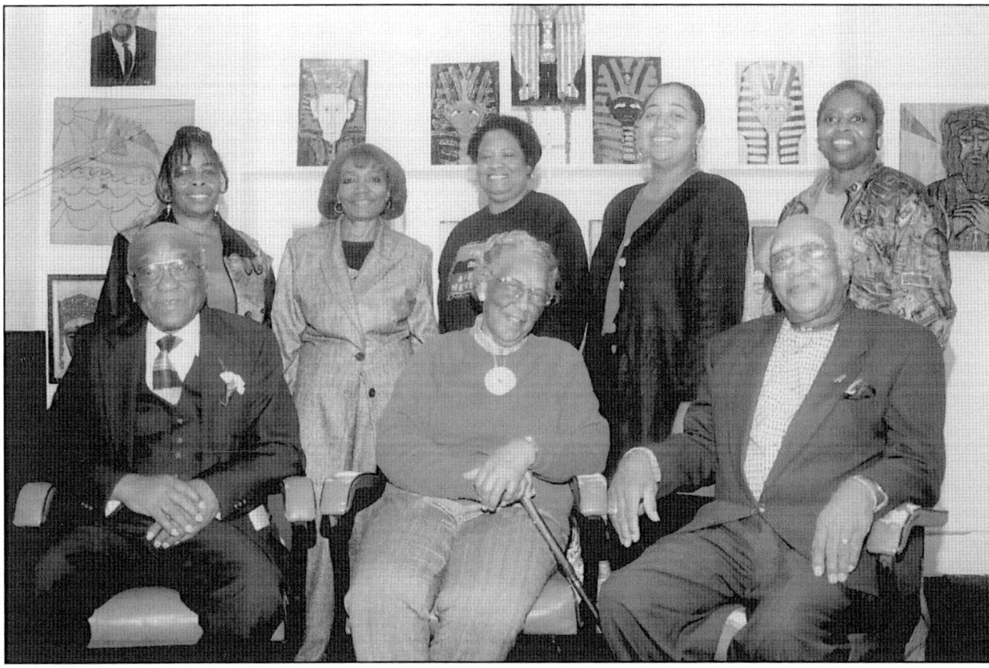

Committee for African-American History Observances Board Members (CAAHO). The board members of CAAHO operate the Dreamkeepers Art Center. Pictured in February 1998, from left to right, are the following: (front row) Nathan Brown, former Pawleys Island magistrate; Florida Yeldell, educator; and David H. Drayton, chairman; (back row) Jacqueline Ross (deceased); Lucille Josey; Thelma Spears, treasurer; Stacey Jemmott; and Lillie Jean Johnson, member of county council.

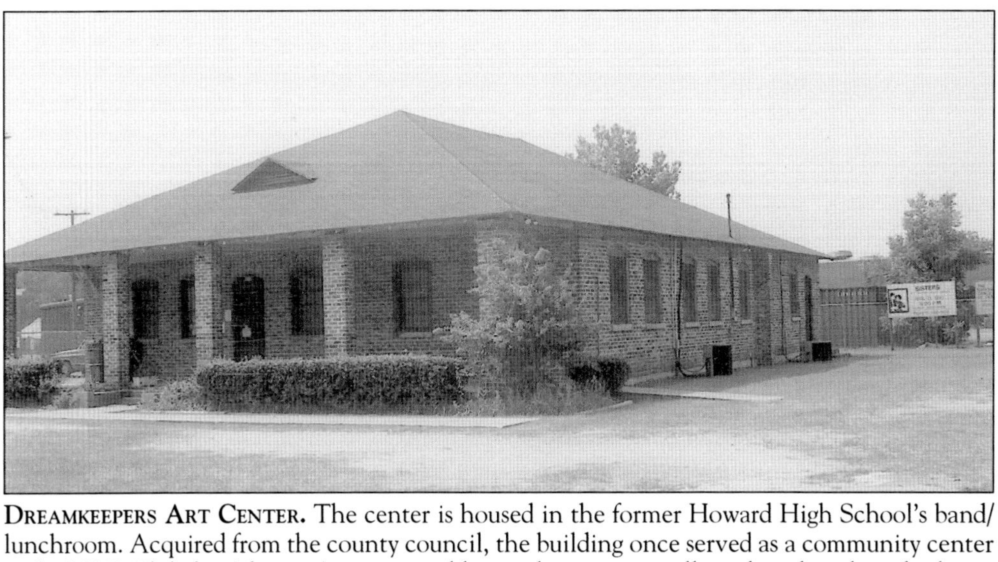

Dreamkeepers Art Center. The center is housed in the former Howard High School's band/lunchroom. Acquired from the county council, the building once served as a community center and a USO Club for African-American soldiers, who were not allowed in the white facilities. The center was constructed by Thomas Clark, a master carpenter and cabinetmaker.

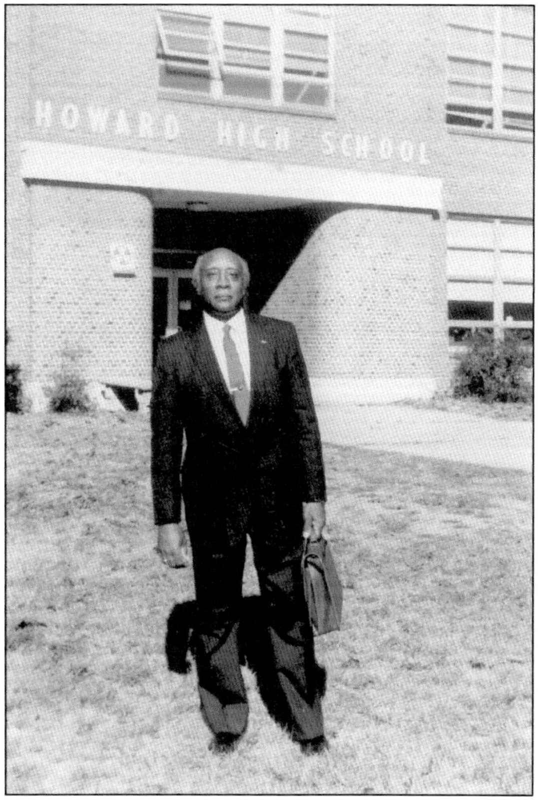

GATEKEEPER DAVID H. DRAYTON. David Drayton is the board chairman of the Committee on African-American History Observances. He provided educational leadership for the 40 years he spent with the Georgetown County School System. A retired principal of Howard High School, he served in that capacity until the school's close in 1983. He is an active steward of Bethel African Methodist Episcopal Church and serves on several boards within the city. (Courtesy of the Committee on African-American History Observances.)

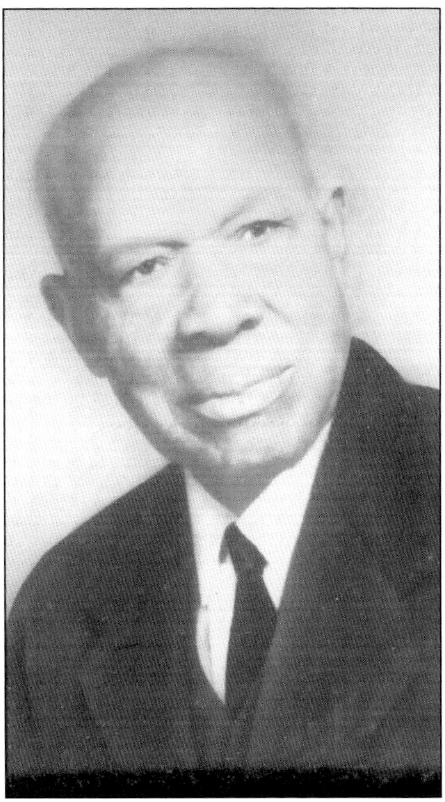

JOSEPH BROWN BECK (1873–1960). Joseph Beck was born in Abbeville, South Carolina. In 1889, he entered Allen University in Columbia, South Carolina; he graduated and went on to attend Hampton Institute in Hampton, Virginia. Even after being employed, it was not unusual for Beck to study during the summer months at such prestigious institutions as Harvard University in Boston, Massachusetts. In 1905, he came to Georgetown, where he married Ella Dunmore. He served as principal of Howard High School from 1907 until 1949, and his insistence on proper academic preparedness, particularly in fields of math and science, often put his students in advantageous positions at the colleges they later attended. A former student of Professor Beck, Frank O. Myers was one of the first African Americans to graduate from Harvard Medical School. Beck was a member of Bethel A.M.E. Church, where he served as a trustee. The professor had three sons, Joseph Elbert, Cornelius Jonathan, and Roswell Beck. His second wife was Leola Atkinson. The J.B. Beck Middle School is named in his honor.

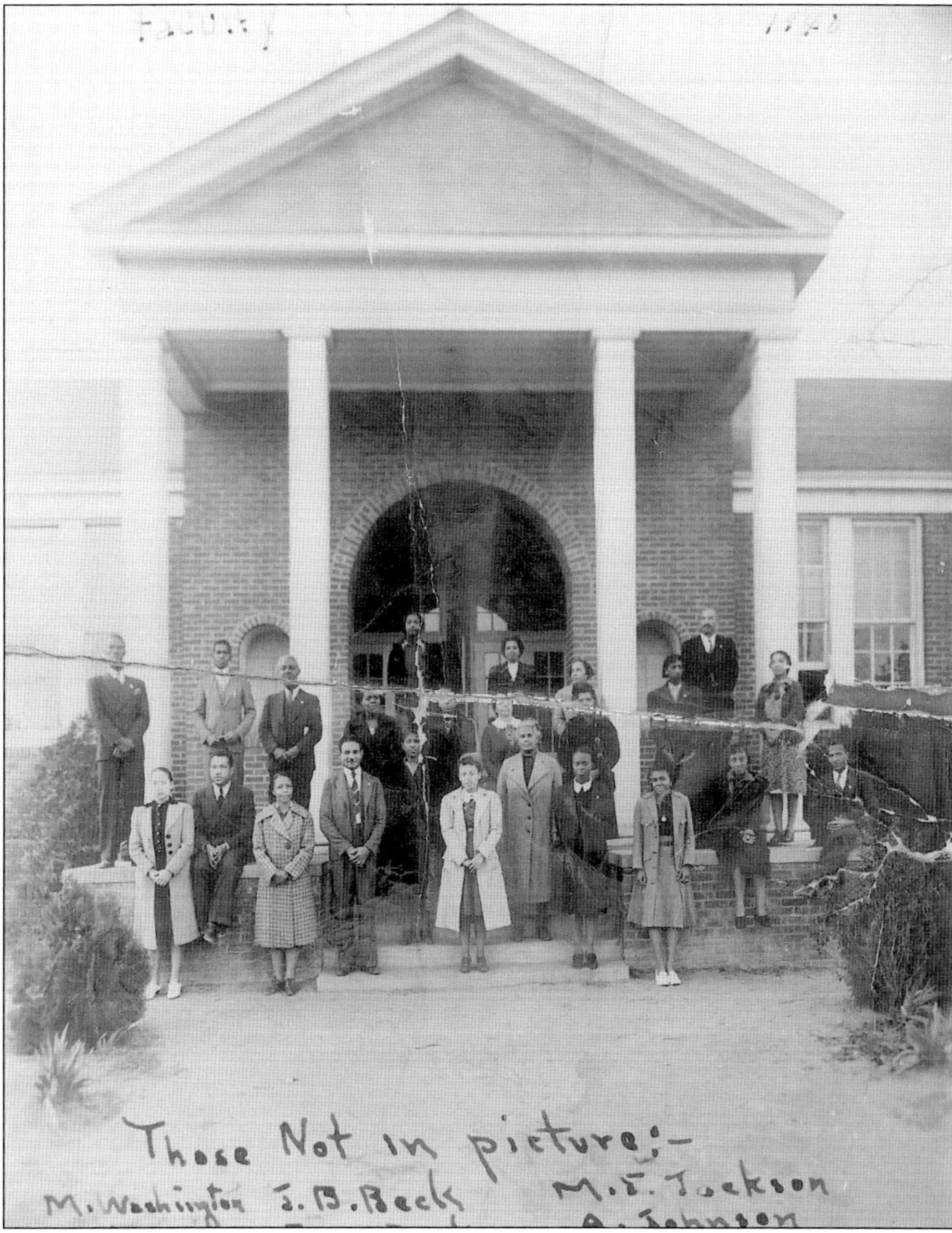

HOWARD HIGH SCHOOL FACULTY, 1939–1940. Pictured, from left to right, are the following: (front row) Camille Moses Barber, Roslyn Beck, Ms. Lawrence, James Prioleau, Carthemina Harper Eliza Howard, Minnie Kennedy, Rosalee Prioleau, and Mrs. Burbage; (second row) Charles Brown, unidentified, Professor Howard, Mrs. Thompson, unidentified, Ms. Ward, unidentified, unidentified, unidentified, unidentified, and Margaret Smith; (back row) unidentified, unidentified, Lillie Fraser, and Professor Boyd. Those not pictured are M. Washington, A.O. Turner, J.B. Beck, E.M. Beck, S.S. Brown, E.E. Holiday, B. Causer, M.E. Jackson, A. Johnson, B. Campbell, F.F. Wilds, J.E. Ward, and M. Robinson. (Courtesy of Minnie Kennedy.)

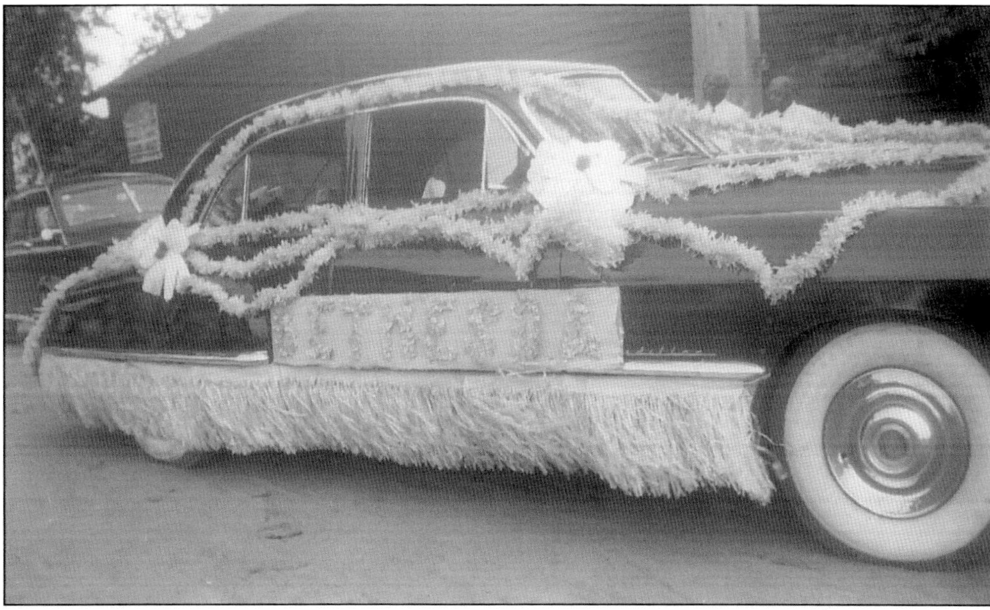

Howard Homecoming Parade. The Bethesda Missionary Baptist Church used the Wilds Funeral Home Cadillac to transport its representatives during the Howard High School Homecoming Parade in 1939. (Courtesy of Barbara W. Huell.)

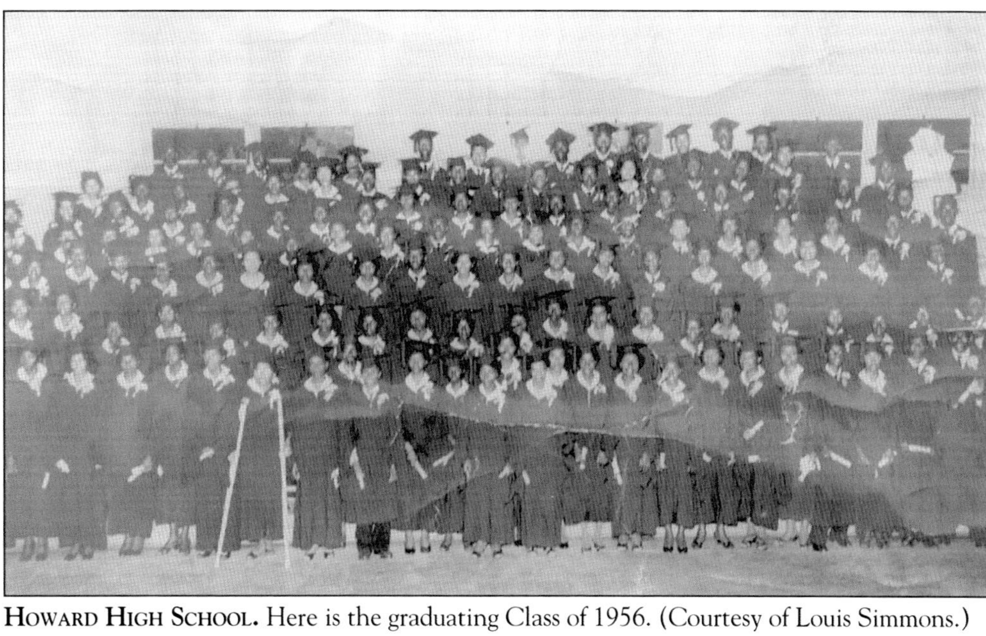

Howard High School. Here is the graduating Class of 1956. (Courtesy of Louis Simmons.)

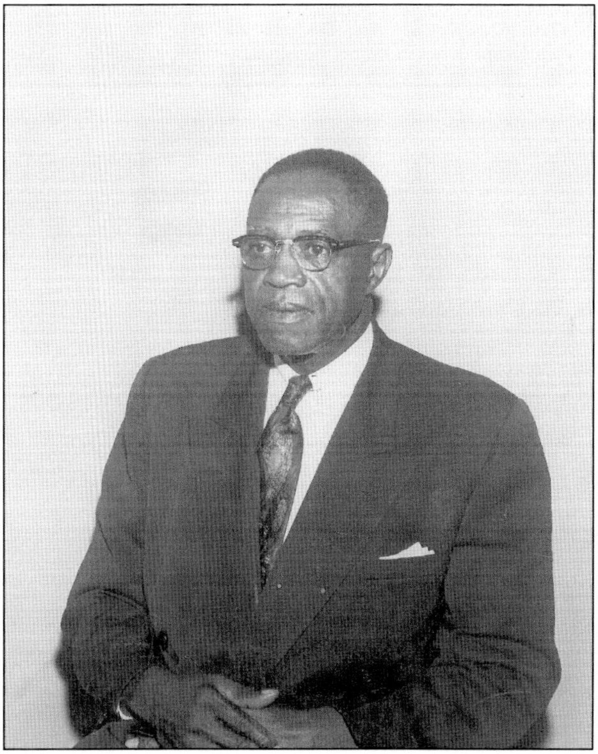

J.E. Smith, Howard High School. Mr. Smith served as the third principal for Howard. He was the former principal of Rosemary School in Andrews, South Carolina. (Courtesy of the Committee on African-American History Observances.)

Minnie Kennedy. Minnie Kennedy attended South Carolina State College at Orangeburg. In 1939, she returned to her native Georgetown, where she taught for one year at Howard High School. The following year she migrated to New York City. A retired early childhood education administrator, she is an active member of Prince George Episcopal Church and the Palmetto Project in Georgetown. Kennedy was born on Christmas Day in 1916 on the Friendfield Plantation of Bernard M. Baruch's Hobcaw Barony. Baruch named the barony "Hobcaw," the Indian word for "between the waters." The land lies on the southernmost part of the Waccamaw Neck peninsula. The first European settlement in North America may have been on the shores of Winyah at Hobcaw Barony. In 1526, Lucas Vasquez de Allyon led a Spanish fleet of six ships from Santo Domingo to North America. According to historian Paul Quattlebaum's book *The Land Called Chicora*, published in 1956, the 600 people on the expedition included Spaniards, Indians captured earlier on Pawleys Island, and black slaves from Haiti. The first landfall was at the mouth of the Cape Fear River in North Carolina. The Native American tribes known to be in the area included the Chicora, Pee Dee, Waccamaw, and Winyahs.

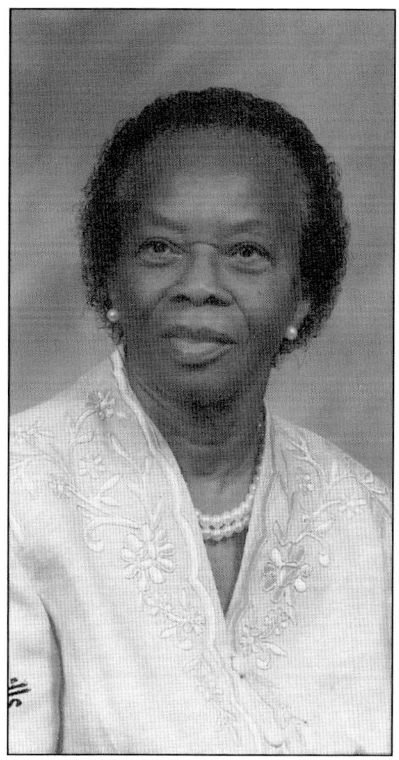

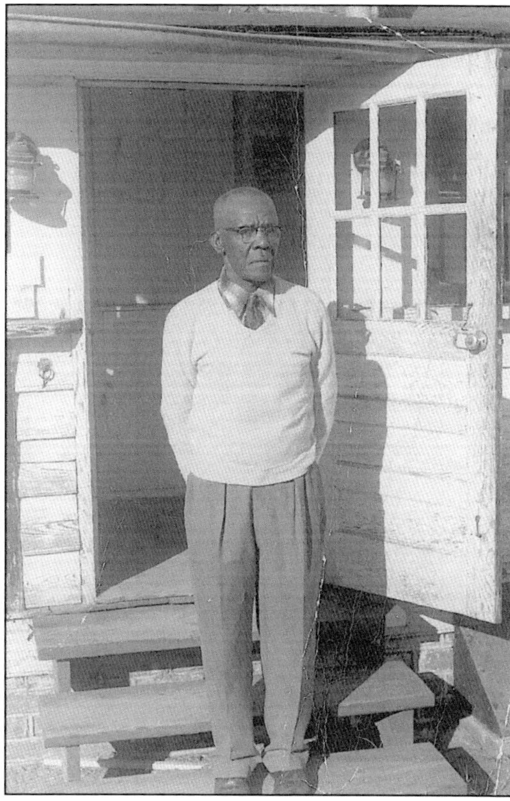

WILLIAM KENNEDY. William Kennedy was employed by Bernard Baruch of New York City for 30 years on the Hobcaw Barony property. This picture was taken in 1956. (Courtesy of Minnie Kennedy.)

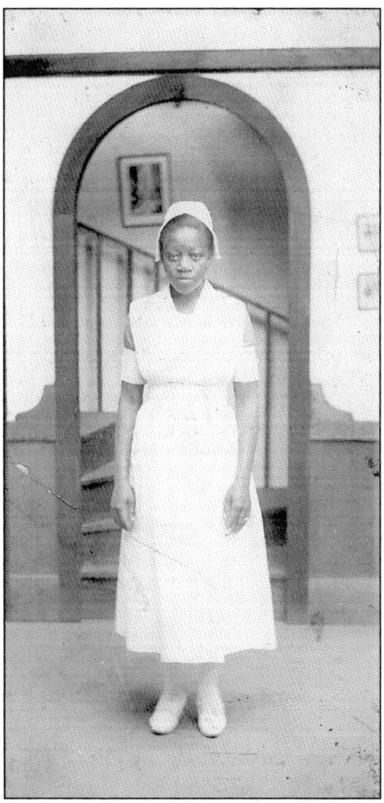

DOROTHY KENNEDY. Dorothy is seen here during her early nursing career in Columbia, South Carolina. She later married and relocated to Jackson, Tennessee. (Courtesy of Minnie Kennedy.)

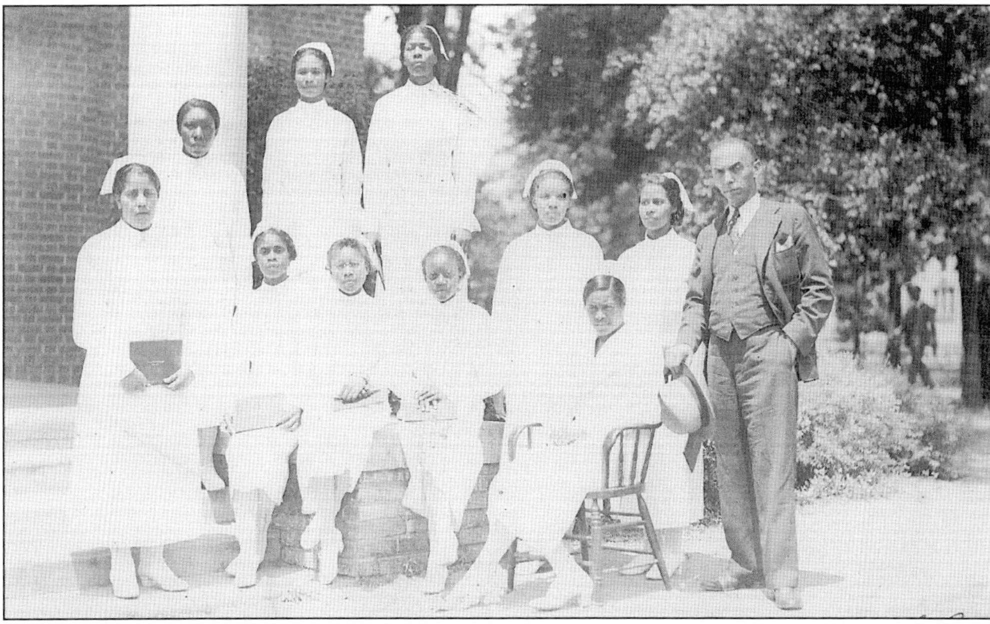

NURSING GRADUATES. Dorothy Kennedy is in the front row, fourth from left, amongst nursing training graduates at Waverly F. Hospital in Columbia, South Carolina, in 1937. (Courtesy of Minnie Kennedy.)

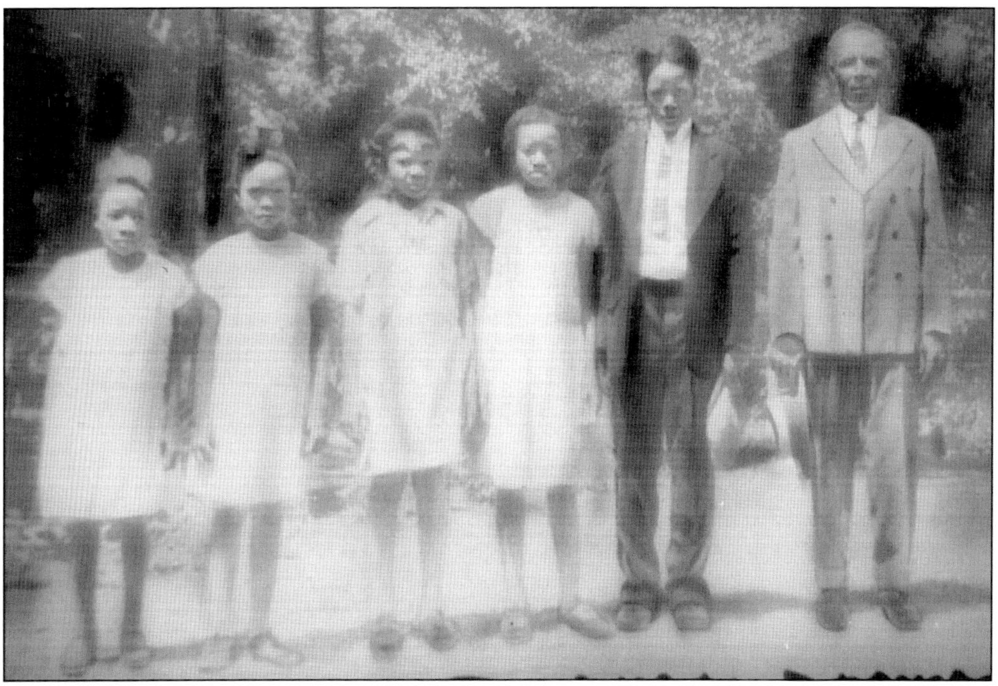

A FAMILY PORTRAIT. Minnie Kennedy's family are on Friendfield Plantation, which was purchased by Bernard M. Baruch during 1905. Pictured, from left to right, are Ida, Minnie, Frances, Dorothy, Edwin, and Minnie's father, William Kennedy. Missing from the photograph are Minnie's mother, Daisy, and sister Nettie. (Courtesy of Minnie Kennedy.)

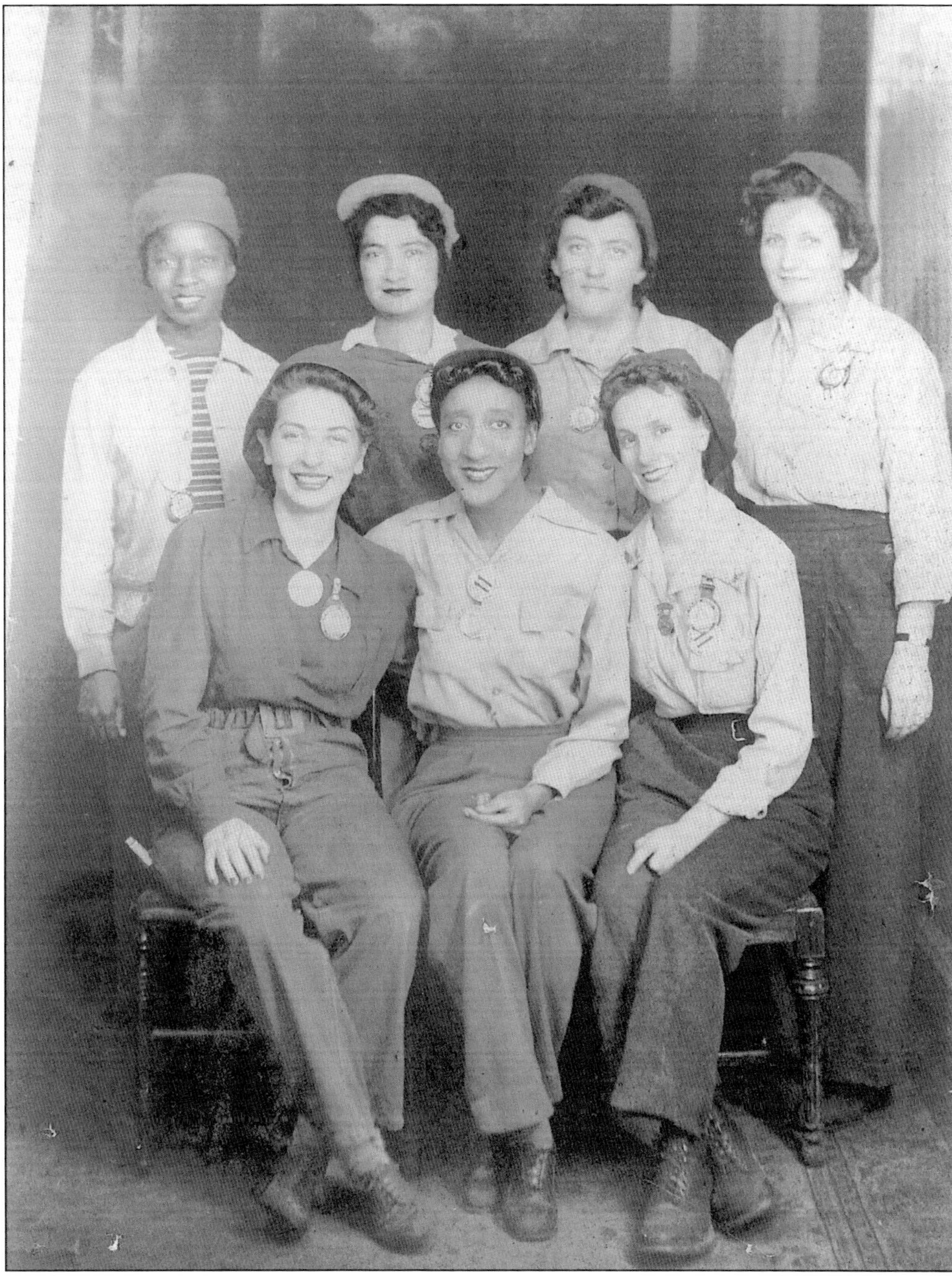

FEMALE SHIPFITTERS. Minnie Kennedy was among the female shipfitters at Brooklyn Navy Yard in New York during World War II. She is pictured in the back row, on the far left. (Courtesy of Minnie Kennedy.)

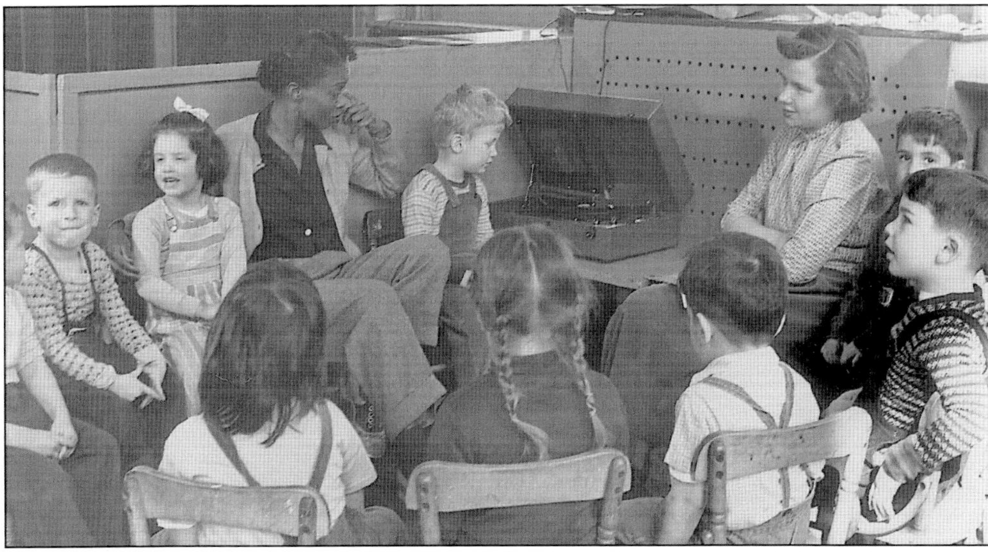

Stop, Look, and Listen. Minnie instructs preschoolers to listen and watch during her first paid teaching position at Rockword Nursery School, a predominately Jewish, private preschool in the Bronx, New York. Minnie began work in a graduate program in mathematics at Teachers College, Columbia University in New York City. Once she began her work with young children, she was so moved by the youngsters that she left the program and transferred to the Bank Street College for Education. She received a graduate degree in early childhood in 1947. (Courtesy of Minnie Kennedy.)

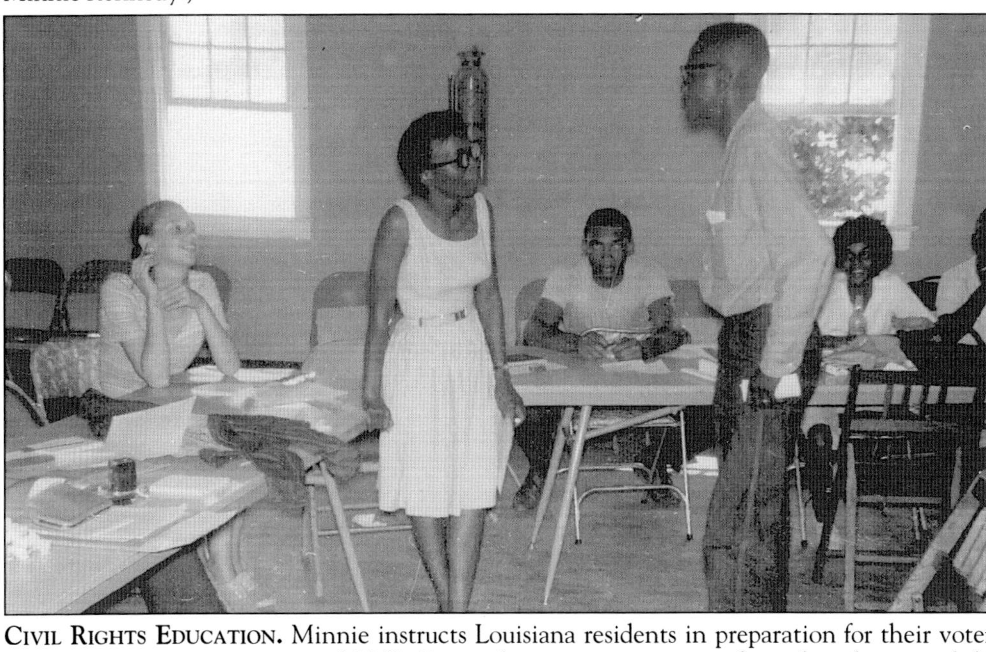

Civil Rights Education. Minnie instructs Louisiana residents in preparation for their voter registration exams in summer of 1963. During her summer vacation from the education field in New York, she served as a political activist. The civil rights project was sponsored by the Congress of Racial Equality (C.O.R.E.). African Americans were required to recite a large part of the Constitution, then they were taken to the courthouse to be tested. If they passed, they were allowed to register to vote. (Courtesy of Minnie Kennedy.)

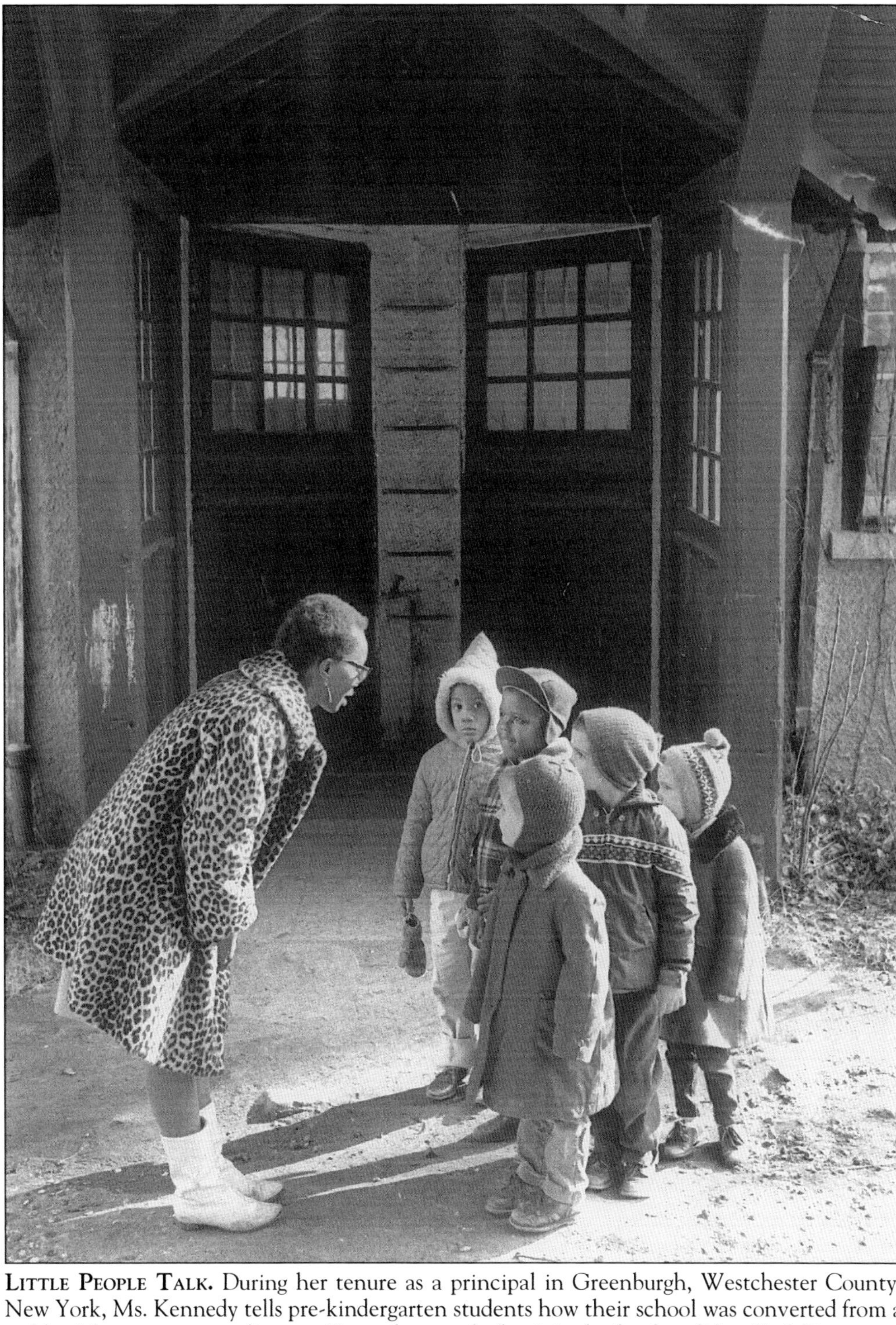

LITTLE PEOPLE TALK. During her tenure as a principal in Greenburgh, Westchester County, New York, Ms. Kennedy tells pre-kindergarten students how their school was converted from a stable. After two years as director, Kennedy was asked to join the faculty of New York University in 1966. (Courtesy of Minnie Kennedy.)

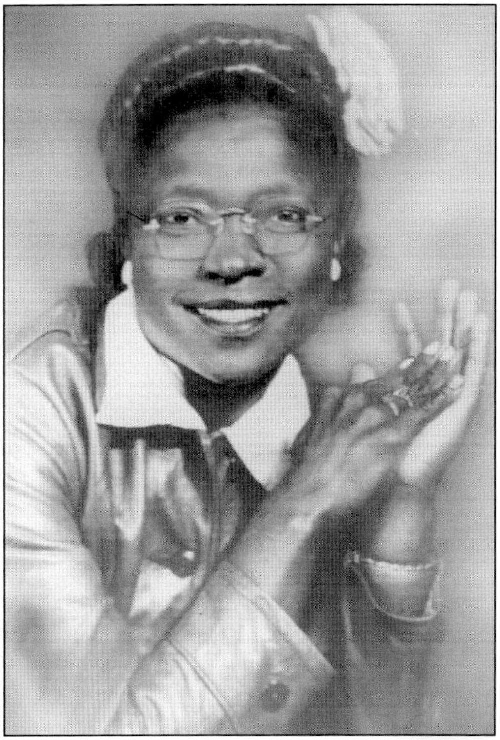

High School Beauty. Pictured here in 1942, Mary Green Covington completed her education at Howard High School. After receiving a Beauty and Culture certificate from the Fan-O-Lin School of Beauty Culture and working briefly in the field, she found the area too competitive—they were only paid $1.50 per head. Mary went on to work at Myrtle Beach, where she met James Covington of Bennettsville, South Carolina. The couple married and migrated to New Jersey. Mrs. Covington returned home in 1985, after a long career as a state facility corrections officer. She is a missionary leader of Bethel A.M.E. Church in Georgetown and is active on its Careteam Ministry and the Georgetown AIDS Task Force. (Courtesy of Mary Green Covington.)

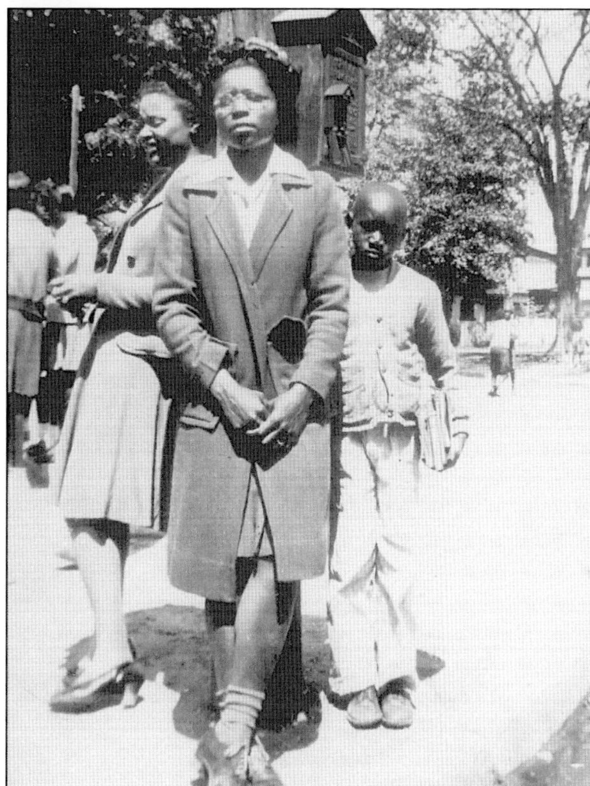

Campus Styling. Derotha Hemingway, Mary Green, and an unidentified boy are seen here on the Howard High School campus in 1943. (Courtesy of Mary Green Covington.)

CENTURIAN. Regina Ward Green (1866–1981) lived 115 years. She and her husband, Rev. David Green, resided on Hazard Plantation in the rural Oatland section, where she is buried. Her daughter, Regina Green Gamble, was married to John Henry Gamble, and the couple had six children: Jesse, Mary, William, James, John Jr., and Henry. Regina died during childbirth, and John Sr., a timber worker, was killed two years later when a tree fell on him. Grandmother Regina raised the six orphaned children. (Courtesy of Mary Green Covington.)

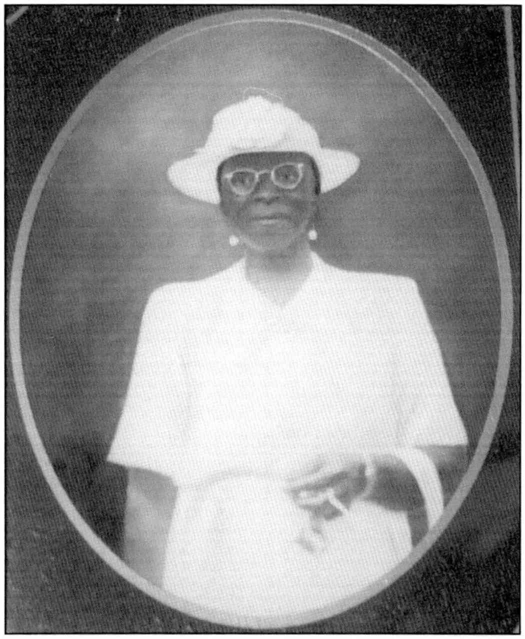

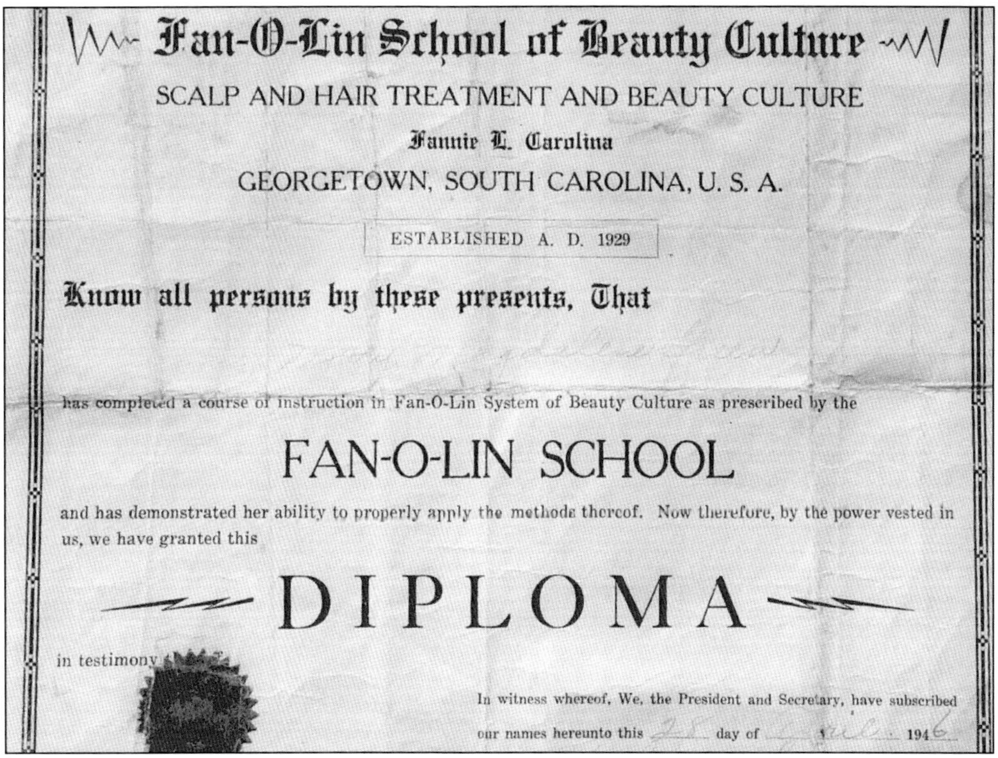

Fan-O-Lin School of Beauty Culture

SCALP AND HAIR TREATMENT AND BEAUTY CULTURE

Fannie L. Carolina

GEORGETOWN, SOUTH CAROLINA, U. S. A.

ESTABLISHED A. D. 1929

Know all persons by these presents, That

has completed a course of instruction in Fan-O-Lin System of Beauty Culture as prescribed by the

FAN-O-LIN SCHOOL

and has demonstrated her ability to properly apply the methods thereof. Now therefore, by the power vested in us, we have granted this

DIPLOMA

in testimony

In witness whereof, We, the President and Secretary, have subscribed our names hereunto this 28 day of April 1946

FAN-O-LIN BEAUTY CULTURE SCHOOL DIPLOMA CERTIFICATE. This certificate was awarded to Mary Magdalene Green on April 28, 1946. The school was owned and operated by Fanny Carolina, and the building formerly stood on the corner of Wood and Highmarket Streets, where the parking lot of Bethesda Missionary Baptist Church is now located. (Courtesy of Mary Green Covington.)

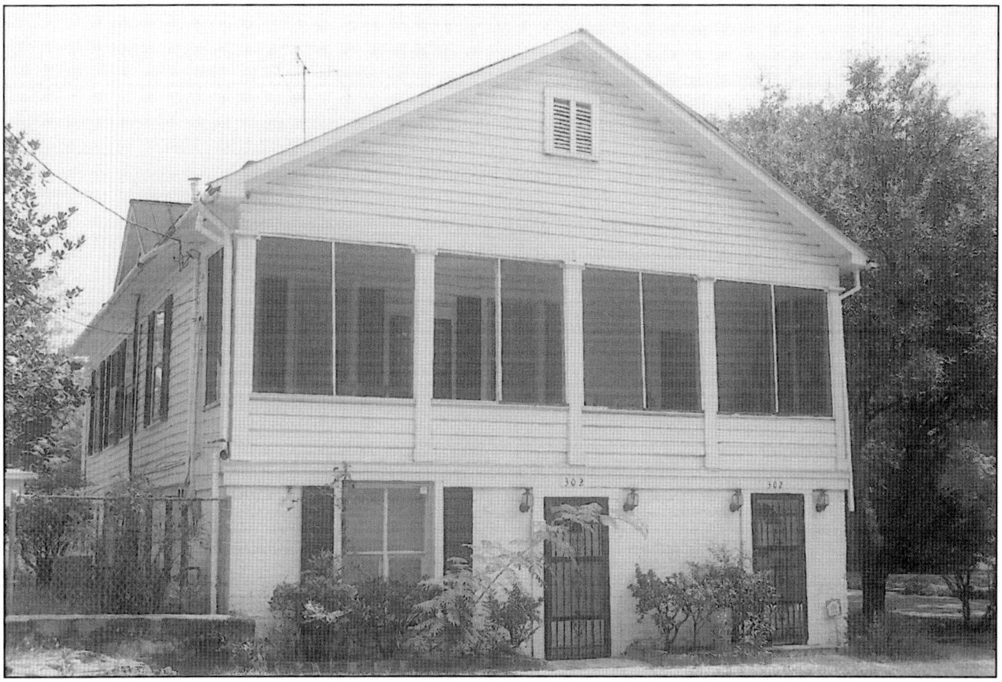

Singleton House. Located at 302 Front Street, this is the site of an old "powder house" used to store ammunition during colonial days. Singleton, an African-American seaman, bought the house and lived there with his family. The family maintains ownership.

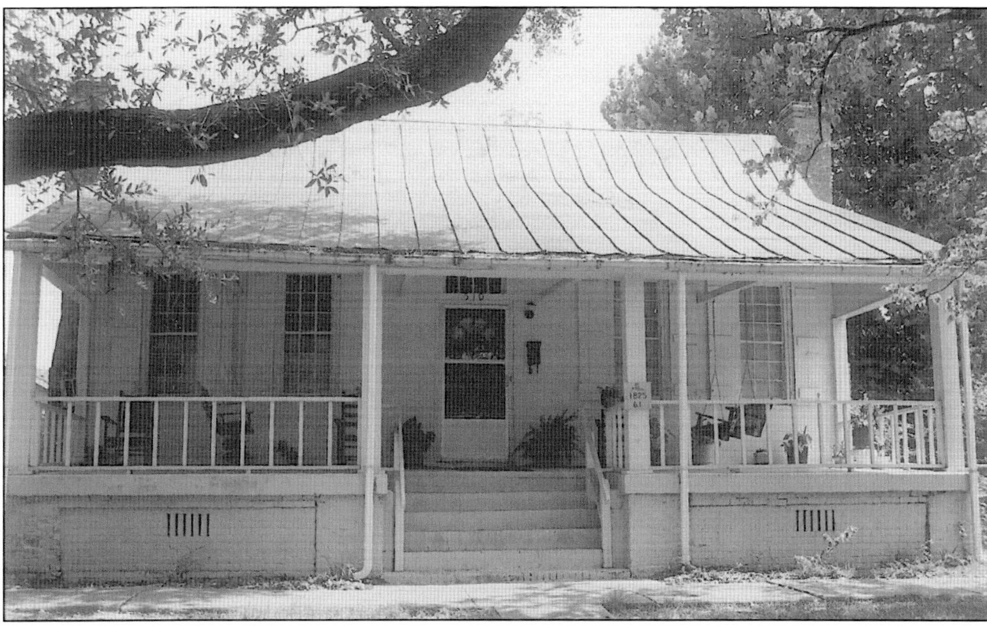

Thomas Jefferson House, c. 1825, at 510 High Market Street. Born after the turn of the century, Thomas Jefferson was widely recognized as the best tanner and shoemaker in the county. Jefferson was known to make good boots and even better conversation. His residence was known locally as "The Speed House."

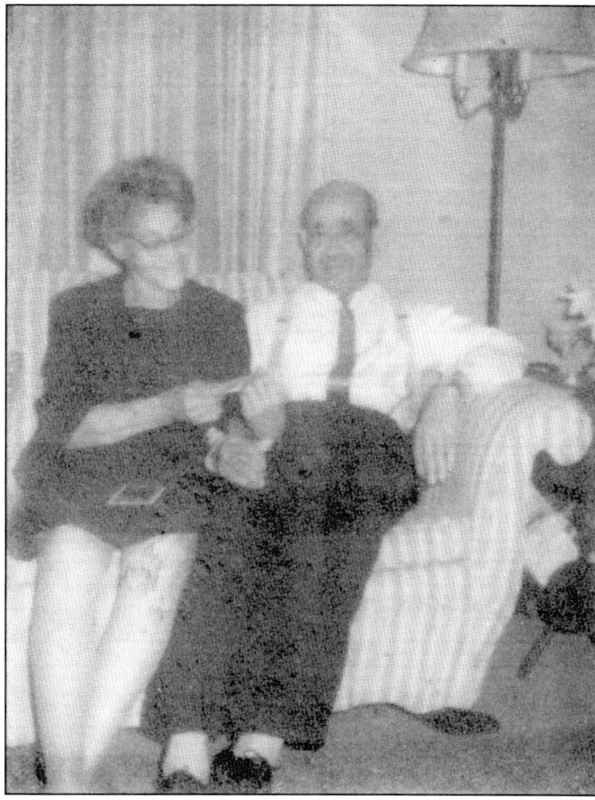

Dr. Ulysses Grant Teele and Mrs. Gladys Cardwell Teele. A 1913 graduate of Shaw University Leonard Medical School in Raleigh, North Carolina, Teele came to Georgetown in 1914 and practiced medicine in the county for 50 years. In the early days of his practice, Teele could be observed making rounds by bicycle or horse and buggy that was rented from mortician W.J. Wilds for county calls. Mrs. Teele, a Raleigh native, was a self-employed seamstress. Her clients included the Kaminski and Huntington families. The couple had no children, but became godparents to Clementine, the eldest daughter of Ernest and Leola Atkinson. (Courtesy of Clementine Atkinson Kelly.)

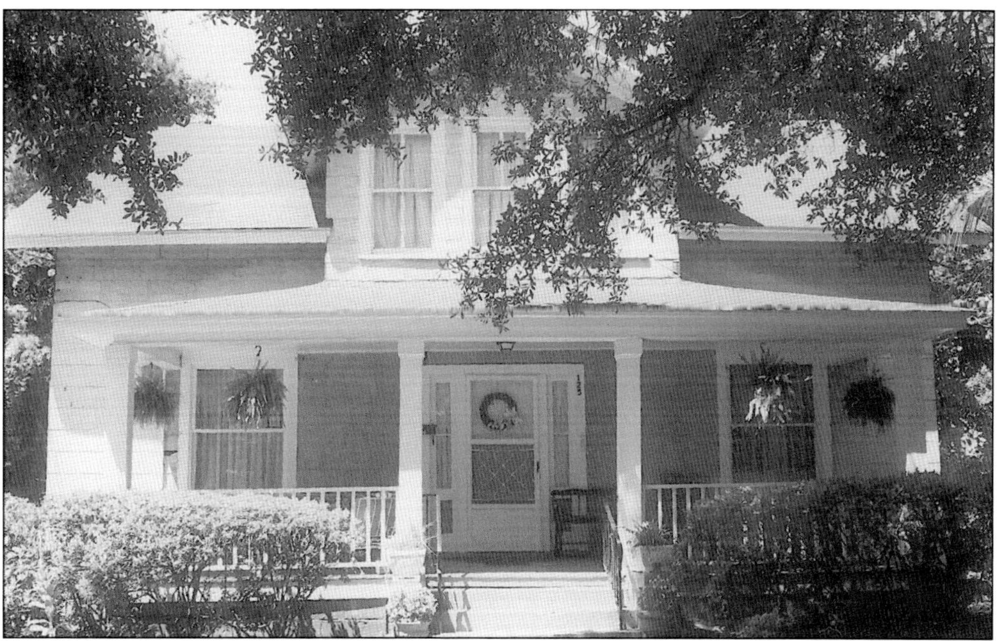

Teele House. Dr. U.G. Teele's house remains intact at 125 Wood Street in downtown Georgetown.

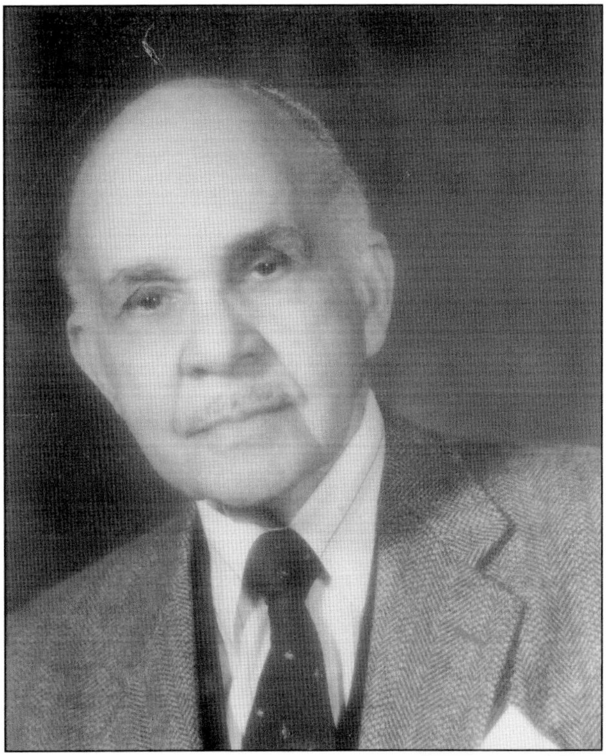

Cornelius Jonathan Beck, M.D. Dr. Beck was the third African-American physician to practice general medicine in Georgetown for 50 years. Long after most physicians had stopped making housecalls, Dr. Beck could be seen visiting patients at their homes. His medical building was located at 1007 Prince Street. In 1980, he became the first African American elected to the Georgetown County Council. (Courtesy of the Committee on African-American History Observances.)

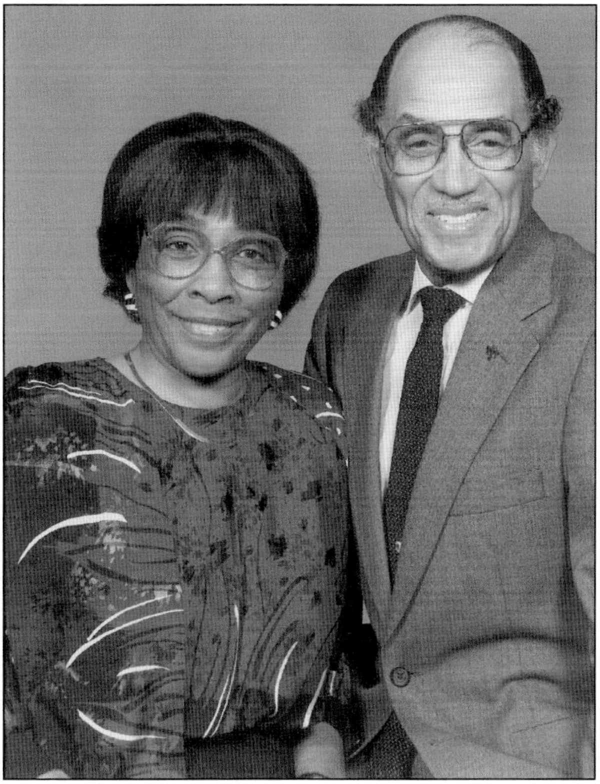

Hudson Enterprises. Samuel Bosket Hudson, the proprietor of Hudson Enterprises, provides real estate management consultant services. A 1943 graduate of the Tuskegee Institute in Alabama, he entered the United States Marine Corps, serving from 1944 to 1946. Sarah Hudson is a retired educator. Pictured are Samuel and Sarah, his wife of 55 years. (Courtesy of Mr. and Mrs. Samuel B. Hudson.)

LITTLE SAMMY. Sam Hudson stands unsupported in bloomers. He was probably two or three years old in this 1924 photograph. This was a luxury, as Sam didn't get another picture taken until he was in high school. (Courtesy of Samuel B. Hudson.)

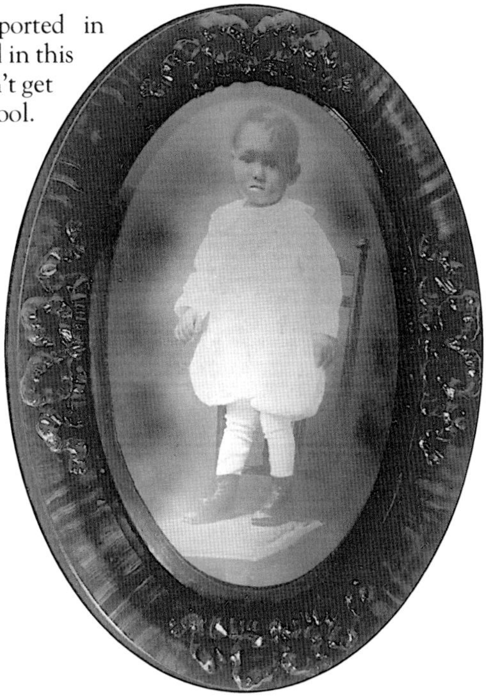

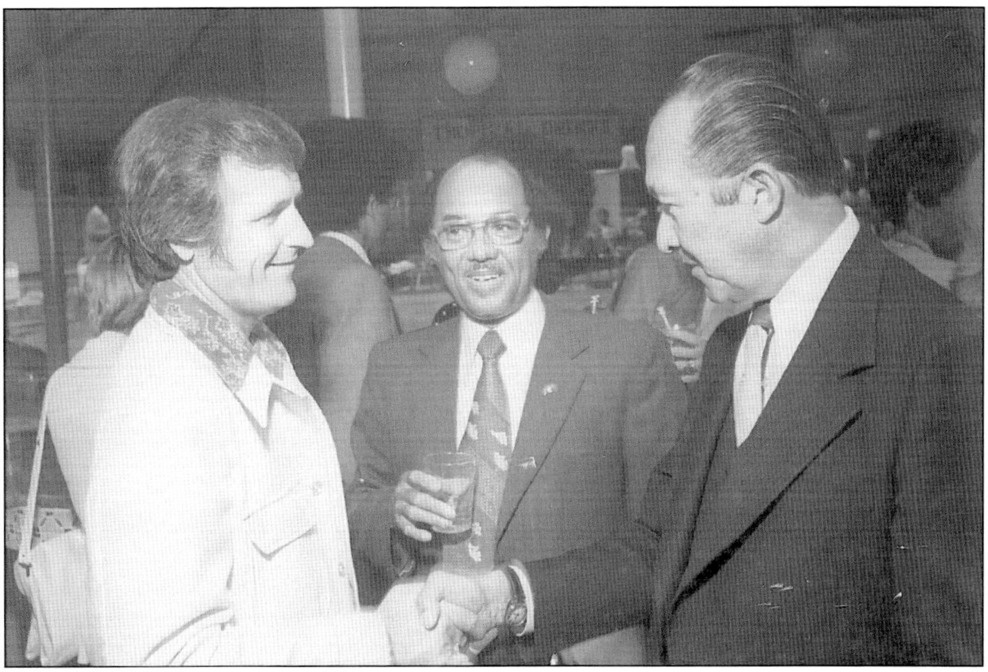

SAM B. HUDSON. Hudson served as the executive director for Waccamaw Economic Opportunity Council, Inc. (WEOC) from 1969 to 1981. Pictured, from left to right, are Dick Elliot, the present senator from Horry County; Sam Hudson; and unidentified national director of Office of Economic Opportunity, who served under President Lyndon B. Johnson. When this photo was taken, Elliot was the chairman of the board of the WEOC. (Courtesy of Samuel B. Hudson.)

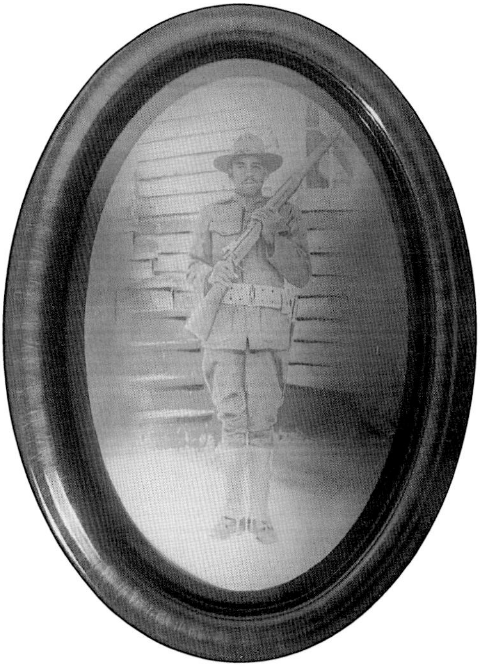

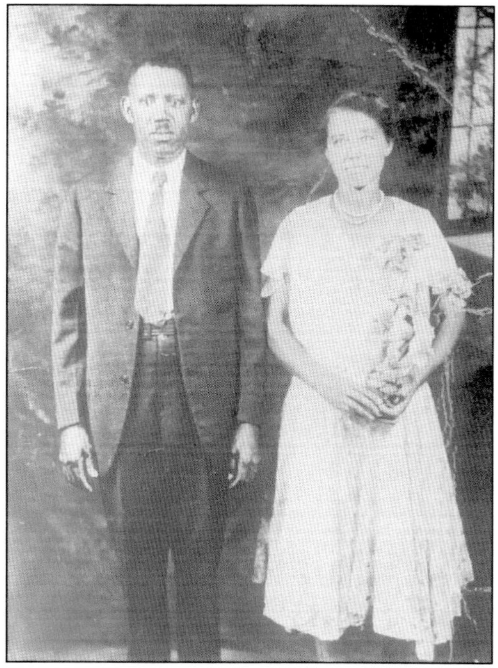

Left: **MELVIN ROGERS HUDSON (1897–1969).** Melvin R. Hudson was raised in Kent, a railroad town just nine miles west of the city towards Andrews. During WW I, Hudson was stationed in France. When he returned from overseas, Hudson received carpentry training in Andrews; he rode a bicycle six miles to work and back each day. He first worked (1926–1928) for Henry Norris, M.D., a surgeon who owned land on Waccamaw Neck, now known as Litchfield. *Right:* **MELVIN ROGERS HUDSON AND WILHEMINA "WILLIE" COMMANDER.** Melvin and Wilhemina are pictured here on their wedding day in 1919. The couple had three children: Samuel, Bernard, and Altamez. The family moved to 408 Wood Street in the city of Georgetown, next to the present Hudson residence. (Courtesy of Samuel B. Hudson.)

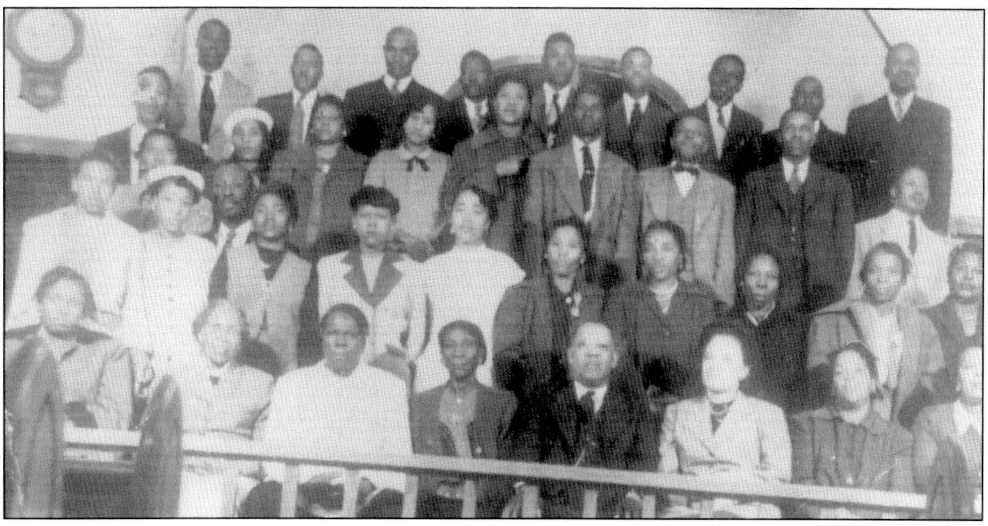

A CONGREGATIONAL POSE. Pictured in the center, over the sign, are Rev. and Mrs. Melvin Rogers Hudson and the Mt. Lebanon African Methodist Episcopal Church congregation of Andrews, South Carolina, on December 28, 1952. (Courtesy of Samuel B. Hudson.)

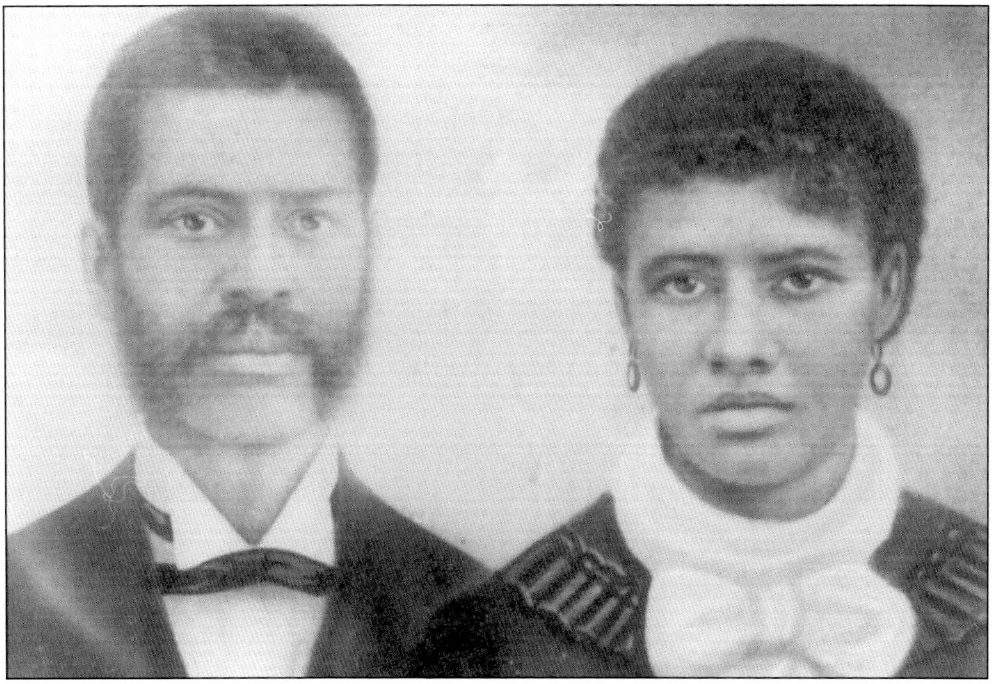

Reverend Meredith B. Hudson and His Wife, Nancy Bennett. This is a photograph of Sam Hudson's paternal grandparents. (Courtesy of Samuel B. Hudson.)

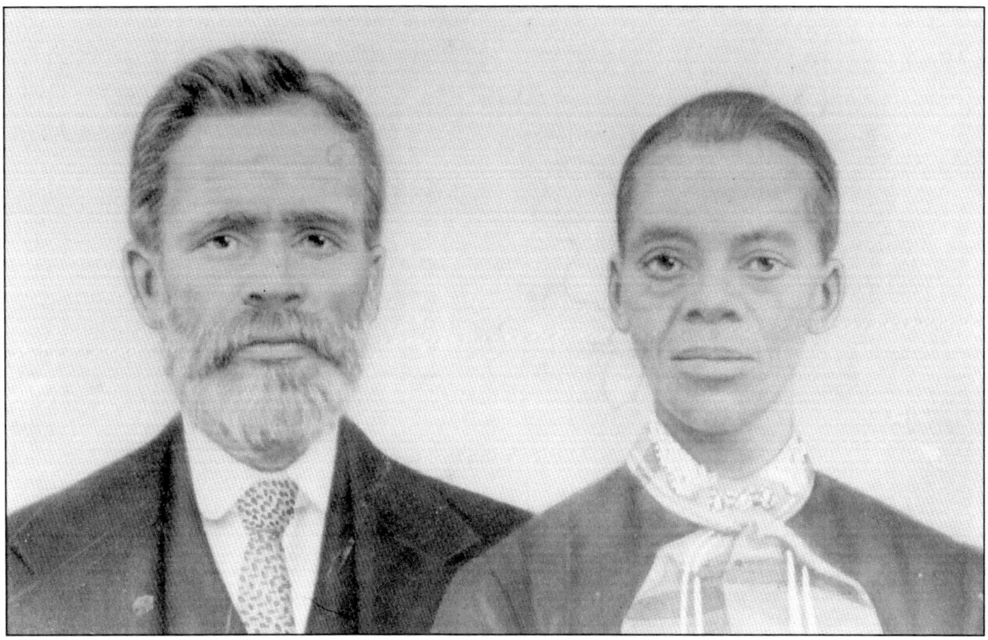

Vincent Hudson and His Wife, Mary Morning Fillmore. This is a photograph of Sam Hudson's paternal great-grandparents from the Kent area, near Andrews. (Courtesy of Samuel B. Hudson.)

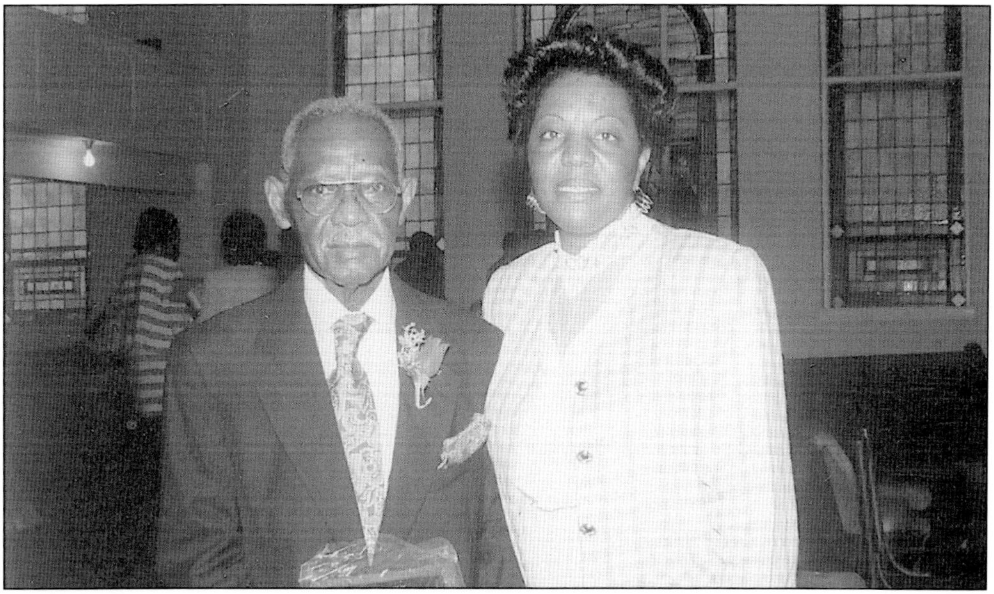

A GRATE HERITAGE. Deacon Samuel King Grate (1912–1994) and Mercedes G. Munnerlyn, his daughter, are pictured here during a commemorative ceremony in his honor. Samuel Grate, having served in World War II, returned and began a lifelong career as a brick mason. He played a significant role in the construction of major schools, hospitals, and hotels in the Carolinas and New York City. Many families enjoy houses built by Sam Grate, and many churches carry cornerstones thanks to Sam Grate. In later years, he taught masonry at Horry-Georgetown Technical College—Georgetown Campus. He was also the vice chairman of the deacon board at Bethesda Baptist Church and an active member of Maceo Lodge #50-Free and Accepted Masons for over 40 years. He and his wife, Juanita, were blessed with three daughters: Daniese Gibbs of New Jersey, Mercedes Munnerlyn of Georgetown, and Alpha Omega of Charlotte, North Carolina.

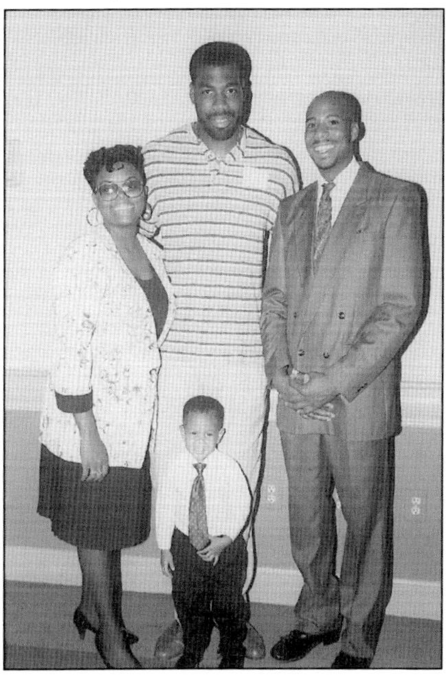

COUSINS. Shondell Munnerlyn Nash (the daughter of Mercedes Munnerlyn) is pictured with her cousin, Mark Bryant, a basketball player now with the Houston Rockets, and Demetric and Ahmez Nash, her husband and son, during the King family reunion of 1992.

SWEETHEARTS. Evelyn and James Grate are pictured in 1944. The couple has a daughter, Cherille Grate Gregg. James is the brother of Samuel Gate.

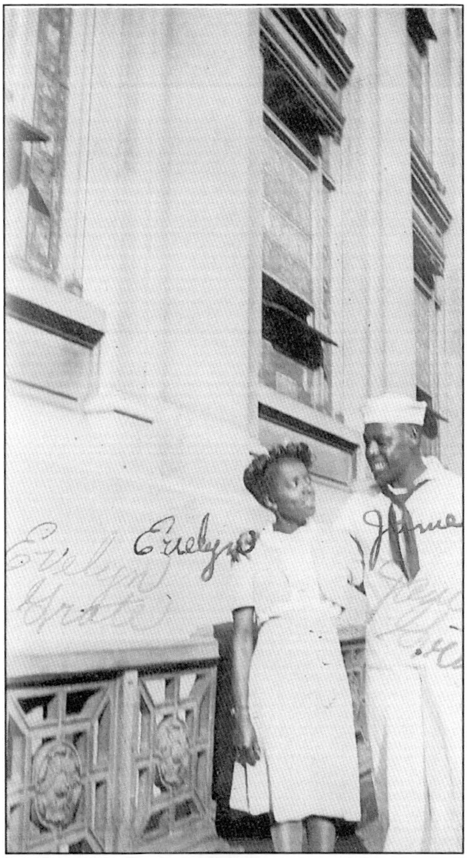

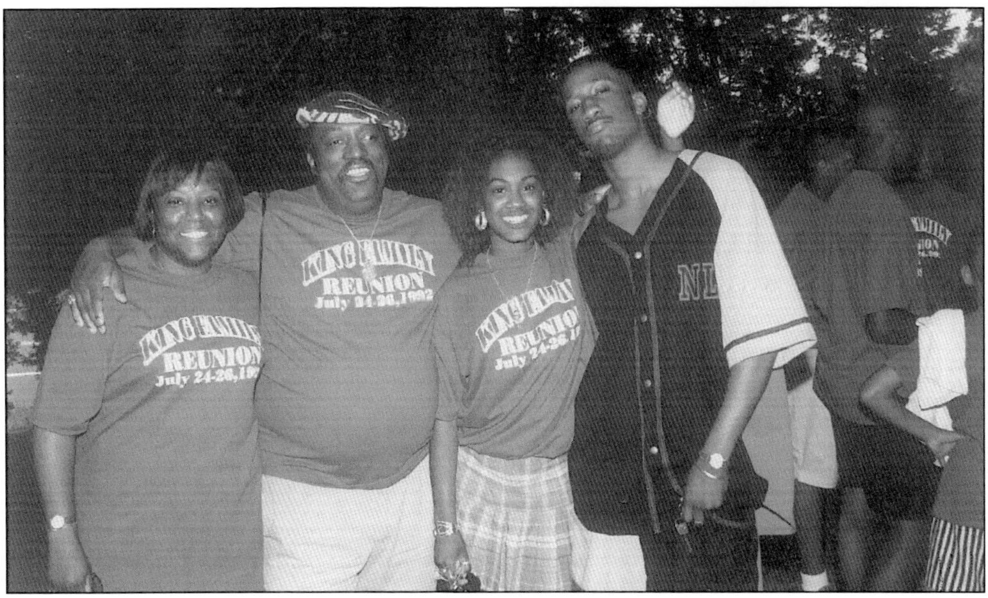

A GRATE TRADITION. The Grate Gregg family poses for a picture during a family reunion. From left to right are Cherille Grate Gregg, David Gregg, and their children, Nikajah and Omari. All reside in New York City.

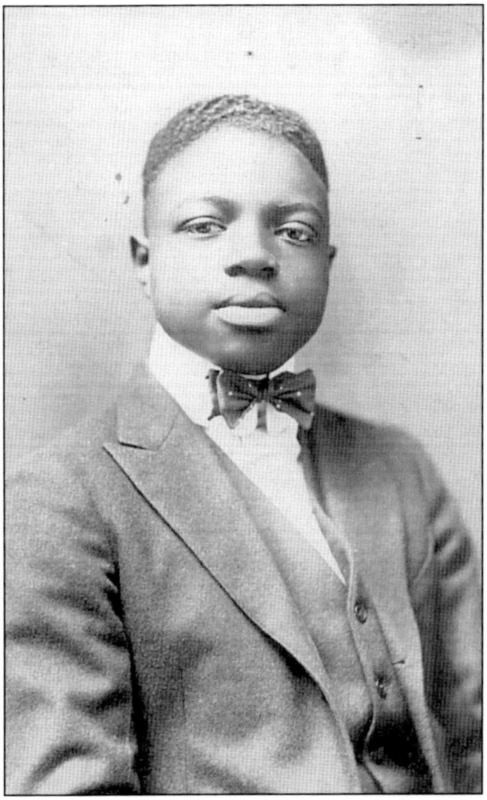

WILLIAM JAMES WILDS JR. (1902–1982). William Jr. inherited the Wilds Funeral Home business upon his father's demise in 1939. The father operated a furniture store in 1903 and went on to establish the funeral business in 1911. The son is pictured during his tenth-grade year at Howard High School, c. 1920. In 1982, the establishment was passed on to his daughter, Barbara W. Huell.

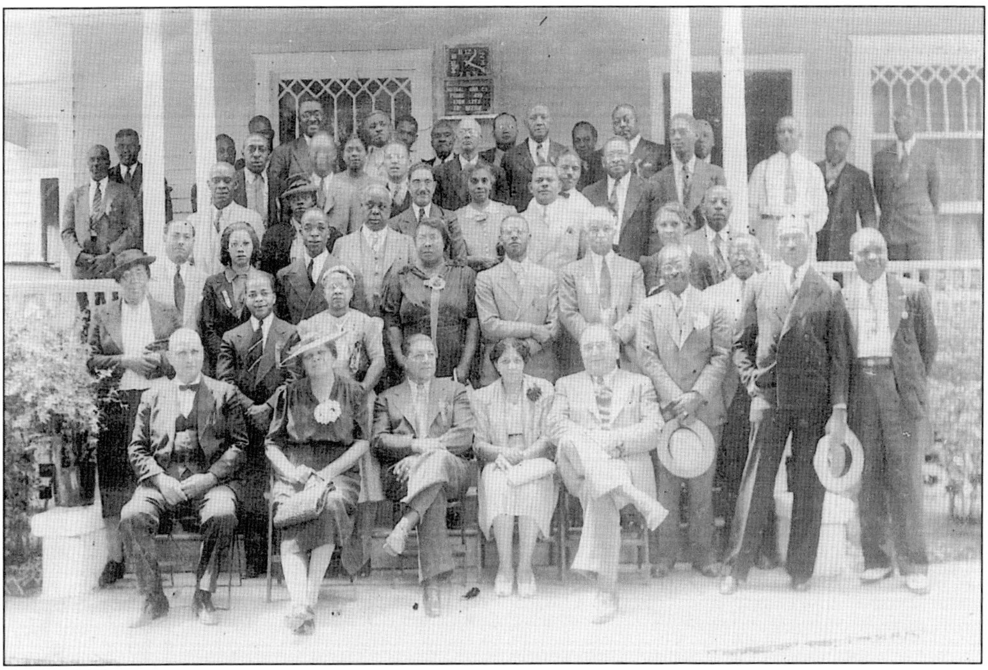

SOUTH CAROLINA FUNERAL DIRECTORS ASSOCIATION. This association meeting occurred in Sumter, South Carolina, in 1945. Wilds Jr. is standing in the front row, on the far right.

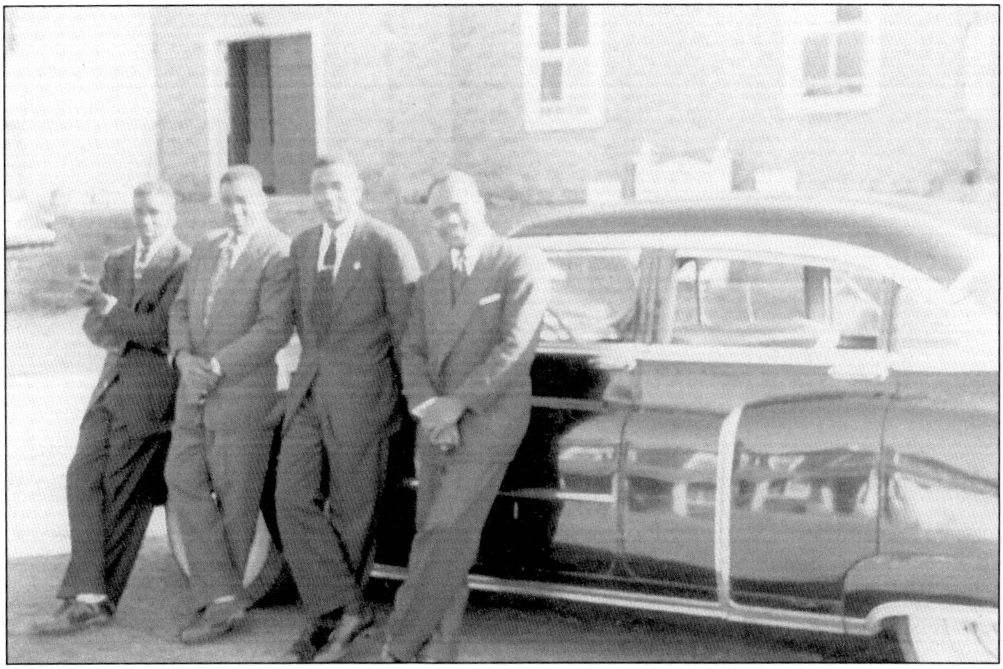

WILDS STAFF. The staff of the Wilds Funeral Home in 1939, from left to right, are unidentified, Willie Deas, Joseph Smalls, and Harold Heyward.

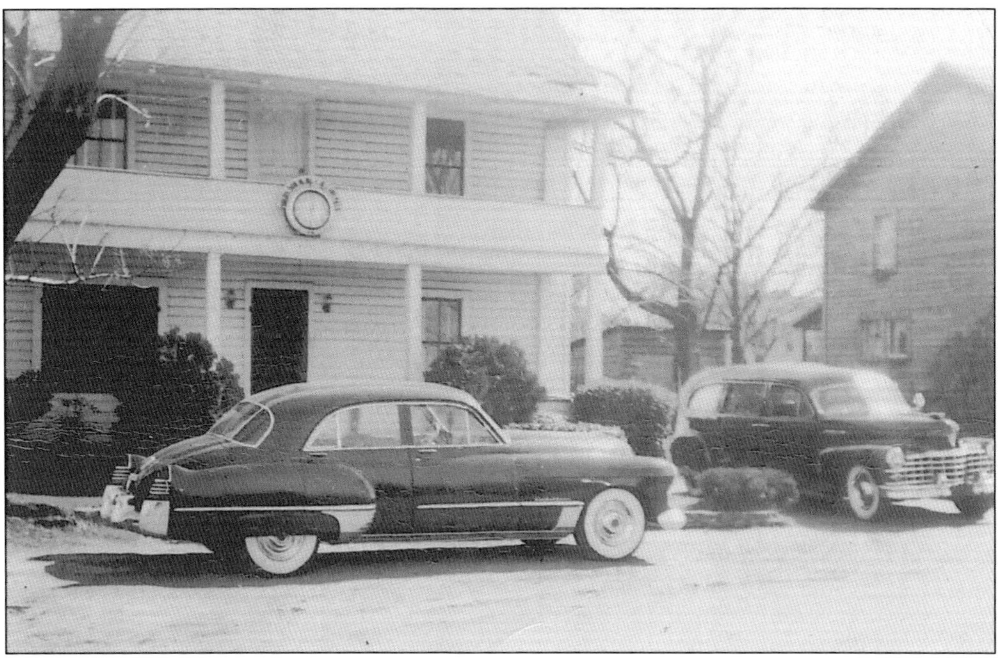

WILDS FUNERAL HOME. The Wilds establishment on Merriman Road is seen here after its first remodeling in 1950. The big clock served as a town clock for the west end community.

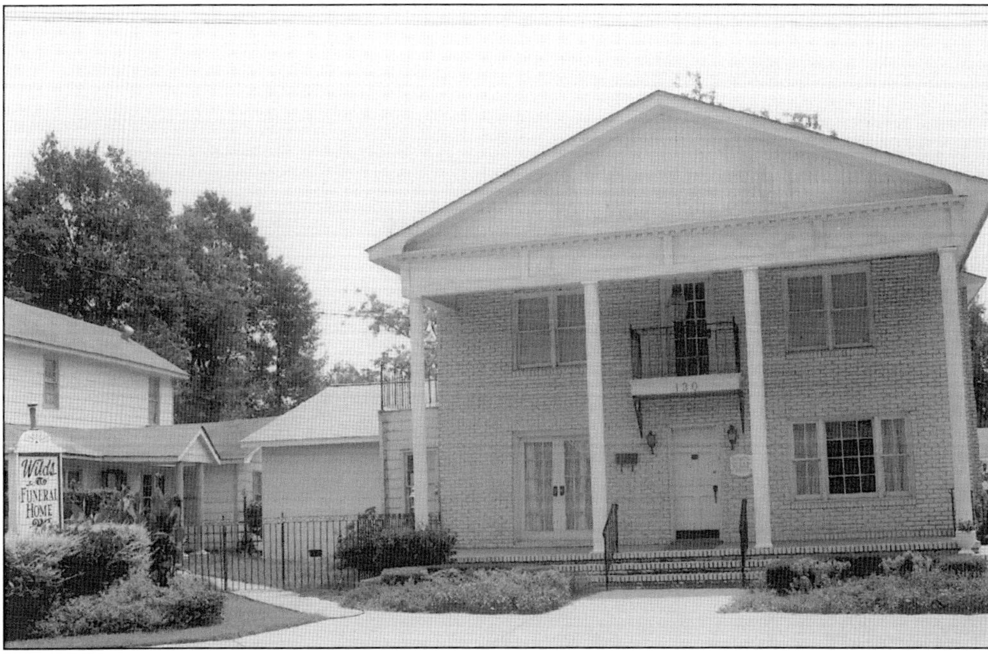

WILDS FUNERAL HOME TODAY.

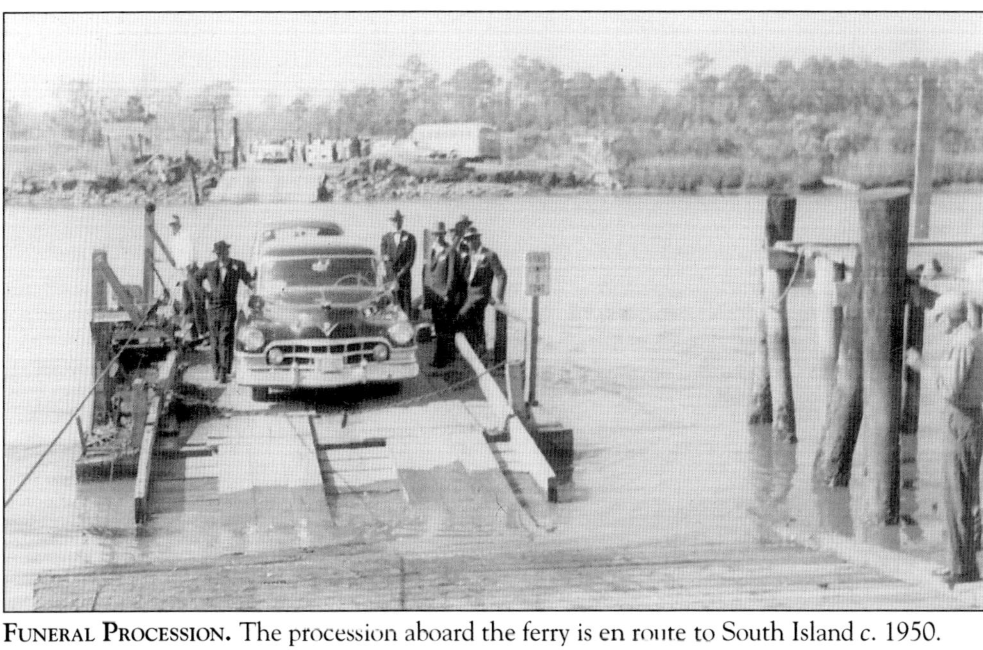

FUNERAL PROCESSION. The procession aboard the ferry is en route to South Island c. 1950.

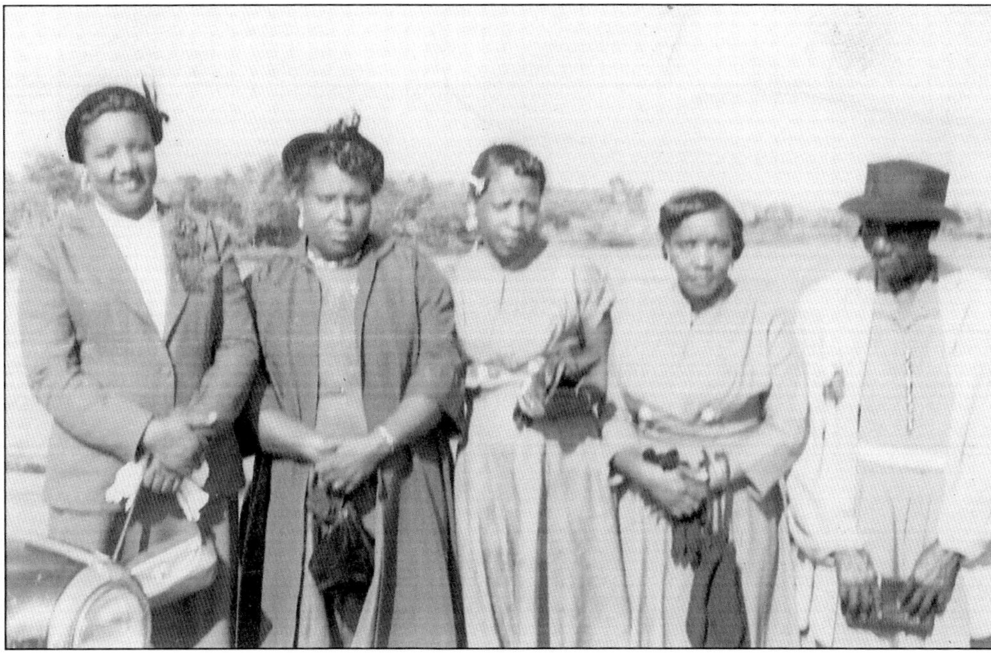

Funeral Procession. These female funeral attendants are pictured aboard a ferry to South Island, *c.* 1950s. (Courtesy Barbara W. Huell.)

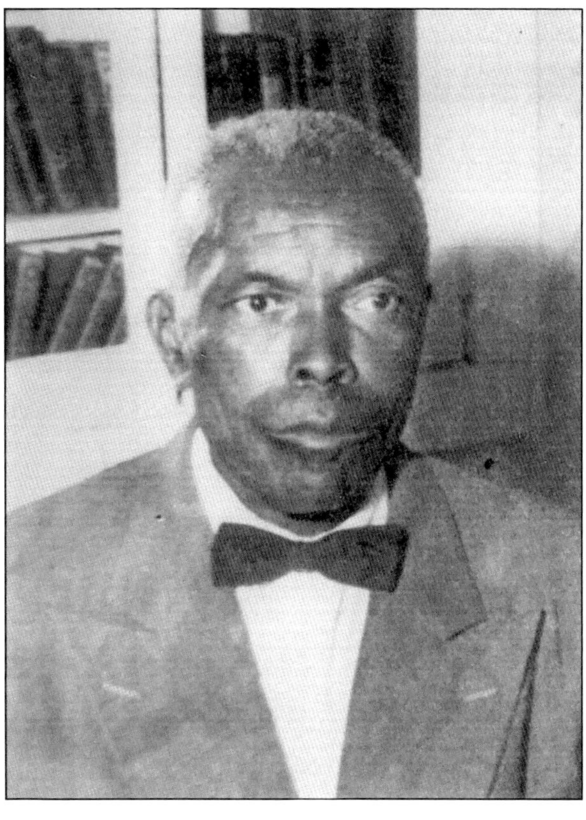

The Progressive Democratic Party. Glennie S. Porcher (1888–1962) founded the first Georgetown Chapter of the National Association for the Advancement of Colored People in 1939. It was said that he came "to resurrect the sleeping Georgetown." He worked to organize the group, whose goal was to encourage African Americans to vote and participate fully in the Democratic elections. Porcher and leaders like Reverend J.E. Prioleau and Alex Alford addressed many state and local issues.

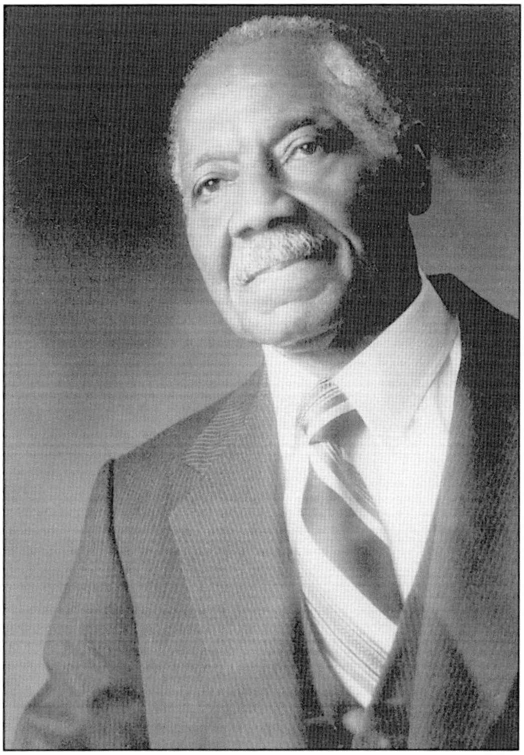

Political Activist. Reverend William Ruben Green Sr. was a member of the election commission and the first African-American vice president of the Georgetown Democratic Party. During the late 1930s, he assumed a leadership role in the community to assist others to successfully complete the "Reading Process," a requirement to obtain a voter registration card. In 1975, Green became an ordained minister and the associate pastor of Cumberland A.M.E. Church.

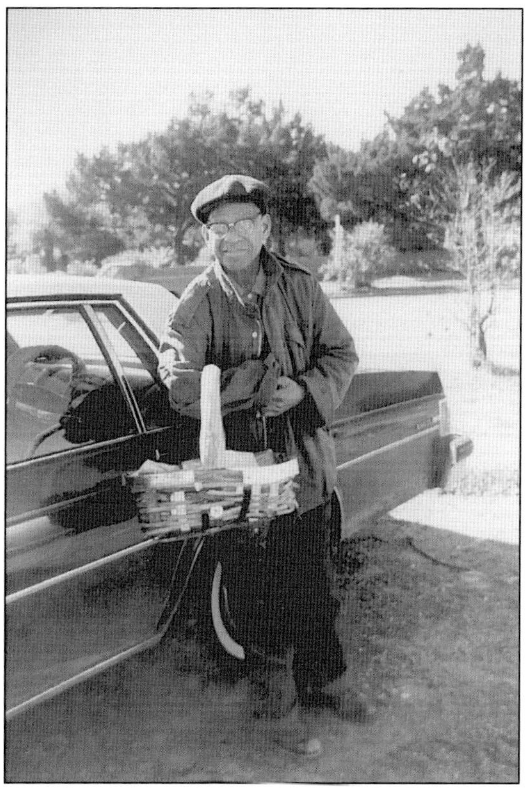

Alexander Alford. Alex Alford was appointed to the Georgetown Voter Registration Board for 15 years. Known for his success in African-American voter registration, this political activist was instrumental in getting the west end annexed into the city limits. This would prove to be a significant political strategy, as the west end area was a predominantly African-American community. "Peanut Alec" was a modest, committed civil rights activist. The former G Street was recently renamed Alex Alford Avenue in tribute to his significant community organizing abilities.

CIVIL RIGHTS ACTIVIST. Houston Parson (1919–1988), a longshoreman by profession, successfully organized African-American citizens to purchase buses and hire their own drivers to transport their children to school in 1950. In 1970, he sought and won election to the Georgetown County School Board. He was the first African American to hold such a position since Reconstruction.

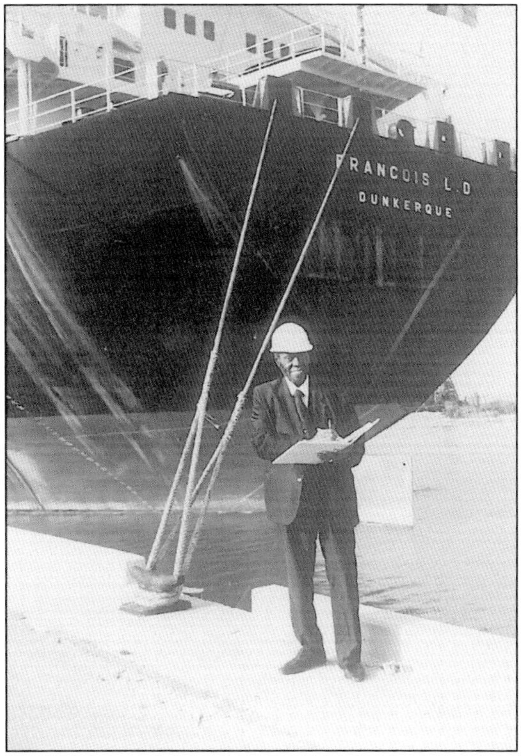

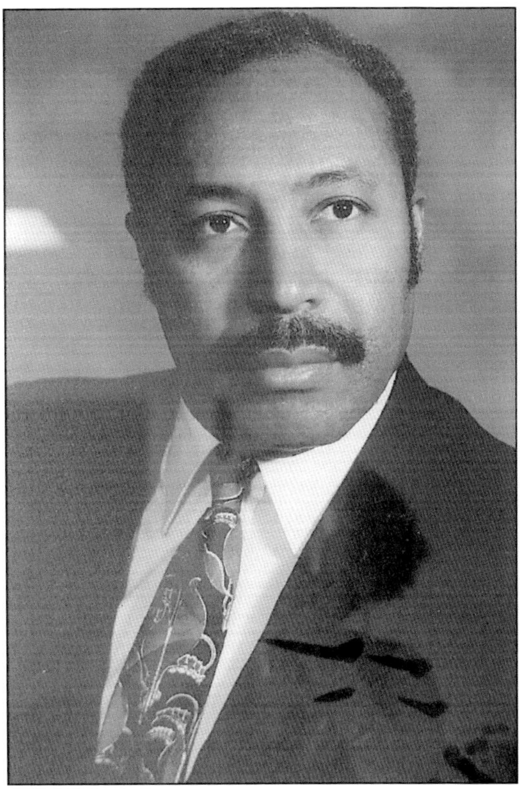

SOUL SAVING STATION. Reverend Richard S. Watkins is the founder and pastor of Soul Saving Station Church. As the chairman of the Committee for Single Member Districts, Reverend Watkins was instrumental in changing the Georgetown County electoral system from "At Large" to "Single Member District" elections. This gave rise to a greater representation of African Americans by African Americans. The church has played a significant role in the empowerment of African-American males and families through its outreach ministry, which addresses such issues as absent fatherhood, incarceration, and substance abuse.

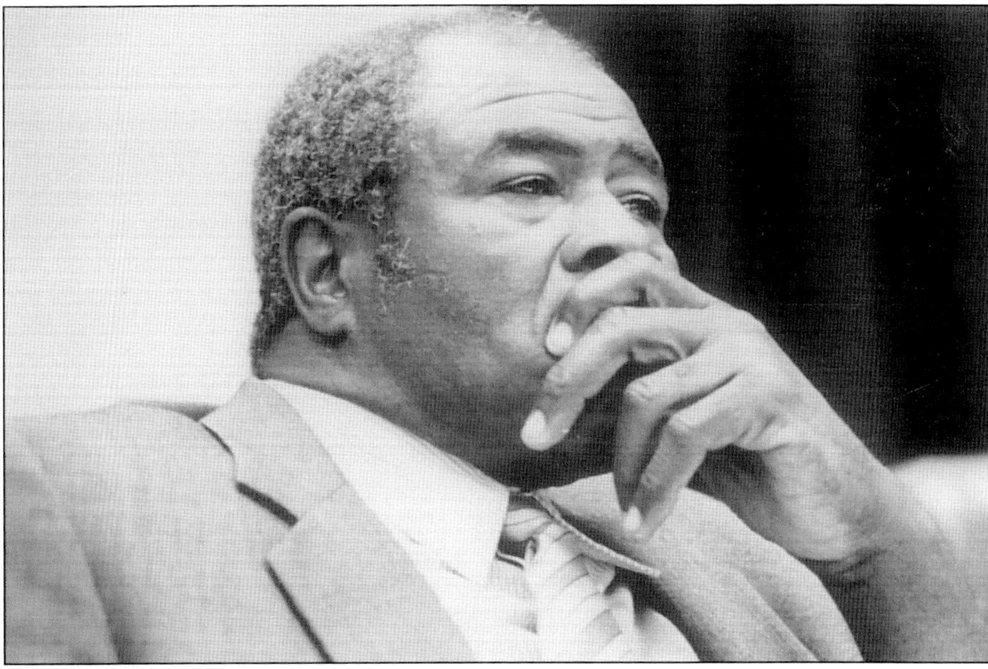

The People's Voice. Sam Bonds, a 1946 Howard High School graduate, was the first licensed city bail bondsman, the first African American appointed to the Welfare Board of Directors, and the second African American elected to the Georgetown City Council (1977–1997) since Reconstruction. Bonds is also the oldest plumbing contractor to serve the city of Georgetown. Bonds, Sam Hudson, and Nathan Brown, the former magistrate of Pawleys Island, were advocates for housing development funds to construct the first three homes for African Americans in the Maryville section of Georgetown in 1963. The houses were financed for the families of David Drayton, Leroy Buttone, and Robert Patterson through the First American Corp. The builders were Lesco Contracting Company. Other African-American families soon followed, and they included the Hemingways, Becks, McGuinnesses, McKnights, Knoxes, Spears, and Wrights.

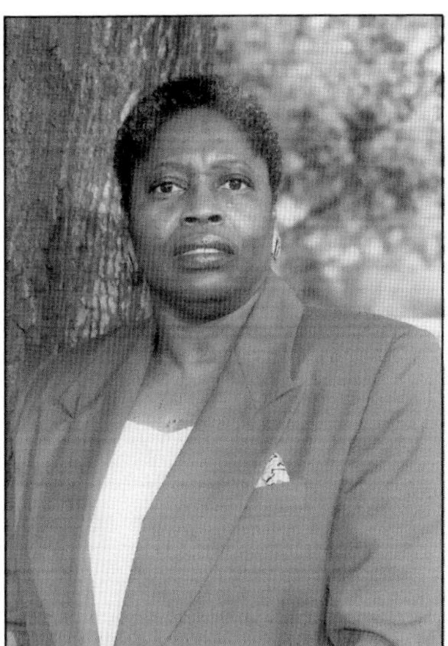

Lillie Jean Johnson, County Councilwoman (1992–Present). Ms. Johnson is the first woman to serve on the Georgetown County Council Board. She is a retired Georgetown High school teacher. The following are present elected officials: Representative Theodore Brown, Morris Johnson (county council member, 1997), Alma White (city councilwoman, 1990), former reporter for the *Georgetown Times* newspaper Brendon Barber (1998), and Darren Holmes (elected in 1998, the youngest African American to serve on the Georgetown County School Board). Holmes is from the Plantersville section.

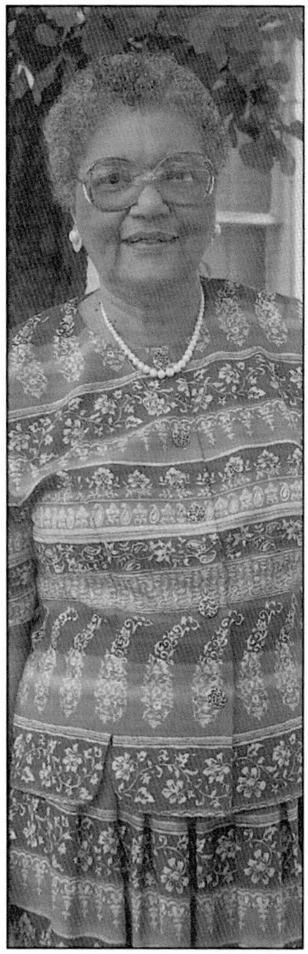

Charles Anne Buttone. Buttone is a member of the Georgetown County School Board. She retired as principal of Kensington Elementary School.

The Brown Family. Harold Jean Brown is a member of the Georgetown County School Board, elected in 1996. She is a graduate of Winyah High School. The first integrated graduating class at this historically white school was in 1968, and Brown, Susan Chatmon Brockington, and Rainey Greene were the three African-American graduates that year. Brown is the first and only African-American secretary at the Georgetown Steel Mill, where she began work in 1972. Her father, Harold James Brown, was born in Charleston, South Carolina, and relocated to Georgetown when he was 15 years old. He first worked for an individual logging company and, later, went on to become the first African-American car salesman in the states of North Carolina and South Carolina. He worked with Divisions of Ford Motor Company, including the Loyal, Bayside Motor Companies, and the Parker Dunn Co., of which he was part owner for three years. His years in this area spanned from 1968 to 1993. In 1993, he established the Harold J. Brown Auto Service Center. He is married to the former Gertrude Youmans, and they are the parents of daughter Harold Jean Brown. Their two sons, Harold Jr. and Dexter Lavoy, are deceased. Pictured, from left to right, are (front row) Gertrude Brown and Harold James Brown, Jean's parents; (back row) Harold Jean Brown; Regina Wragg, her daughter; Jacquelyn Brown, her niece; and Jawahn Wragg Ware, her daughter.

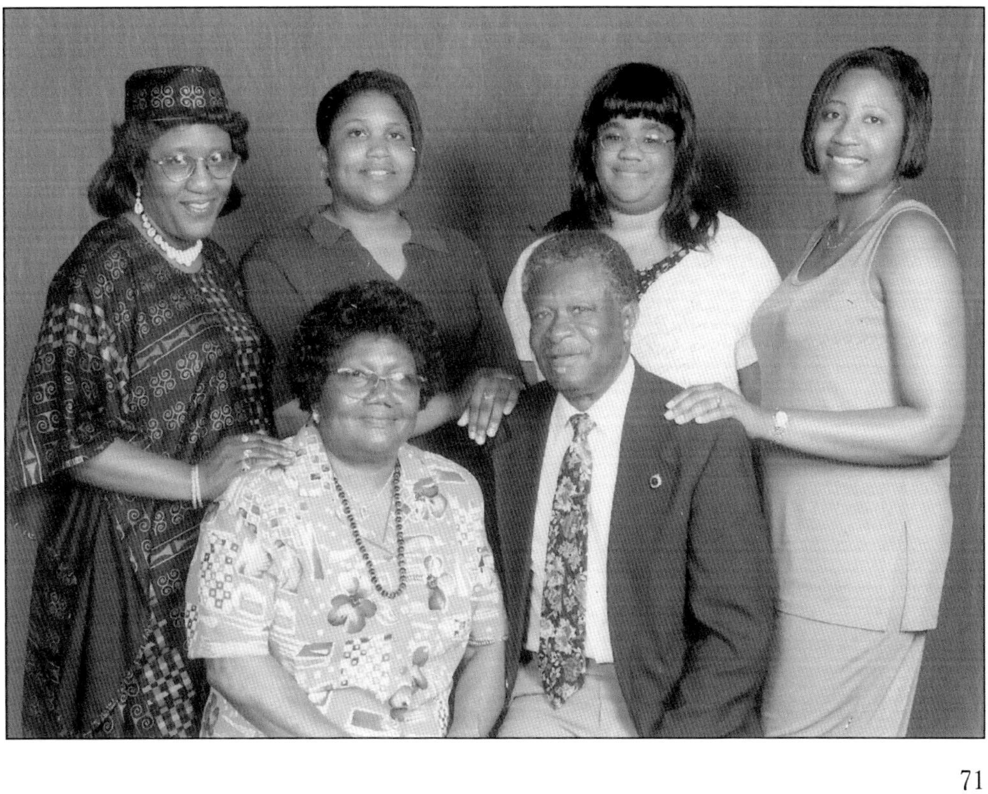

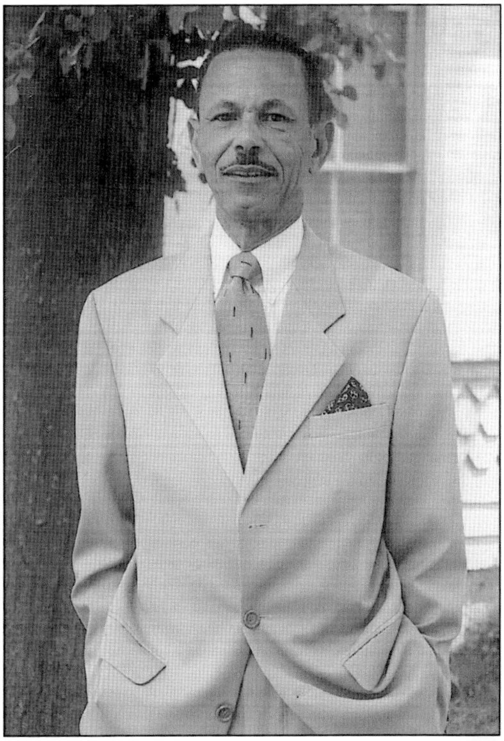

PETE HEMINGWAY. Pete Hemingway is currently the chairman of the Georgetown Chapter of the NAACP. An Air Force retiree, he is married to Mattie Daniels Hemingway, a retired media specialist of Choppee High School. They are the parents of Peter Henry IV, George Thomas Sr., Walter Samuel, and Marilyn Laverne.

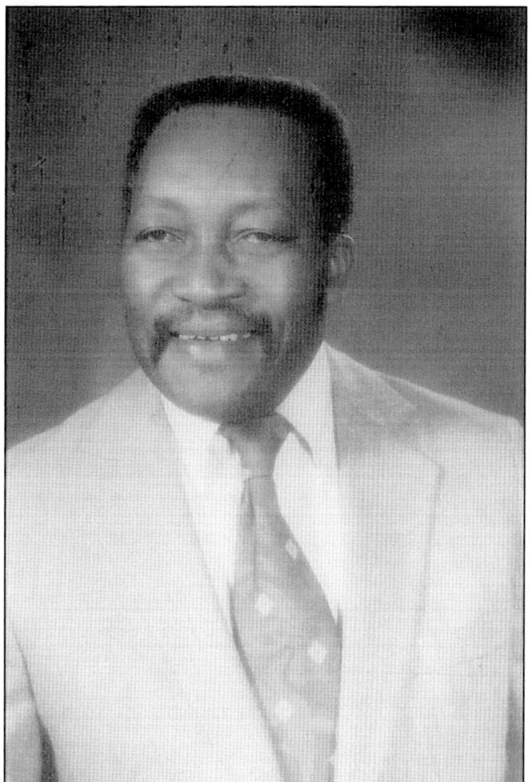

JEROME NICHOLAS HOLMES. Holmes was the first president of the Brown's Ferry Water Company. He played an instrumental role in acquiring the sewer and water system in his own and neighboring communities.

"THE MAYOR OF SANDY ISLAND." Prince Washington (1895–1975) was a community activist from Sandy Island. For many years, he transported students by boat to the mainland to board buses to Georgetown County schools. A fireman for ships at sea, he served as the captain of the *Old Brookgreen*, which sailed the Intracoastal Waterway. He was an active member of New Bethel Baptist Church, a trustee and an ordained deacon for 35 years. He also served as the president of the Home Charity Lodge and was a board of trustees member of Morris College in Sumter, South Carolina. He and his wife of 61 years, Rebecca, have two children, Laura and Benjamin, as well as foster children, Julia and Richard.

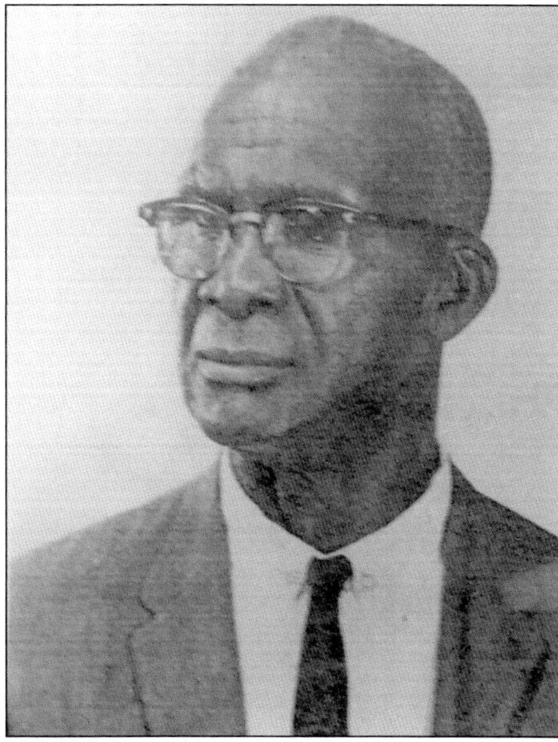

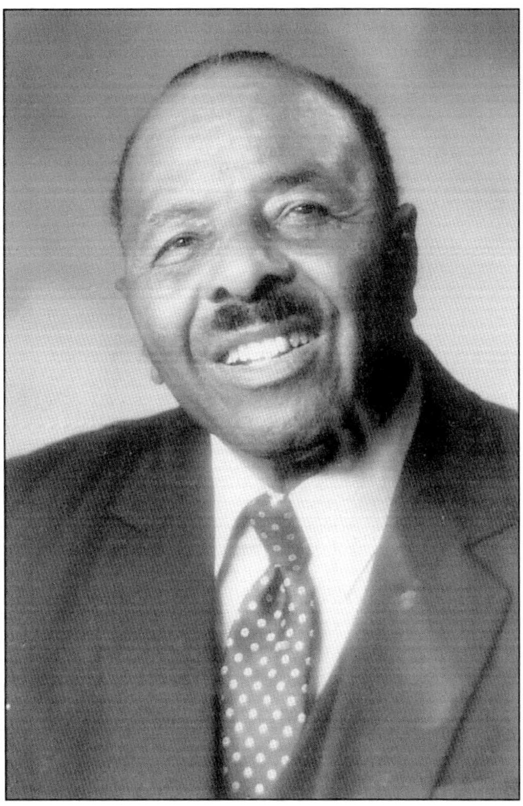

ROSS STAFFORD. Ross Stafford is recognized as one of the founders of the Sampit Elementary School; he donated his own acreage for the school. He was also largely responsible for the extension of the Georgetown mail route to the Sampit community and the erection of mailboxes in front of individual homes. (Courtesy of the Committee on African-American History Observances.)

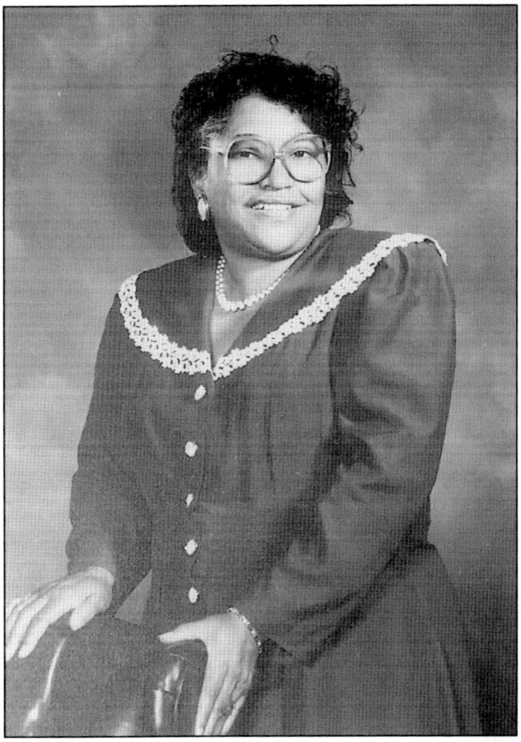

Florrine Linnen. With a long history of community activism, Florrine Linnen plays a significant role in the health education and prevention of diabetes in the African-American community.

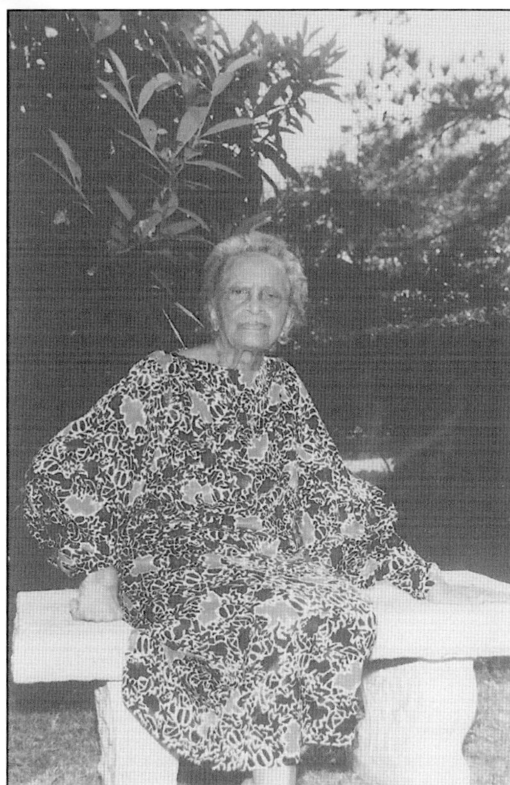

Maudest Kelly Squires (1903–1989). Squires was the first African-American woman to hold an elected seat on the Georgetown County School Board. She was a former supervisor of rural schools and the principal of Choppee High School. The impressive "gymtorium" at the high school is named in her honor.

Pauline Dunmore Lawrence (1903–1993). Pauline Dunmore Lawrence taught from 1928 to 1975 and was a classic example of a dedicated educator, a productive woman, and a dynamic force. She was the mother of Charles Anne Buttone.

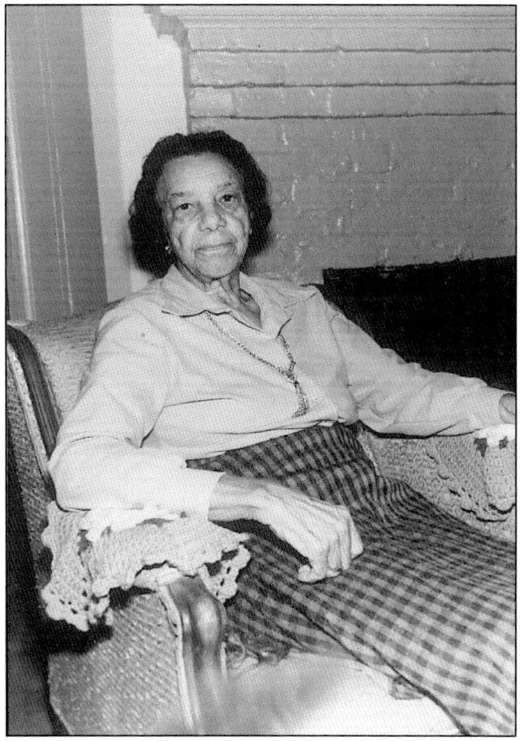

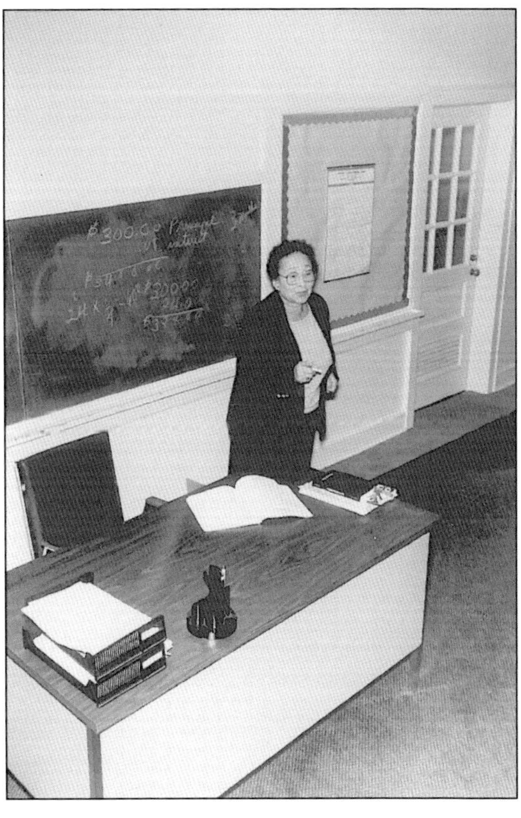

Camille Barber (1917–1998). A superb educator, Barber's philosophy and her life were inseparable. "All students should be educated to the limit of their capacities."

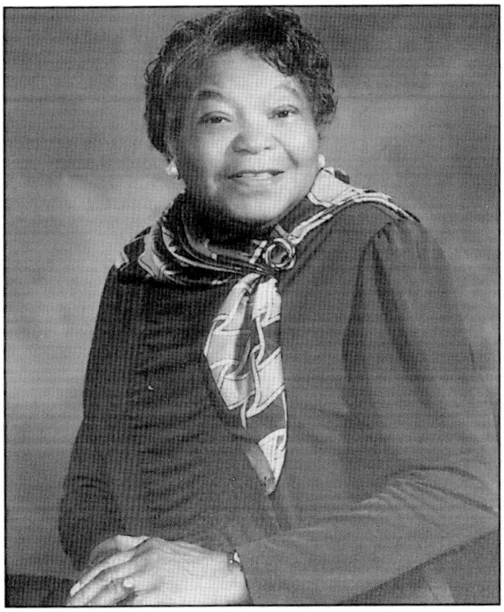

Etta Thompson. Thompson was the first African-American woman elected to the city council of Andrews, South Carolina. A dedicated educator for over 40 years, Thompson served for 34 of those years in Rosemary High and Middle Schools in Andrews.

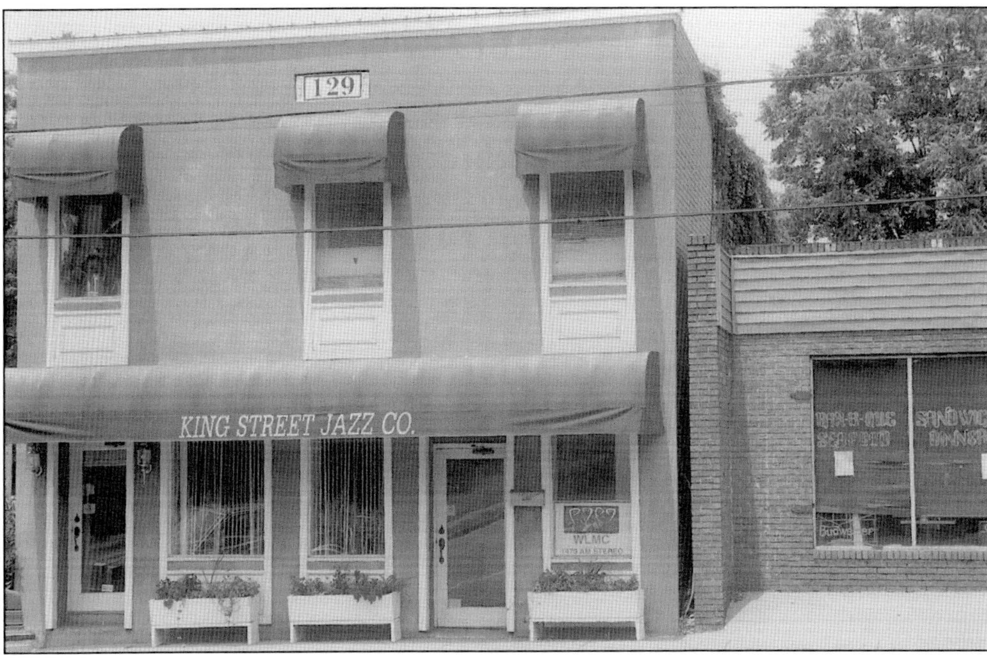

Radio and Jazz, A Hand in a Glove. WLMC 1470 AM Radio provides a gospel ministry and serves as a vehicle for positive and educational voices of the African-American community of Georgetown County. Shows cover events ranging from fire safety to health issues, such as breast cancer, AIDS awareness, and diabetes prevention. Founded by Barbara and Melvin Huell in 1994, the station is managed by Toby Smith, and Vergie Alston Tennyson serves as the announcer. Vanessa Greene served as the general manager for WLMC radio from 1995 to June 1999. She is the founder and director of Global Media Arts and has served on many executive boards, including the United Way of Georgetown, the Cultural Council of Georgetown County. She also spearheaded the most recent Winyah Auditorium Project, which seeks to develop a new civic center for the county. She is the daughter of Alvin and Cleo Greene. The ground level of the building houses the King Street Jazz Club, which is also operated by the Huells.

ELOISE V. COOPER. After retiring from Bellevue Hospital in New York City with 25 years of psychiatric service, Cooper returned home, organized, and became the first president of a community senior citizen club, which offered recreation and other social activities to the elderly.

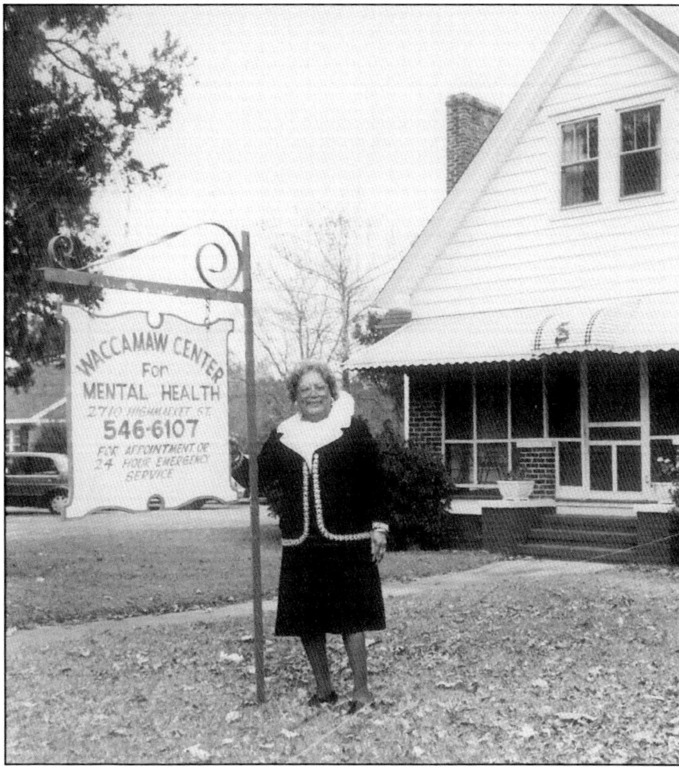

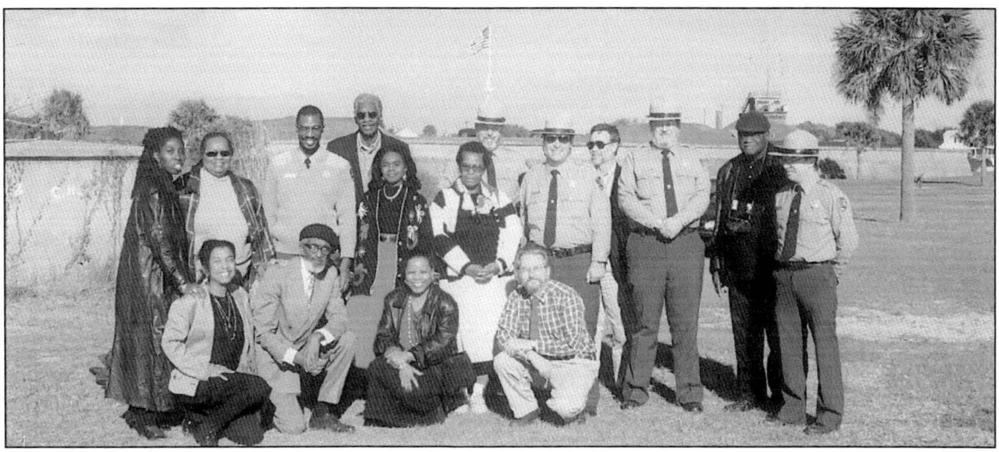

SOUTH CAROLINA AFRICAN-AMERICAN HERITAGE COUNCIL. Members of the council pose for this photograph during a meeting and tour of Fort Moultrie on Sullivans Island near Mt. Pleasant, South Carolina. The council is currently collaborating with the National Parks Service in their endeavors to interpret the Gullah culture of the Lowcountry. Pictured, from left to right, are (front row) Ramona La Roche, Family Tyes, Georgetown; Andrew Rodrigues; Vanessa Greene, WLMC Radio, Georgetown; and unidentified; (back row) Marquetta Goodwine, Gullah Geechee Sea Island Coalition, St. Helena Island; Vermell Rodrigues, Gullah Ooman, Pawley's Island; Michael Allen, president, SCAAHC, National Parks Service (NPS); Emory Campbell, Penn Center, St. Helena Island; Joyce Cokely, Mt. Pleasant; Roslyn Saunders, Sandlewood Associates; John Tucker, NPS; unidentified, NPS; Joe Opallo, Penn Center; unidentified, NPS; unidentified; and unidentified, NPS.

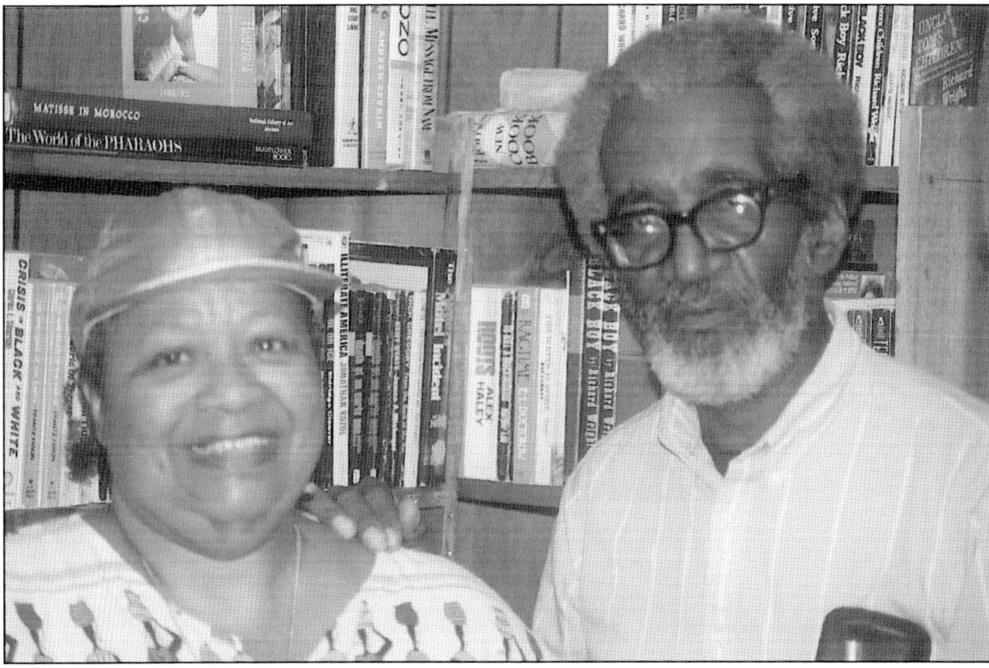

GULLAH OOMAN. Vermelle "Bunny" and Andrew Rodrigues are the proprietors of the Gullah Ooman Shop of Pawleys Island. The shop features unique items, gifts, and collectibles. Among them are quilts, Gullah t'ings, African-American collectibles and memorabilia, art and antiques, as well as books and historical papers. Pictured below is Bunny describing her African-American Story Quilt.

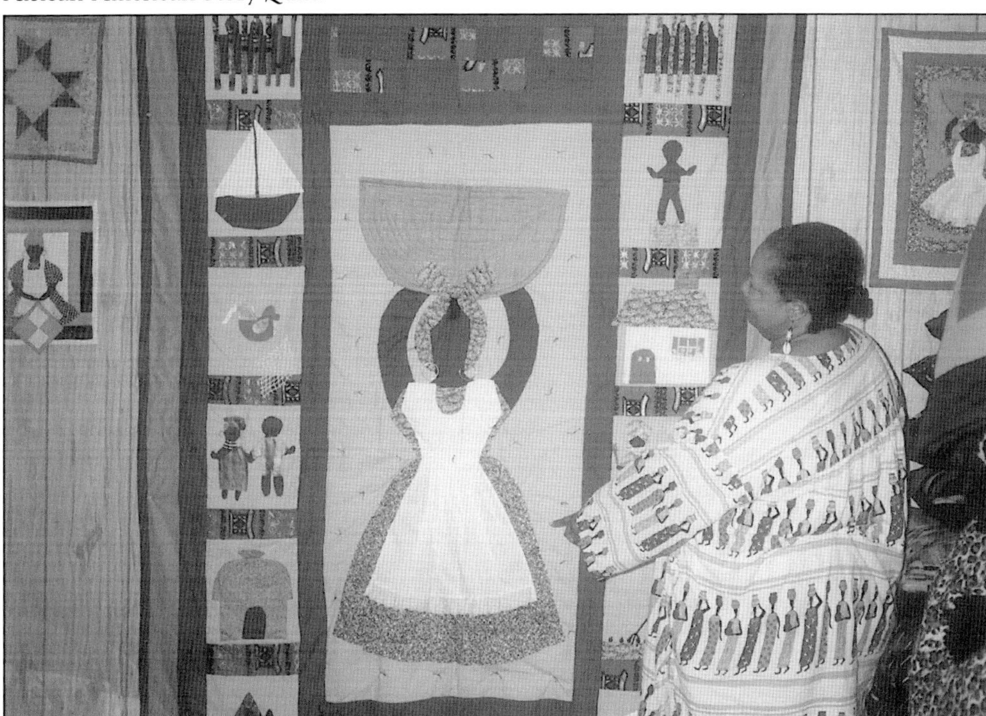

A CHEROKEE ANCESTOR. Edward Smith was Vermelle Smith Rodrigues's paternal great-grandfather. "Bubba Ed," a Cherokee Native American, lived in Back Landing, near High Market and Howard Streets.

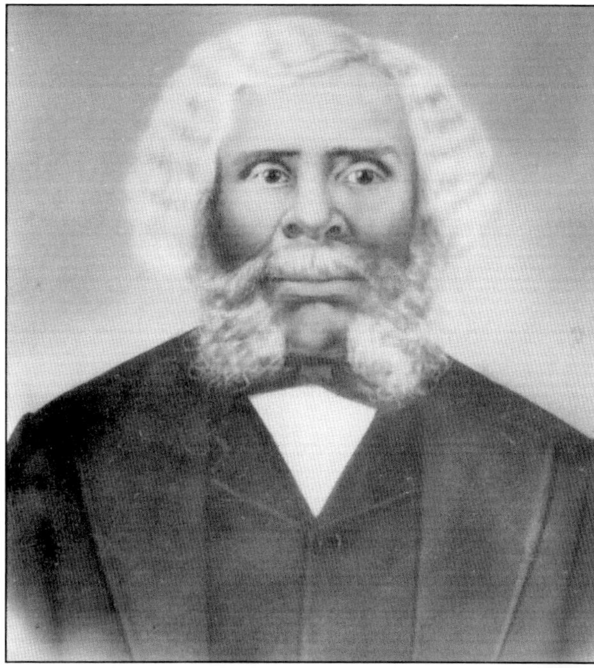

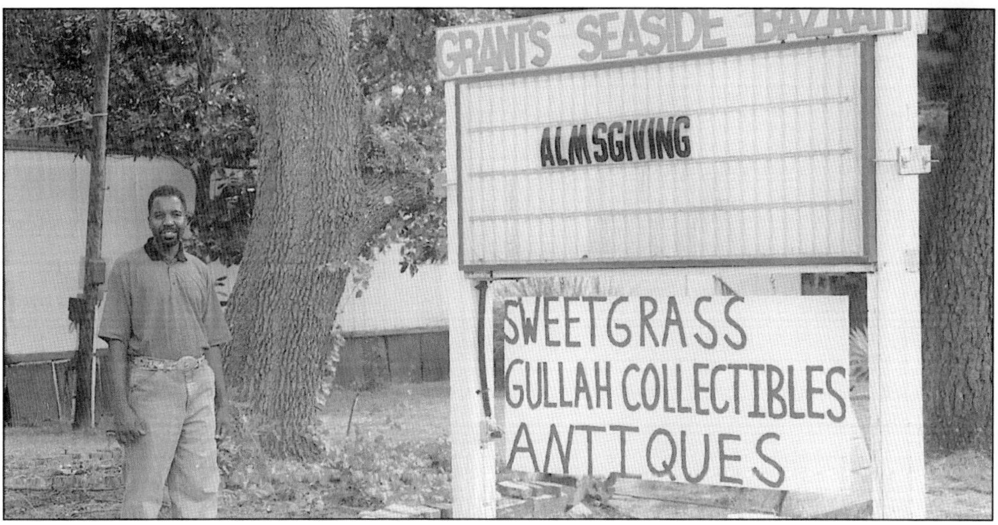

GRANT'S SEASIDE BAZAAR. Charles Edward Grant is the proprietor of Grant's Seaside Bazaar on Pawleys Island, and he is married to Blondell, a real estate agent. His business opened in 1994 and sits on heirs' property passed on to him by his paternal great-grandfather, Robert Grant. His paternal grandfather, Charles Grant (1893–1955), established the original family grocery store, the Eagle's Claw, in 1946. The store closed and the building went unused since the late 1950s. Charles Grant worked for Dr. Henry Norris at the former Litchfield Plantation, and Janie Baker (1901–?), Grant's fiancée, courageously left for Charleston alone in 1923. There she was employed as a housekeeper for Mayor Gilbert Rhett. She later returned to Pawleys Island to marry Charles in 1924; the ceremony was performed by Reverend S.J. Dobbins of St. Stephen A.M.E. Church. The couple resided in what was then known as the Waverly Mills section on Shell Road, so named for the oyster shells of which it was made. The area is now the location of Waccamaw Elementary School.

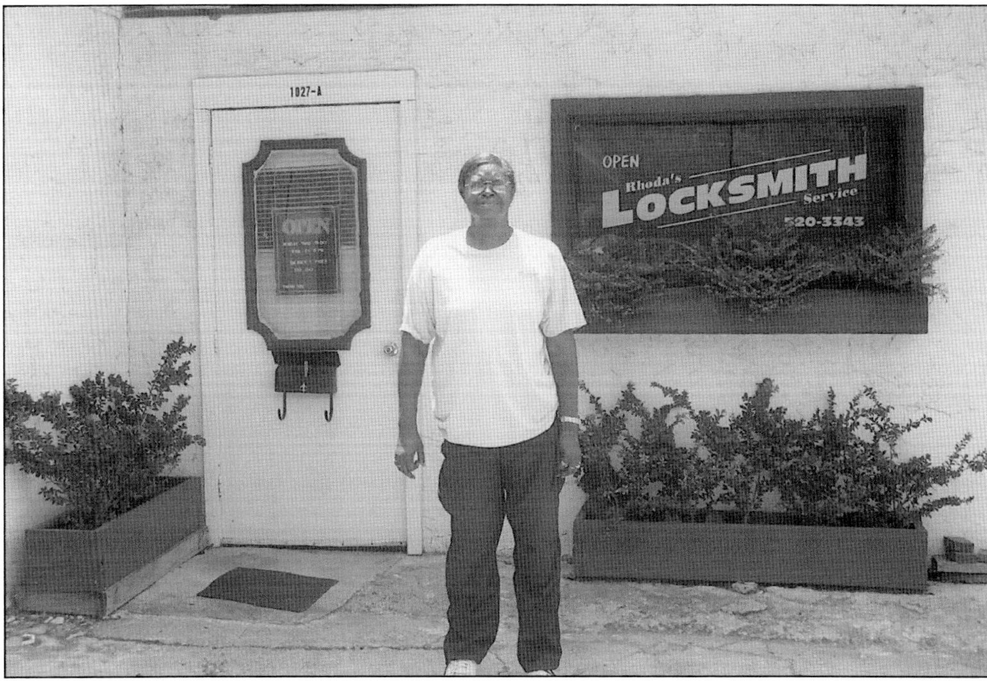

RHODA'S LOCKSMITH. Rhoda McClain is the proprietor of Rhoda's Locksmith. In 1988, she became the first African-American female locksmith in South Carolina. Voted "Locksmith of the Year" by her professional peers in 1997, McClain is indeed a leader in her field. Her establishment is located on Wood Street, and she is a resident of Andrews.

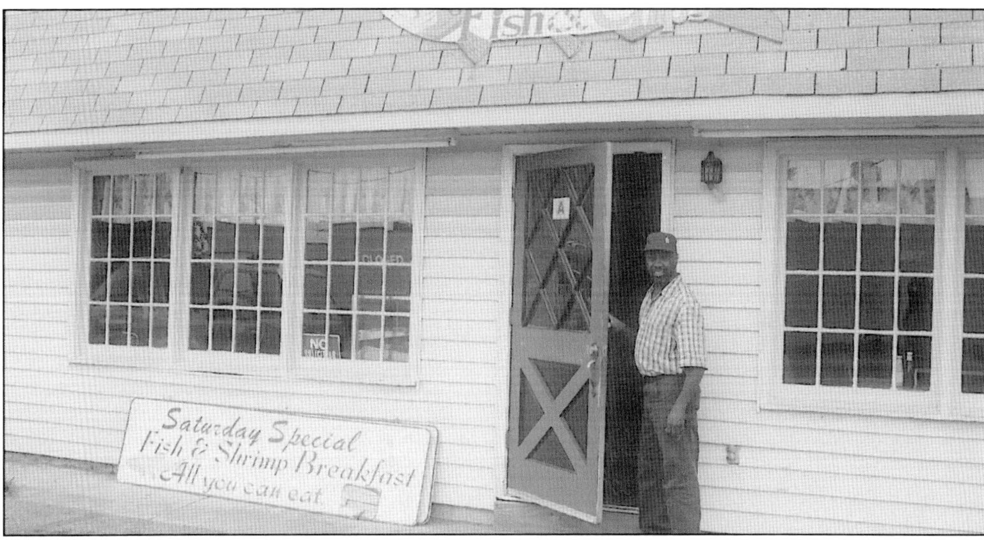

LAMAR'S FISH AND CHIPS. Lamar Iszard, the son of Viola King and Ed Iszard, took over the family's fish business upon his return from the military in 1972. He purchased property on South Merriman Road, relocated the business, and continues to lease to several businesses in the Lamar's Square location. The original Kings Fish Market, restaurant, and liquor store at 1214 1/2 Church Street was begun by Sam King III. His wife, Thelma, had family connections to fishermen from McClellanville, South Carolina. The couple sold the business to Sam's sister, Viola, and her husband, Ed Iszard. Sam and Thelma migrated to Brooklyn, New York, in 1954.

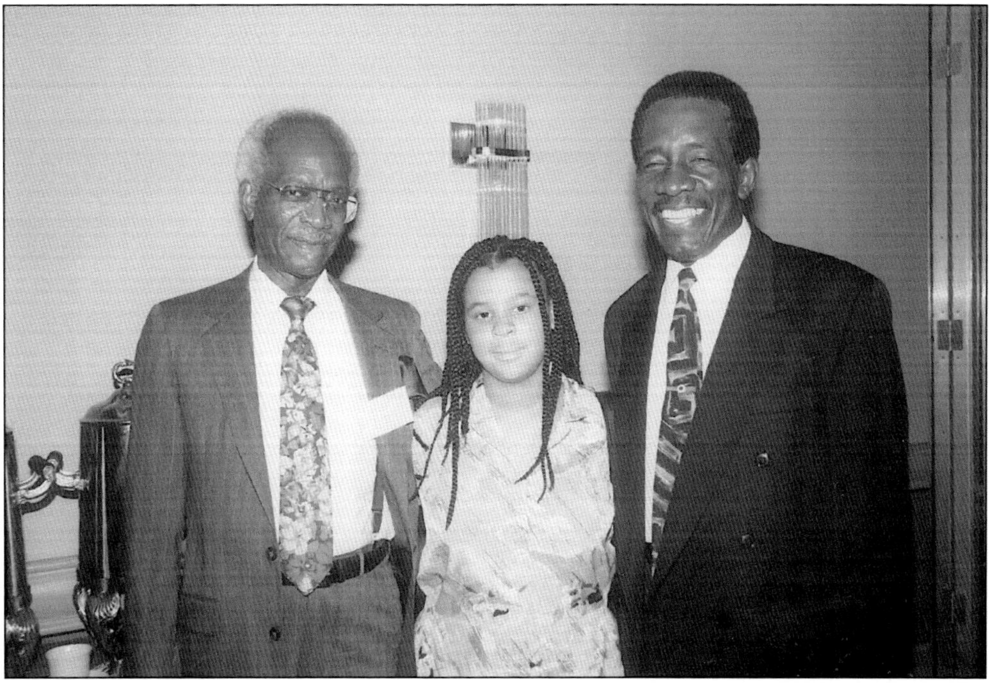

KING FAMILY REUNION. Reverend Harold King (1925–1999), the pastor of the Cornerstone Baptist Church of Baltimore, Maryland, his granddaughter, and cousin Stanley Iszard (Lamar's brother) are seen here during the King family reunion in 1994.

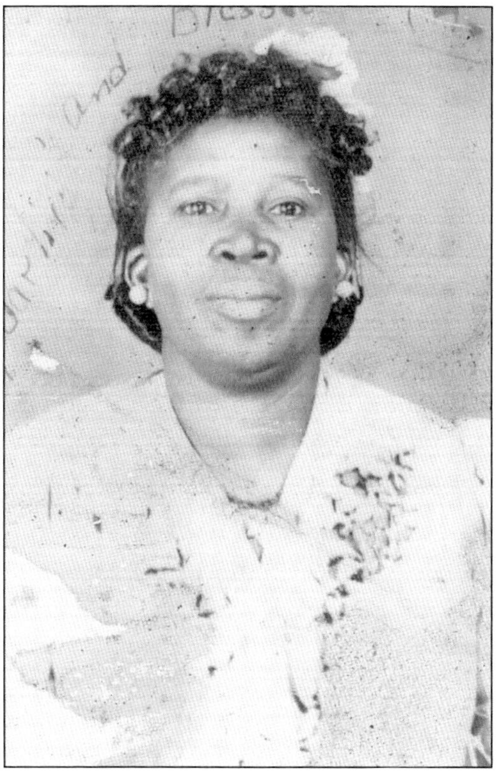

FLORENCE B. LOGGIE (1898–1955). Florence was wife of Rev. Samuel King (1884–1941), and the family resided in Bettsville Village. Their seven children were Sam, Joe, Viola, Arthur, Herbert, Harold, and Charlotte. (Courtesy of Myrtle King.)

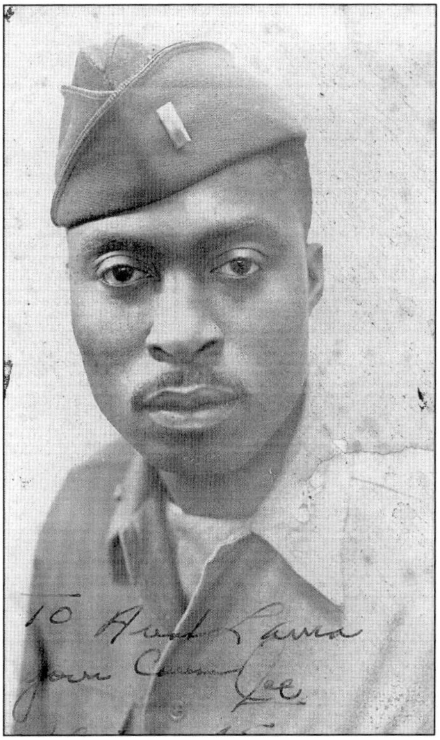

Captain Joseph Elias King (1917–1952). Joe King is pictured here during World War II. After the war, he returned and taught algebra at Howard High School. His wife is Addie of Greenville, South Carolina, and his daughter Jo Anne lives in New York City.

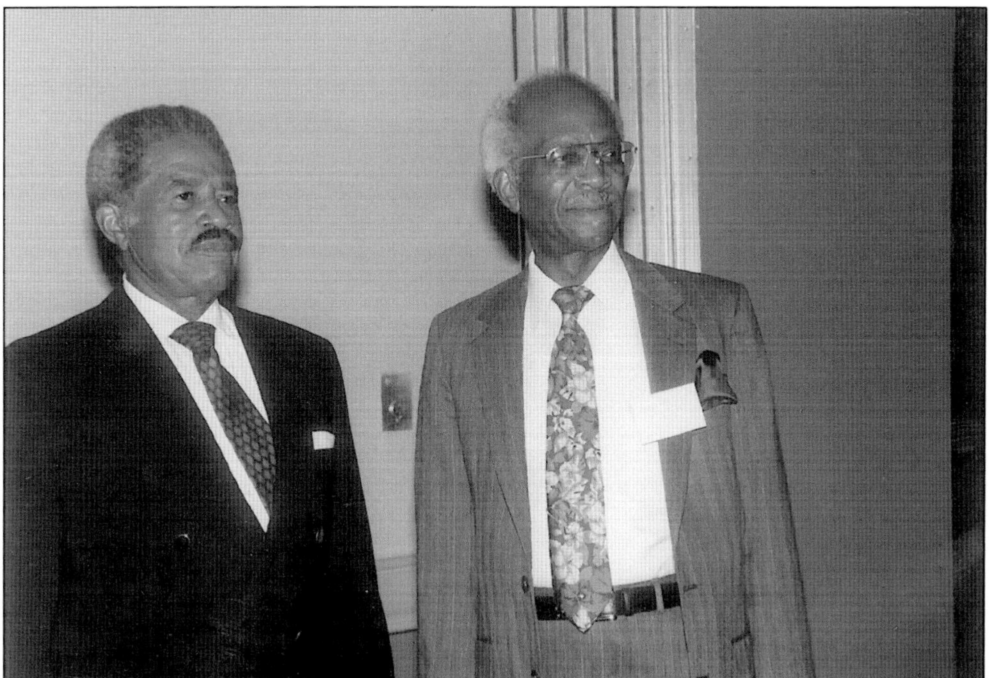

Brothers Arthur and Reverend Harold King. Arthur King is pictured with his brother Rev. Harold King during a family reunion in 1992. Arthur serves as a deacon for Bethesda Missionary Baptist Church. Reverend King died in 1999.

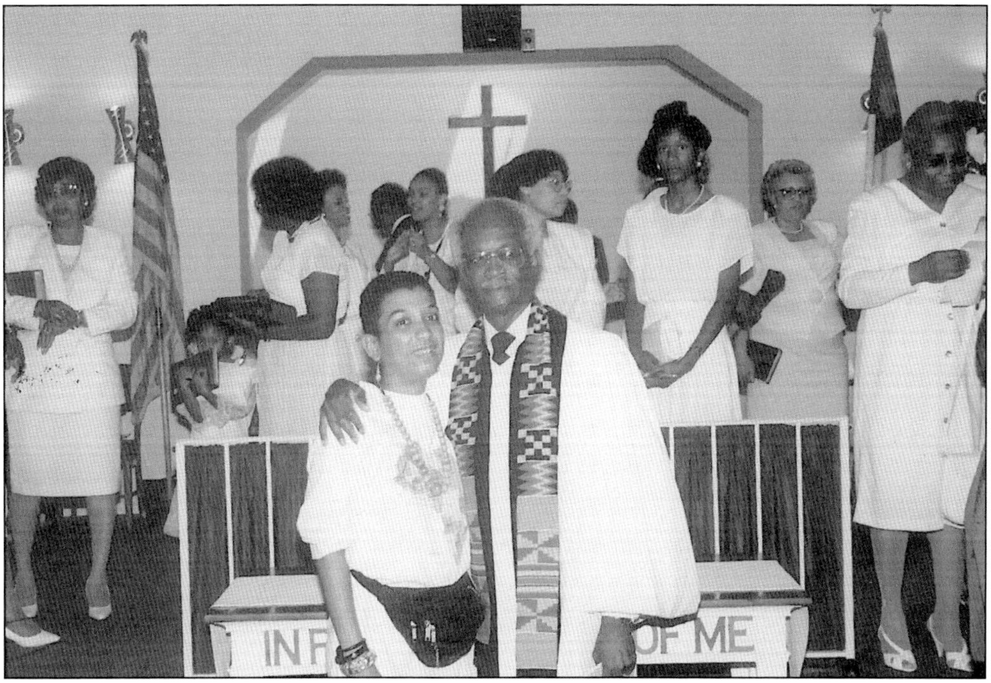

COUSINS. Cousins Ramona La Roche and Reverend Harold King, the pastor of the Cornerstone Baptist Church of Baltimore, Maryland, pause to record a moment in time during family reunion church service in 1992.

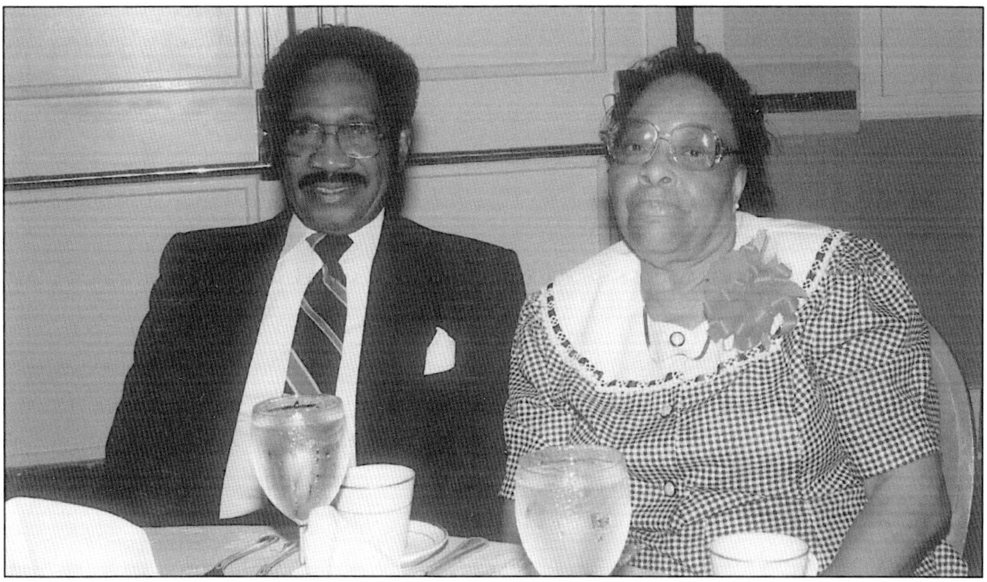

DEACON HERBERT KING. Herbert King, an elder deacon of First Calvary Missionary Baptist Church, is a retired alum plant worker. He and his wife, Katherine, are the parents of Alex, Bernard, Herbert Jr., Ronald, and Sonia.

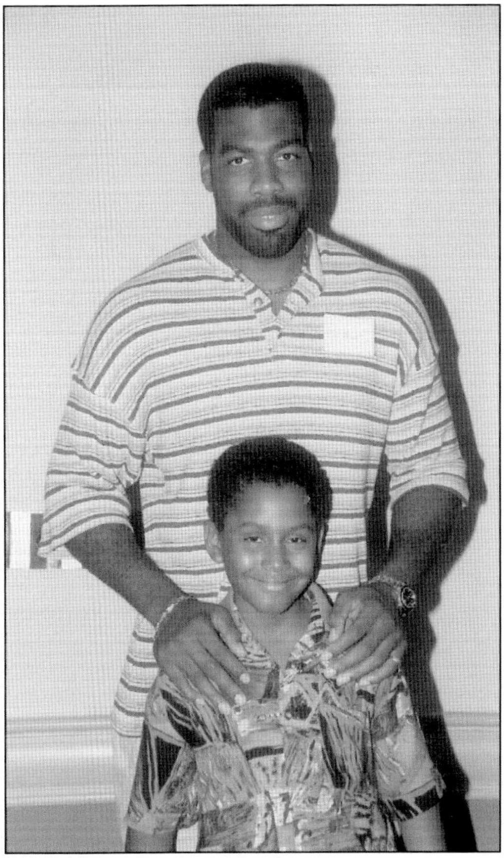

Sports Dreams Turned Reality. Ojas La Roche proudly smiles during his first meeting with his cousin and renown professional basketball player Mark Bryant.

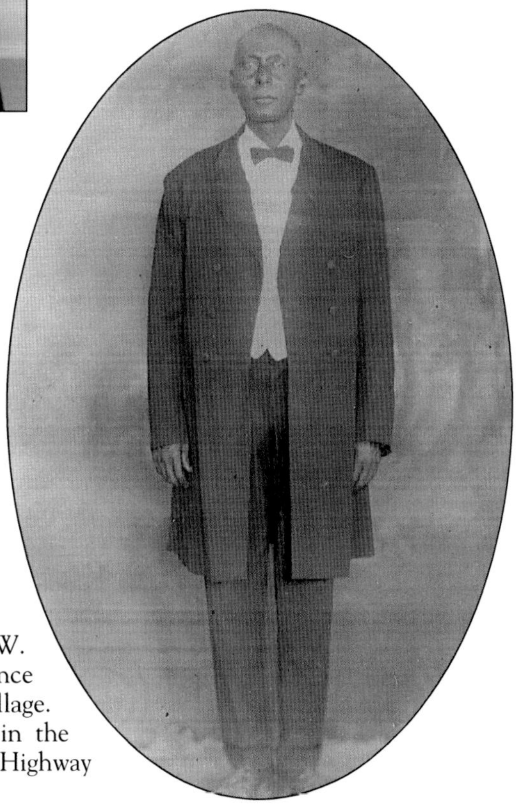

A Real Soul Stirrer. Reverend Abraham W. Wright was the founding pastor of Providence Missionary Baptist Church of Bettsville Village. The church, originally organized in 1891 in the village, later relocated to its present site on Highway 17 North. The rebuilding occurred in 1965.

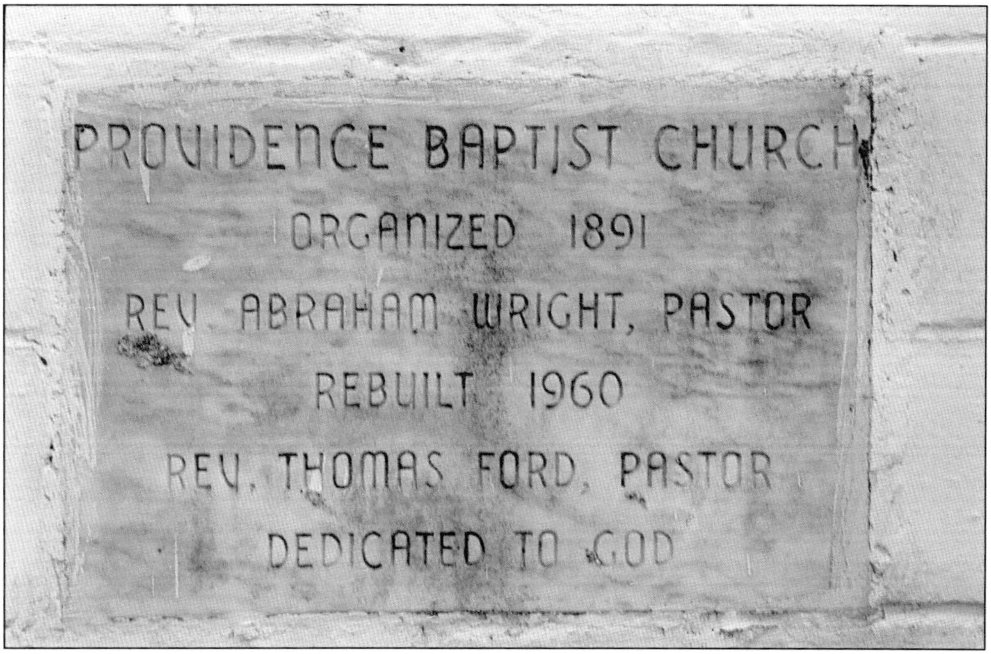

Heritage of a Village. Providence Baptist Church was originally located in Bettsville, an African-American village east of the Waccamaw River. Approximately 25 families resided in the community. Beginning in 1938, property owners began to leave the area. By the end of the 1940s, all families had left the village, and the property was bought by George Vanderbilt of New York City. Pictured are Providence Missionary Baptist Church and its cornerstone, which reads, "Providence Baptist Church was organized in 1891 by Rev. Abraham Wright, Pastor. Rebuilt 1960 by Rev. Thomas Ford, Pastor. Dedicated to God."

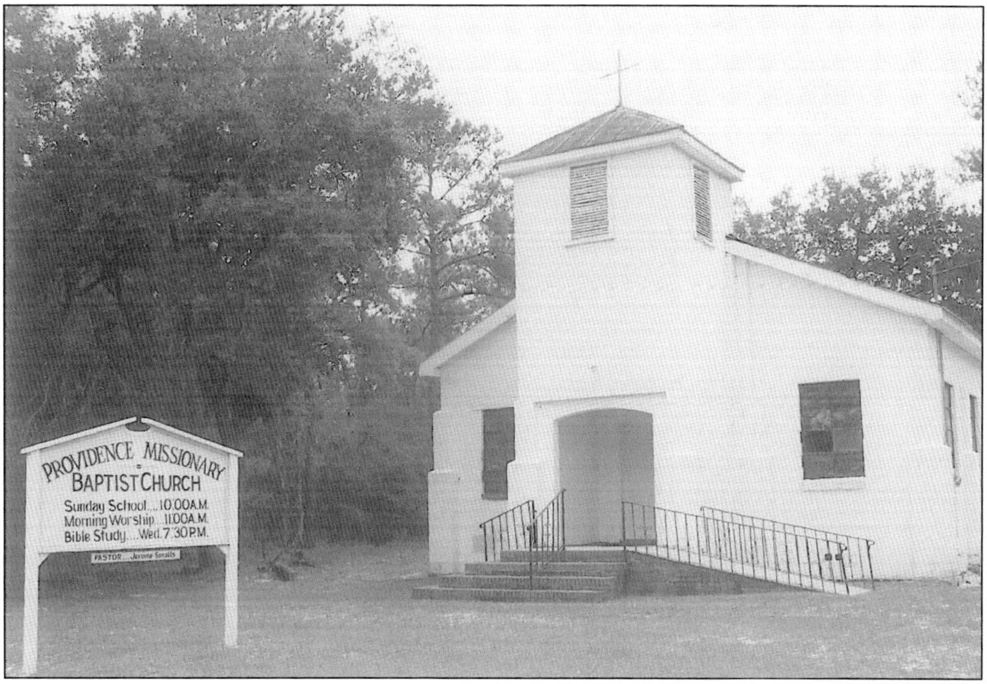

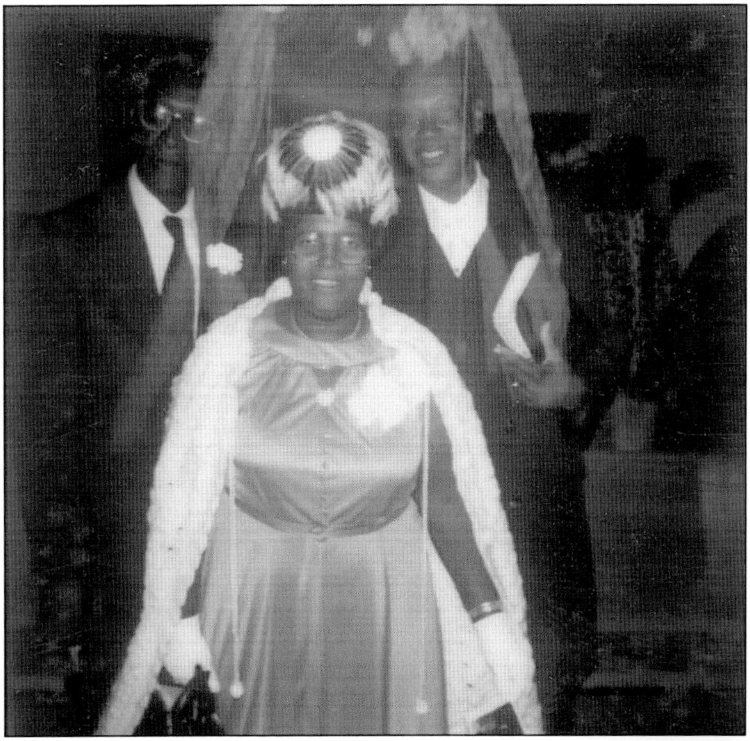

A Real First Lady. Pictured, from left to right, are Reverend Braves, the former pastor of Providence Baptist Church who is now deceased, his wife, Mary, and unidentified.

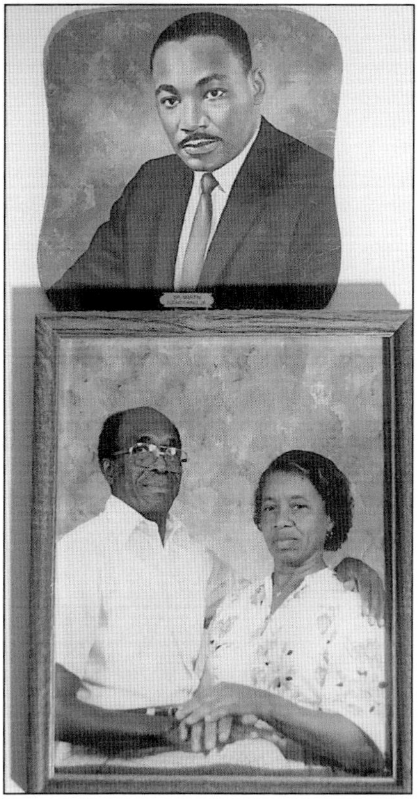

Together We Stand. Deacon Peter Small Jr. and Annie Gardner Small, his wife of 62 years, are former Bettsville Village residents. They attend Providence Baptist Church. Mr. Small is a member of a Masonic Order and the United Order of Home Charity Society, #28. The couple has a daughter, Mable Small Jenkins. (Courtesy of Mr. and Mrs. Peter Small.)

SUPERINTENDENT GARDNER. Ben Gardner, the father of Annie G. Small, served as the superintendent for Beneventum and Springwood Plantations. Annie was born on the former Beneventum Plantation. (Courtesy of Annie Small.)

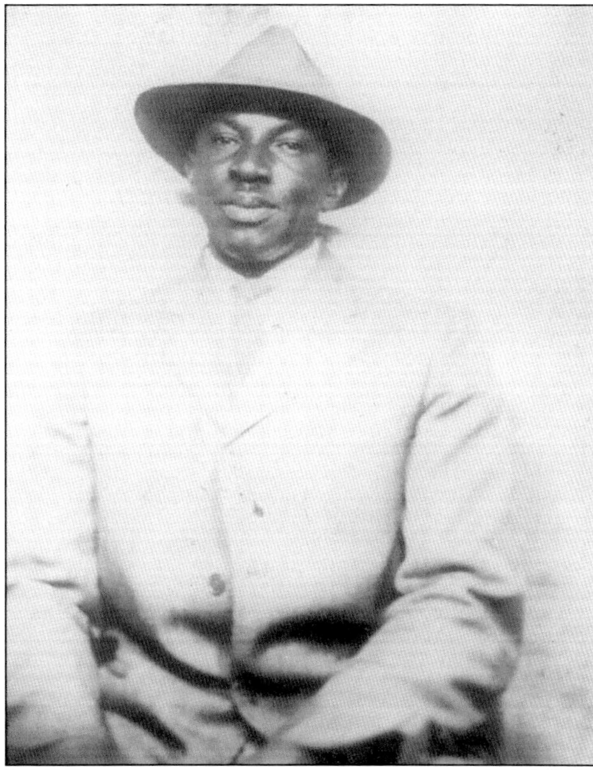

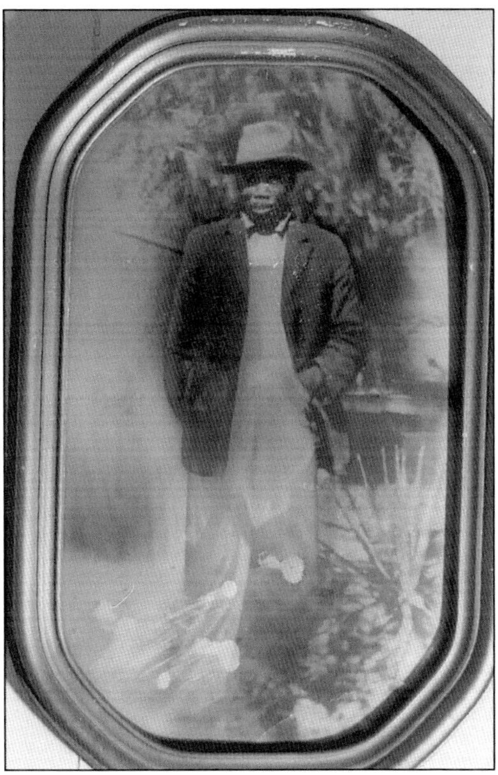

SOLID. Peter Small Sr. (?–1922) stands tall for a portrait on his property in Bettsville Village on Waccamaw Neck. His wife was Martha Gilliard Small of Fairfield, and the couple had 12 children: Andrew Sr., James, Prince, Arthur, Lue, Rebecca, Ethel, Louise, Gertie, Peter, Guy, and Elizabeth. (Courtesy of Peter Small Jr.)

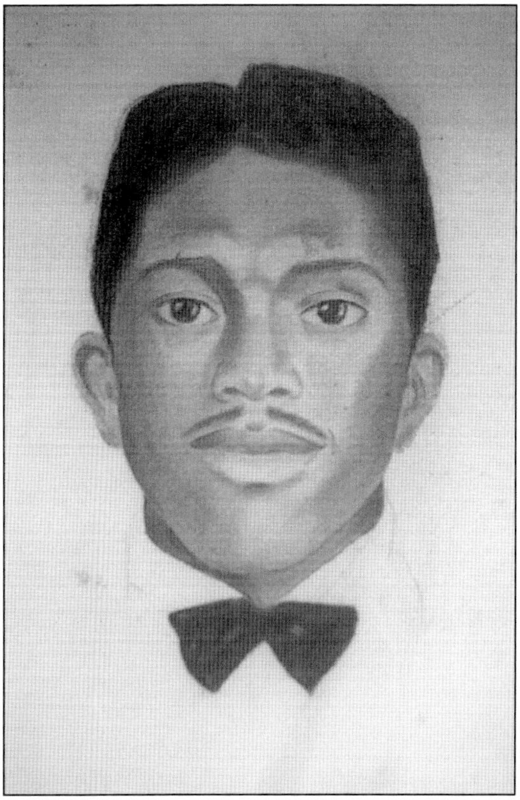

Portrait of a Butler. Peter Smalls Jr. was employed as a butler for three families during his working career. Here, he is depicted as a young butler in the early years of his career in a drawing done by a guest of his employer. (Courtesy of Peter Small Jr.)

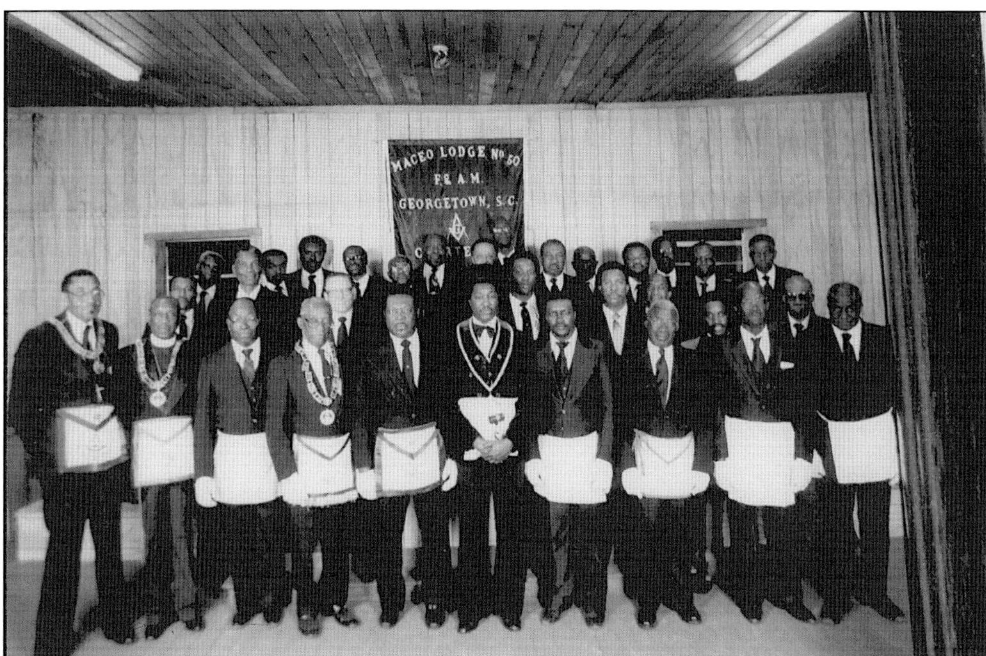

Masonic Order. Peter Small Jr. is a member of the Maceo Lodge No. 50 F. & A.M. (Free & Accepted Masons) of Georgetown, South Carolina. (Courtesy of Peter Small Jr.)

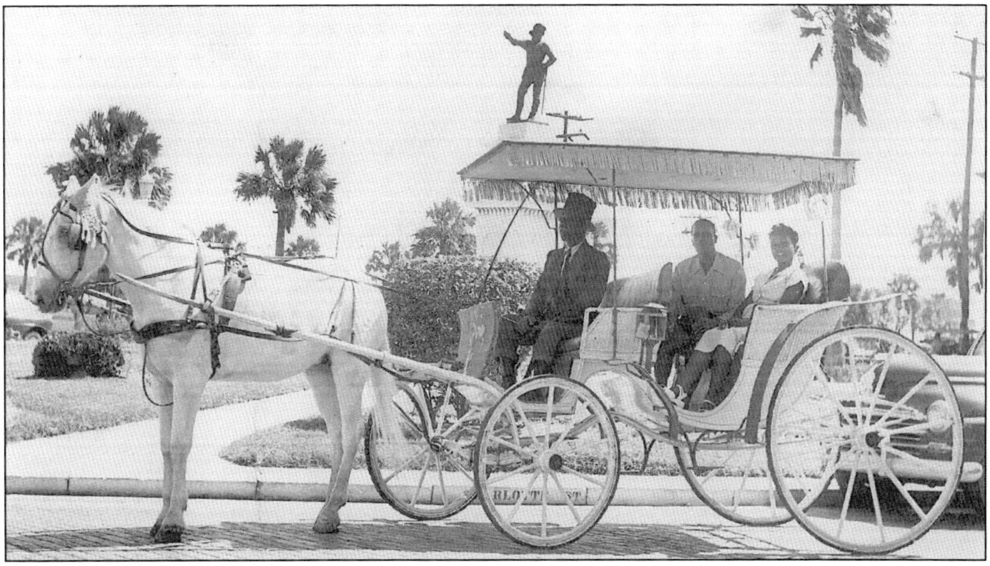

NEWLYWEDS. Joe Weathers Sr. (1905–1998) and Thelma Hughie traveled by bus to St. Augustine, Florida, for their marriage in 1950. Mrs. Weathers is the granddaughter of Reverend Abraham Wright and the daughter of Lucinda Hughie, a midwife. The Weathers' children are Betty Adams, Loretta Welborne, Arnetta Campbell, Catherine W. Cuberthson, DeLorise Weathers, Joan W. Smith, Sharrell W. Hankins, Lucinda W. Harris, Benjamin Washington, Herbert Dennison, Percy, and Joe Jr. They also have 20 grandchildren and 10 great-grandchildren. (Courtesy of Thelma H. Weathers.)

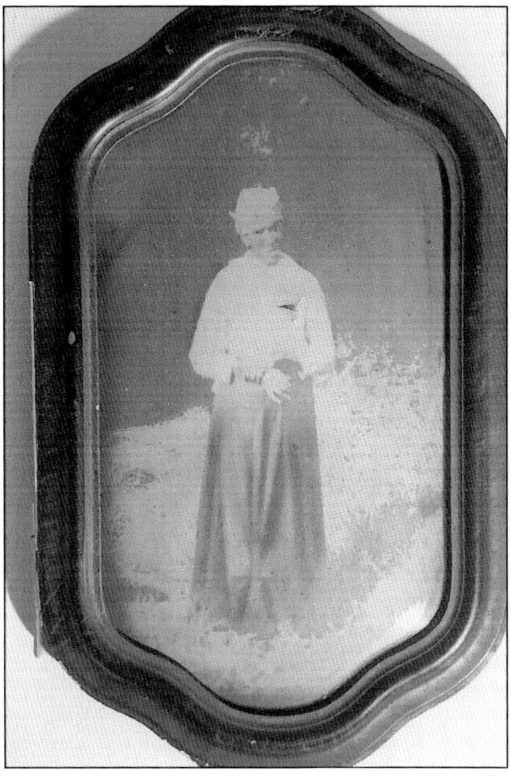

MARTHA BURRIS. Joe Weather's maternal grandmother was from Mansfield Plantation. (Courtesy of Thelma H. Weathers.)

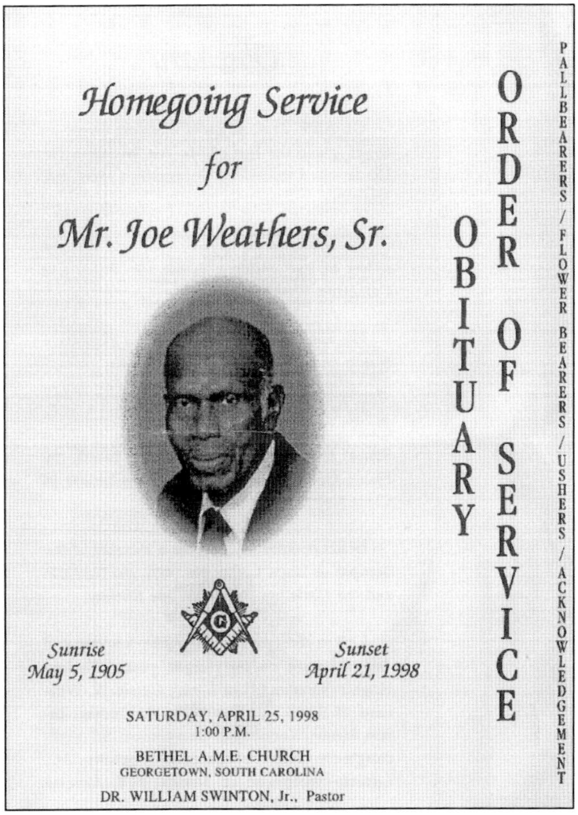

Homegoing Service

for

Mr. Joe Weathers, Sr.

Sunrise
May 5, 1905

Sunset
April 21, 1998

SATURDAY, APRIL 25, 1998
1:00 P.M.

BETHEL A.M.E. CHURCH
GEORGETOWN, SOUTH CAROLINA

DR. WILLIAM SWINTON, Jr., Pastor

OBITUARY

ORDER OF SERVICE

PALLBEARERS / FLOWER BEARERS / USHERS / ACKNOWLEDGEMENT

Joe Weathers Sr. Joe Weathers Sr., the son of Frank and Catherine Weathers, was employed by Mansfield Plantation for 52 years. He was a member of Bethel A.M.E. Church, the Temple of Hope Lodge No. 426, the NAACP, and the Christian Friendly Aid Society.

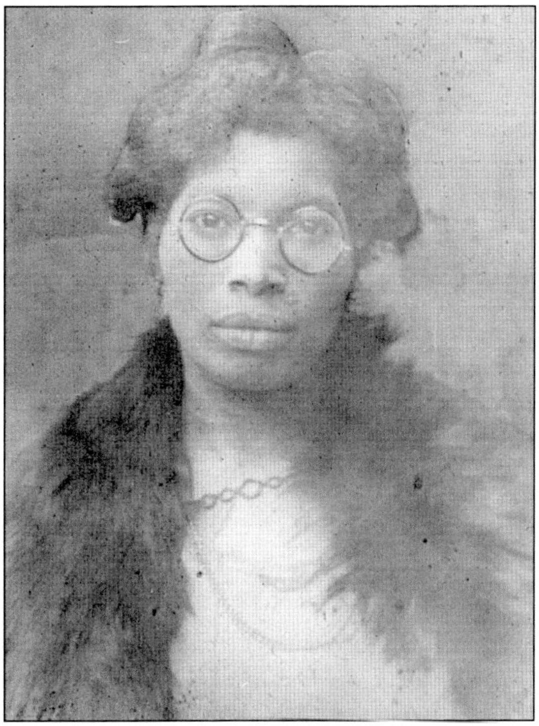

Big Sister. Etta Weathers was Joe's older sister. (Courtesy of Thelma H. Weathers.)

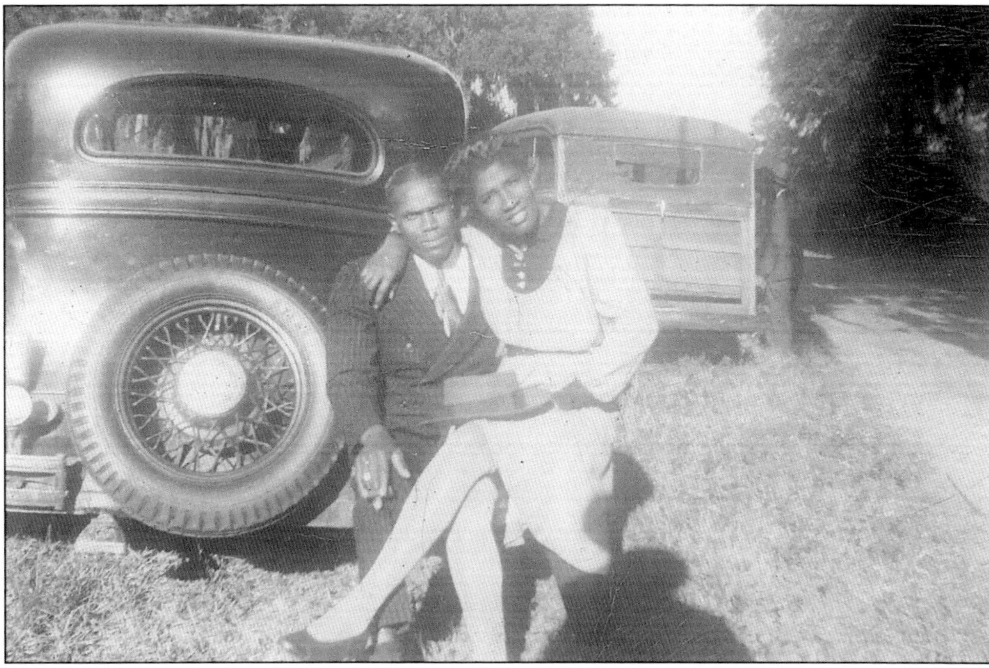

Joe and Bessie. Joe Weathers and Bessie Evans, his former girlfriend, take time for a photograph in front of a classic auto. (Courtesy of Thelma H. Weathers.)

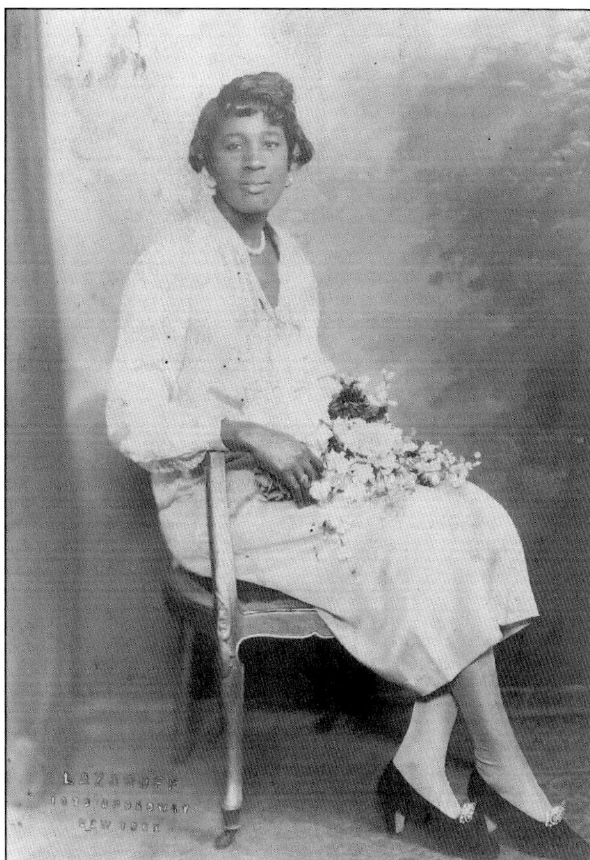

Emily "Min" Toomer, 1929. "Min" was the eldest daughter of Emmaline "Linnie" Shaw and Jacob Toomer, and her family, including siblings Jerry, Laura, John, and Lucille, resided on High Market Street between St. James and Meeting Streets. Emily migrated to Harlem, New York. She retired from Bellevue Hospital Food Service Department. (Courtesy of Myrtle King.)

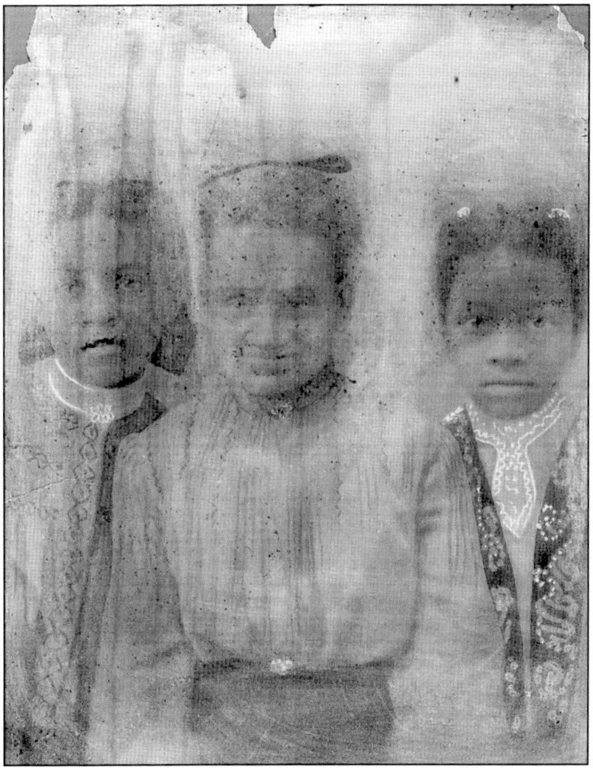

Mother and Daughters. Pictured from left to right are Carey Smalls Williams; "Ma" Lucy Shaw Smalls Holmes (d. 1937), Carey's mother; and Lucille, perhaps a surrogate daughter. The family resided in the Slab Town area of the city. Lucy's siblings were Emmaline, Mariah, Anthony, and the Reverend William "Bubba" Shaw. She also had a son, Cato, who was said to be an excellent singer in the church. He would often venture to Bettsville by boat to hear the sermons and to sing at Providence and Browns Chapel Baptist Churches on the Waccamaw Neck. Lucy's daughter, Carey, was the first of the family to migrate to Harlem, New York. She was gainfully employed as a dressmaker and a beautician.

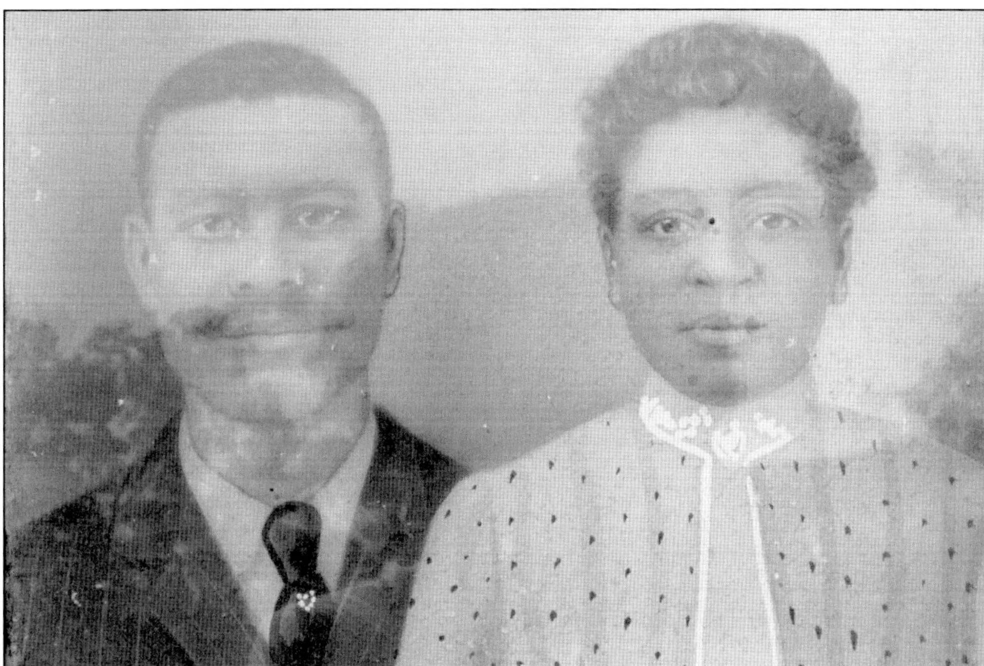

A Handsome Pair. This couple may be Emmaline Shaw Toomer's brother Anthony Shaw and his wife.

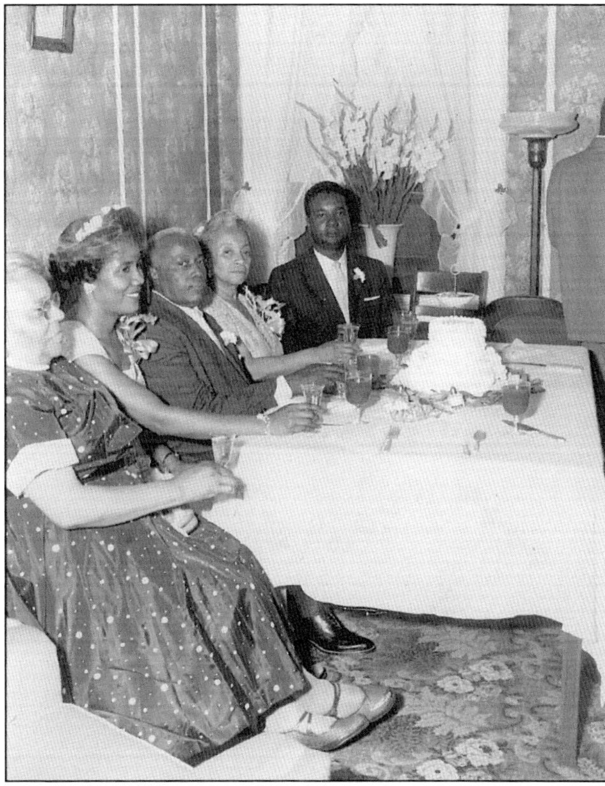

JERRY TOOMER. Above, the eldest Toomer boy, Jerry, is pictured during a social event (third from left) with his wife, Edith. Below, Jerry is pictured in his Baltimore, Maryland residence in 1980.

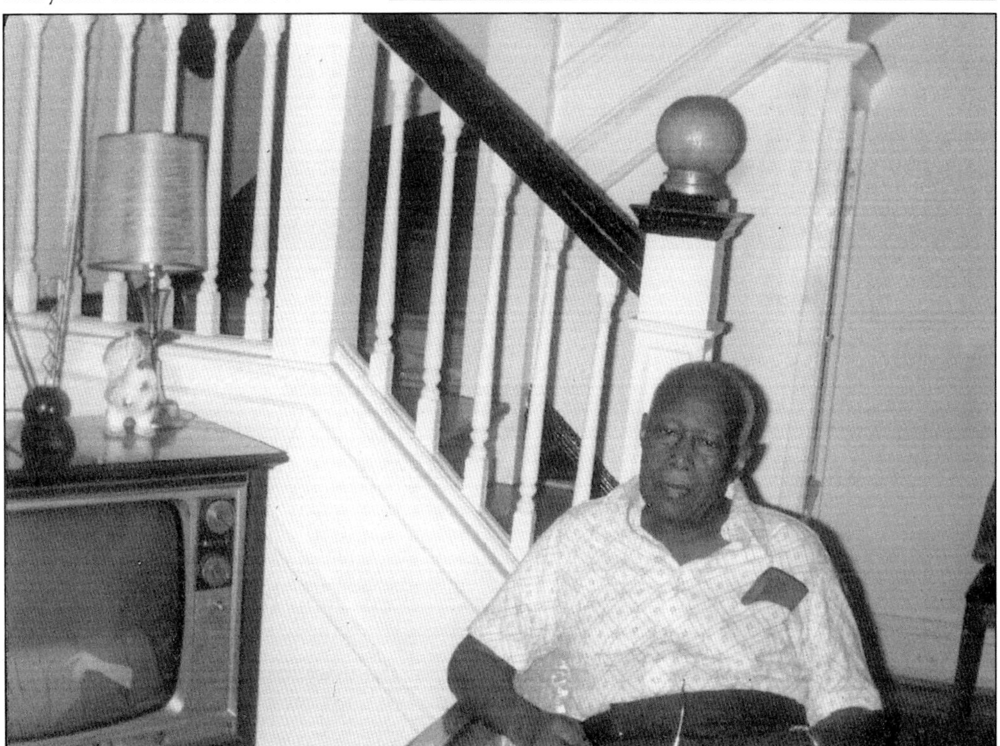

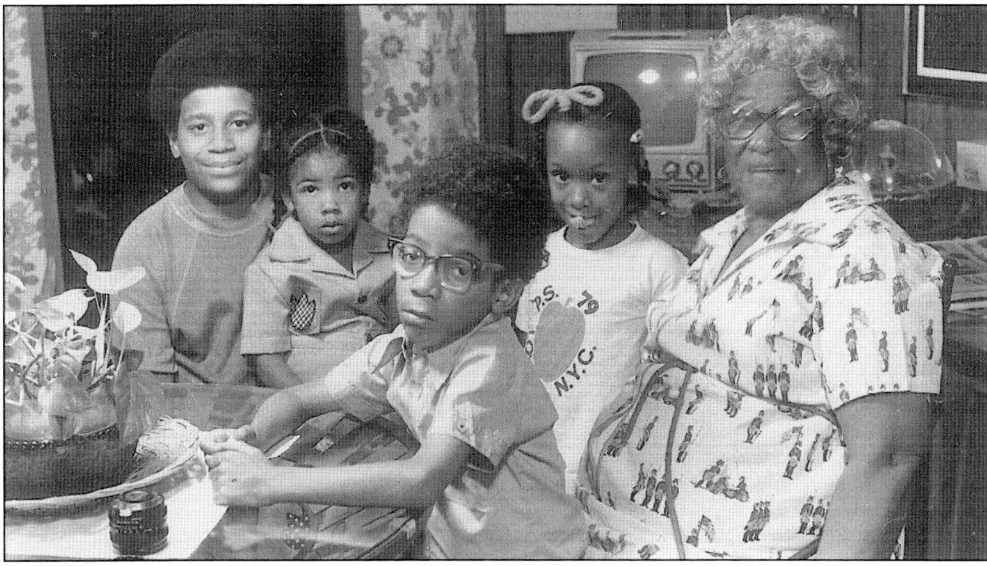

Grandma Laura. Laura Toomer King Armstrong (1900–1984), the wife of Albert King Sr., bore nine children during her marriage to King. The children were Albert Jr., Myrtle, Emily, Alberta, Edna, Herman, Pearl, Thelma, and Ernest, all of whom began their education in the one-room schoolhouse at the Brown Chapel Baptist Church in Bettsville, east of the Waccamaw River. Pictured, from left to right, are Fred Dailey, grandson; Azana and Ramon King, great-grandchildren; and a neighbor in 1977.

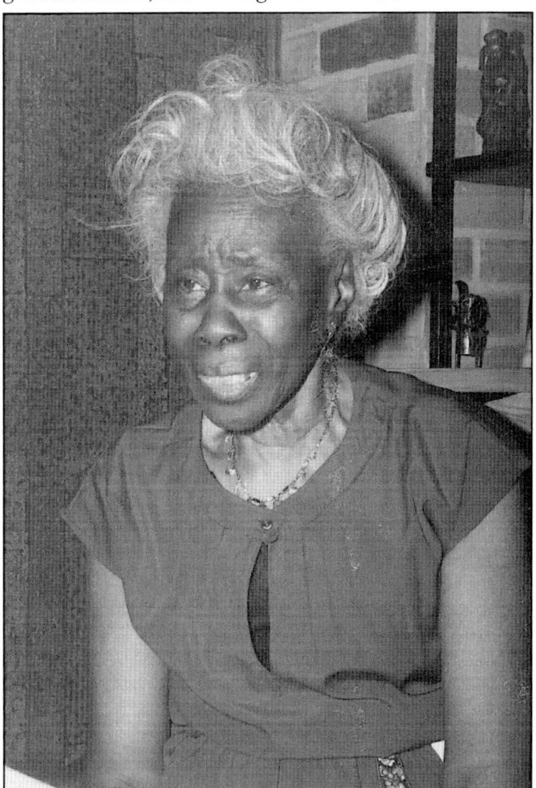

Matriarch Aunt Lue. Lucille Toomer Francis is seen here during a family holiday gathering at her niece's home. Lucille, a retired seamstress and a multi-talented craftswoman, was an extremely active leader at her local senior citizens program.

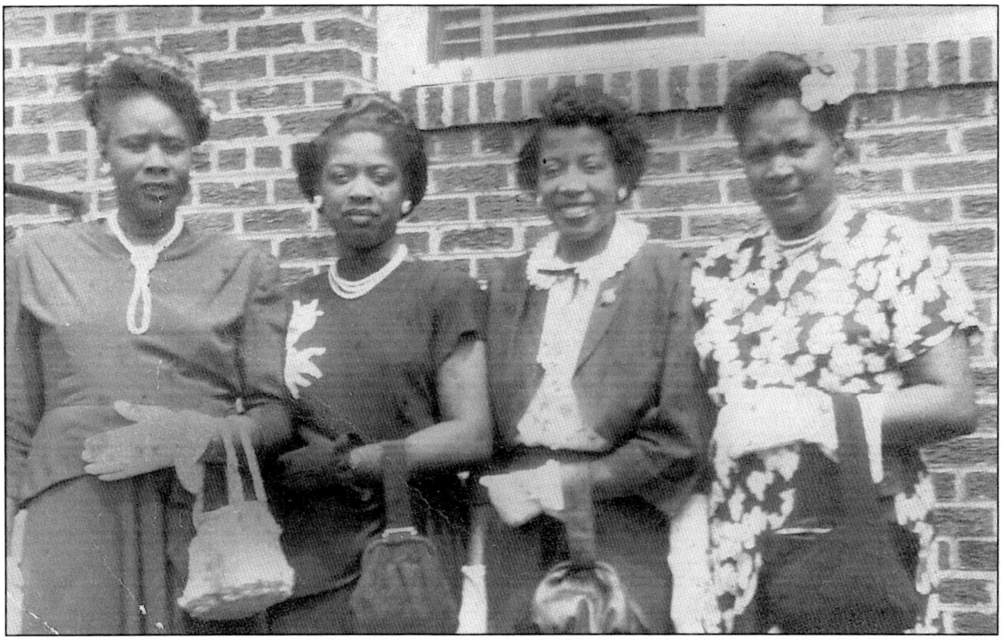

AN OUTING WITH AUNTIE. A Sunday outing features, from left to right, Lucille Toomer Francis (1912–1990), and her nieces Alberta, Emily, and Myrtle King in the 1940s.

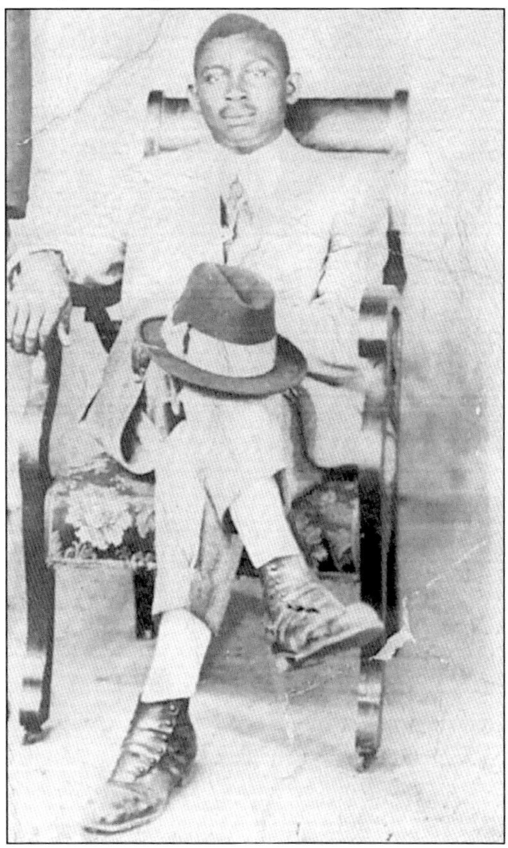

ALBERT KING (1898–1937). Albert King Sr. sold animal skins as his primary profession but also worked in carpentry and sold mail-order products from his home and his "Tin Lizzy" Ford automobile. These goods included straightening combs, comb heaters, heart-shaped perfume bottles, cosmetics such as Orchid hairdressings, Sweet Georgia Brown foundations, Watkins products, Sloans liniment, Brilliantine (a shiny slick-effect hair conditioner), lotion foot softeners, and vanishing and cold creams. Albert also played the accordion. He was a resident of Bettsville Village on the Waccamaw Neck, east of the river, near Arcadia.

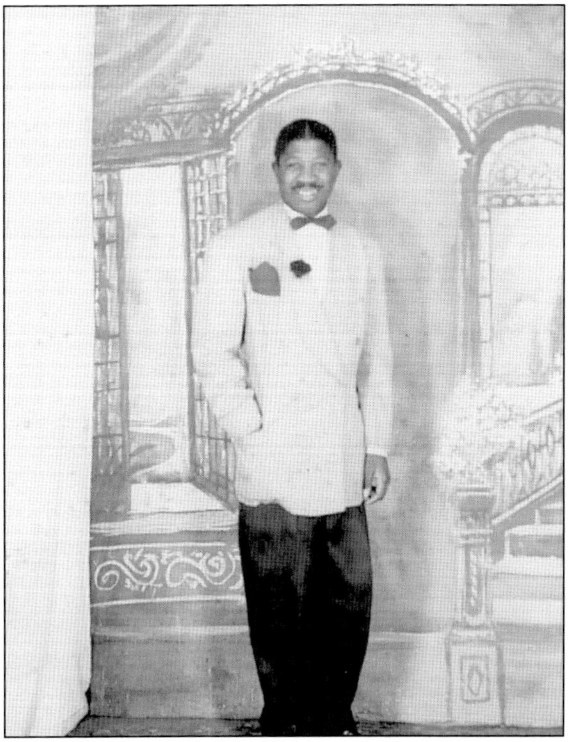

ALBERT "TINY" KING JR. (1917–1984). "Tiny" was the eldest son of Albert and Laura King. He began his lifelong musical career as a saxophonist in Georgetown. Later, he relocated to New York City, formed jazz bands, and played throughout the eastern seaboard.

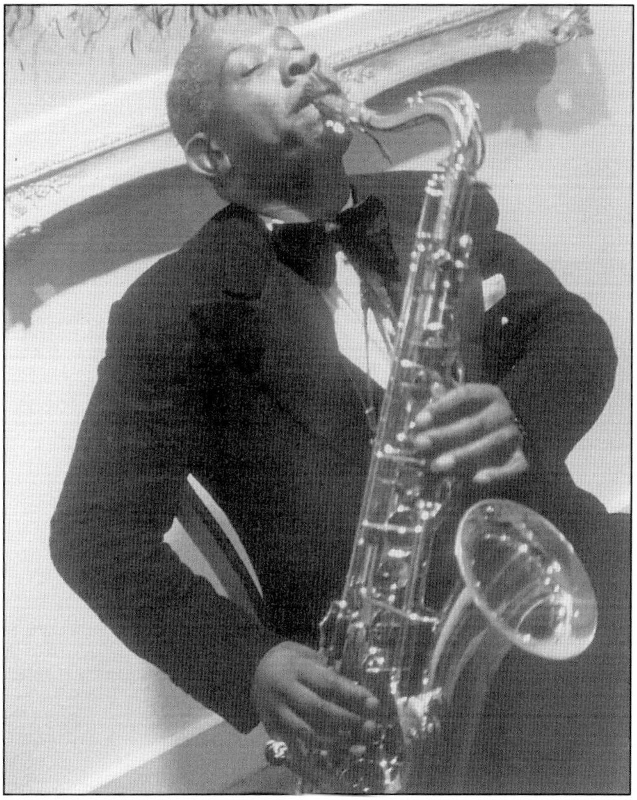

LIKE FATHER, LIKE SON. Robert King, Albert Jr.'s son, is an accomplished musician and photographer. This picture was taken in the 1950s. Today he is known as Wali Obara Rahman, a percussionist and flutist. He and his wife, Andara, manage the Saba Aru Afrik Music and Dance Ensemble in New York City, a troupe that performs throughout the United States. The group recently served as musicians for a national cultural gathering held at Penn Center on St. Helena Island, near Beaufort, South Carolina.

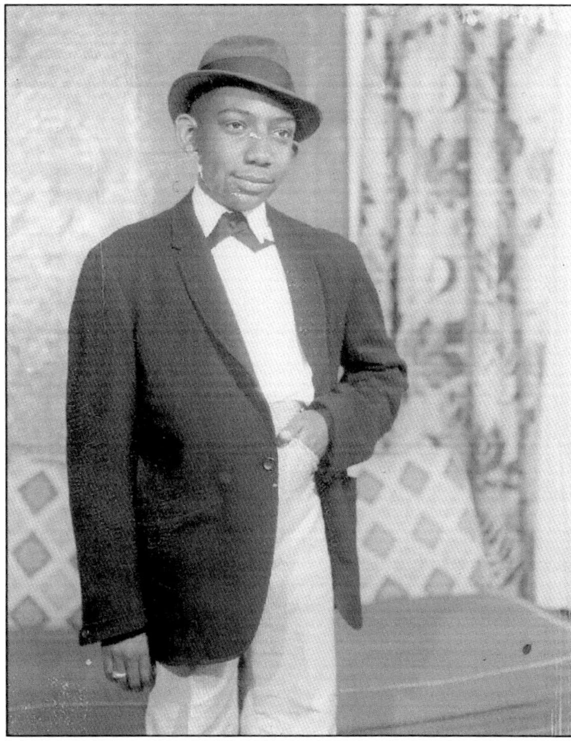

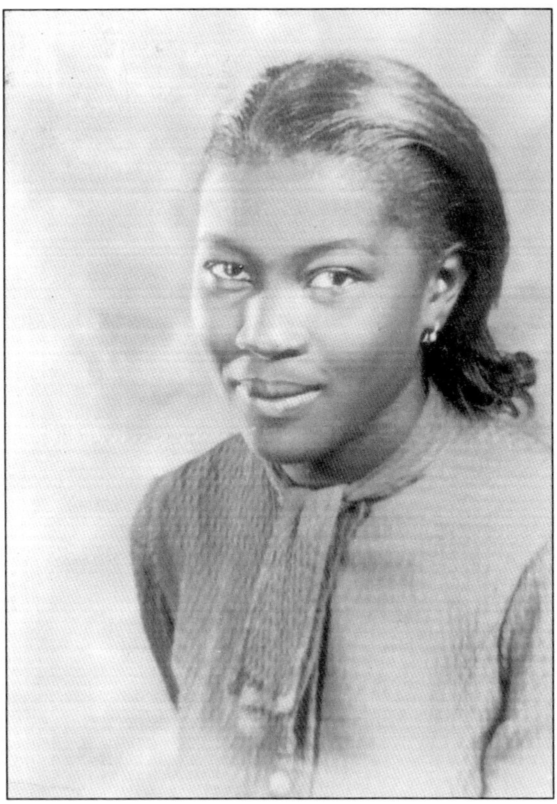

MYRTLE KING. Myrtle, Laura and Albert's eldest daughter, is pictured during her Howard High School years in 1938. With a keen interest in the medical field, Myrtle began training at Florence Williams Hospital, where Dr. Beck removed tonsils and Dr. Bell delivered babies. The hospital was located next door to the original Howard building. (Courtesy of Myrtle King.)

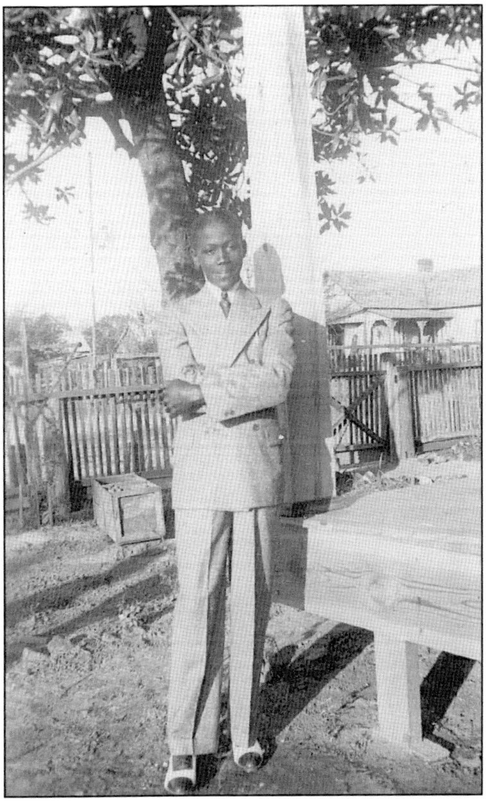

AN ADMIRER. Isaac Fishburne is patiently posing for this picture as he waits to spend time with Myrtle King on a Sunday afternoon during high school days, 1939. (Courtesy of Myrtle King.)

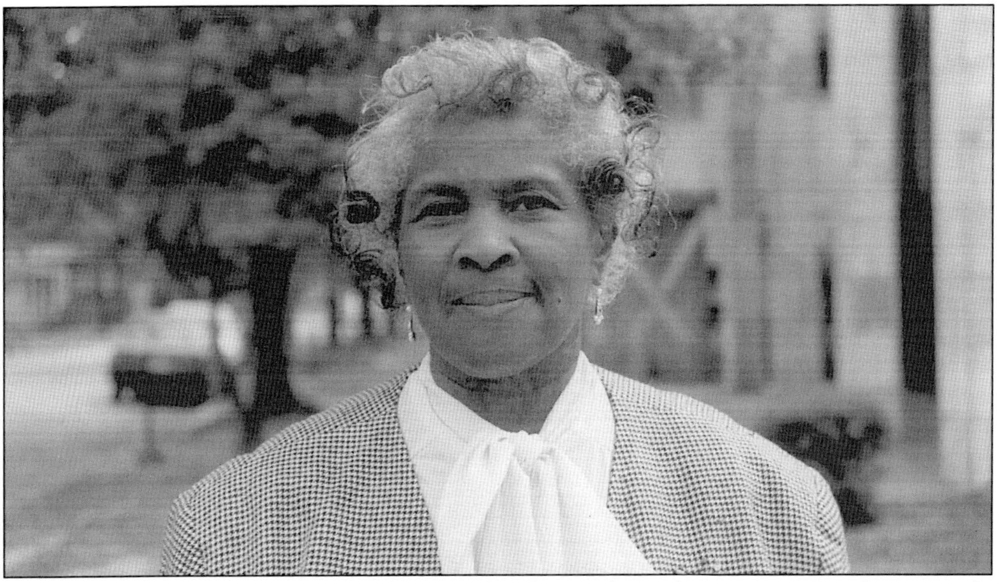

MOM. Affectionately called "Mom" by most family members, the name truly reflects Myrtle King's nurturing qualities. She is a retired pediatric nurse. After leaving St. Lukes/Woman's Hospital, she returned home to Georgetown in 1977. King is an active member of First Calvary Missionary Baptist Church, and she is pictured here on Easter Sunday, 1992.

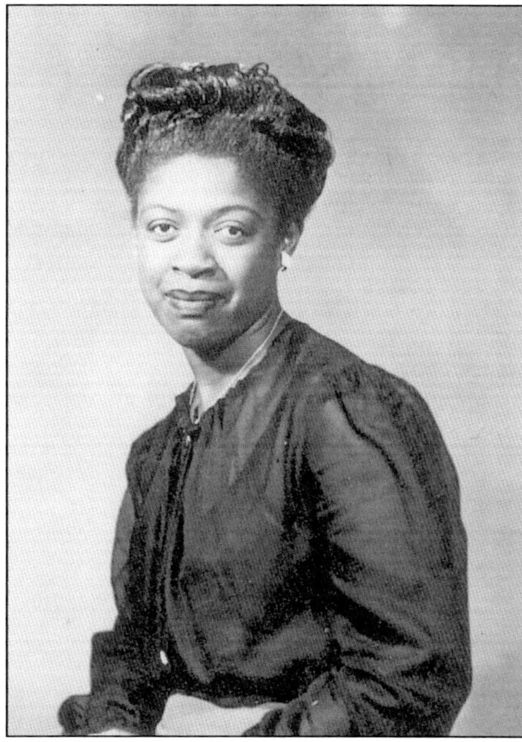

TRANSITIONS. Alberta King Byrd (1922–1978) is depicted here before her migration south, after residing in New York City.

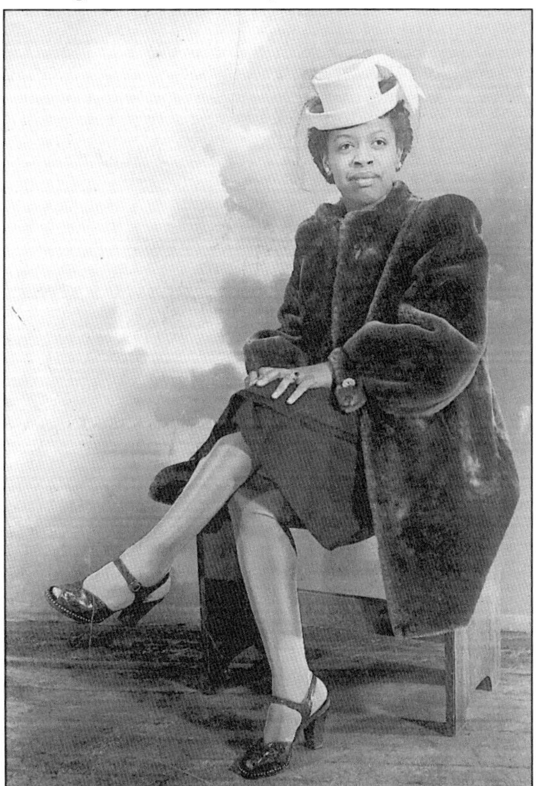

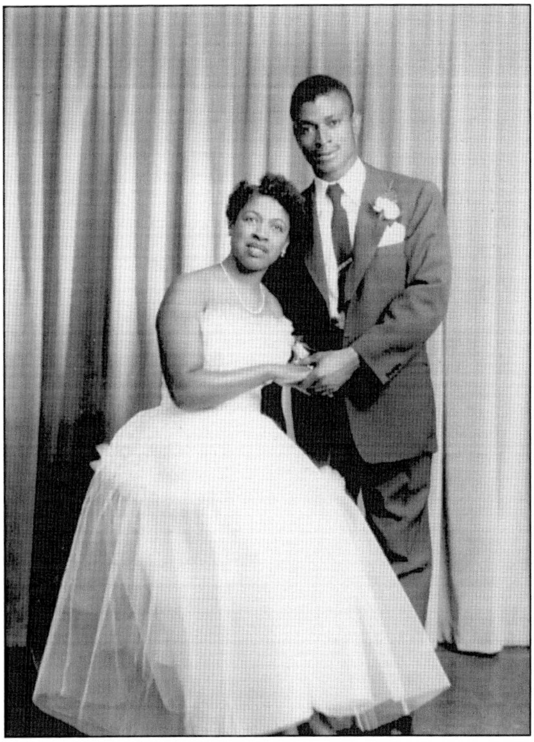

AN EVENING BALL. Alberta King and Washington Byrd pose during an evening ball in the late 1950s.

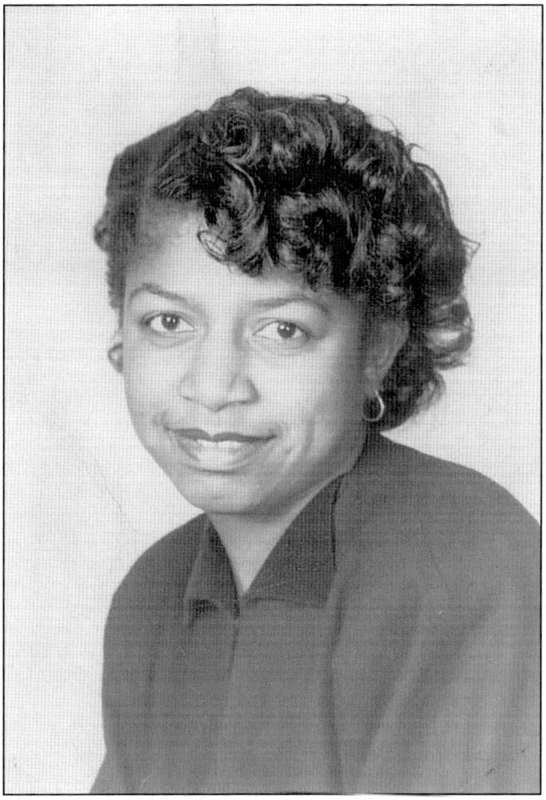

EDNA KING (1925–1991). Edna King graduated from Benedict College in Columbia, South Carolina, in 1949.

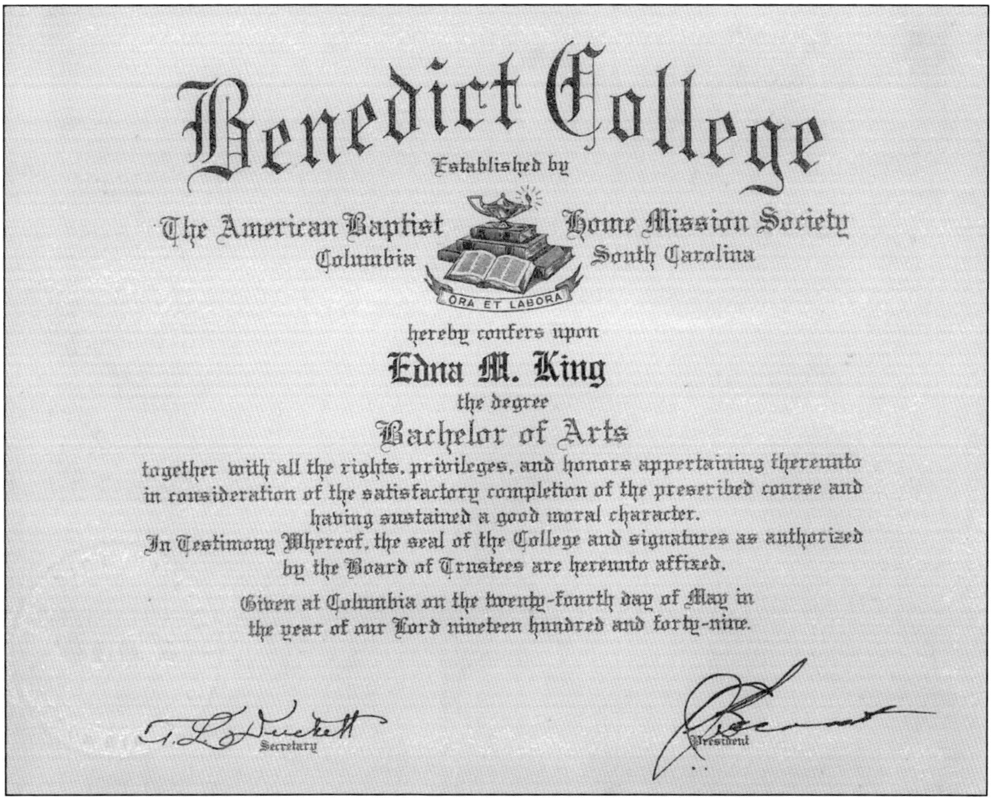

Benedict College

Established by

The American Baptist Home Mission Society

Columbia South Carolina

ORA ET LABORA

hereby confers upon

Edna M. King

the degree

Bachelor of Arts

together with all the rights, privileges, and honors appertaining thereunto in consideration of the satisfactory completion of the prescribed course and having sustained a good moral character.

In Testimony Whereof, the seal of the College and signatures as authorized by the Board of Trustees are hereunto affixed.

Given at Columbia on the twenty-fourth day of May in the year of our Lord nineteen hundred and forty-nine.

T. L. Duckett
Secretary

President

BACHELOR OF ARTS DEGREE. This degree was authorized by the American Baptist Home Mission Society and bestowed upon Edna King.

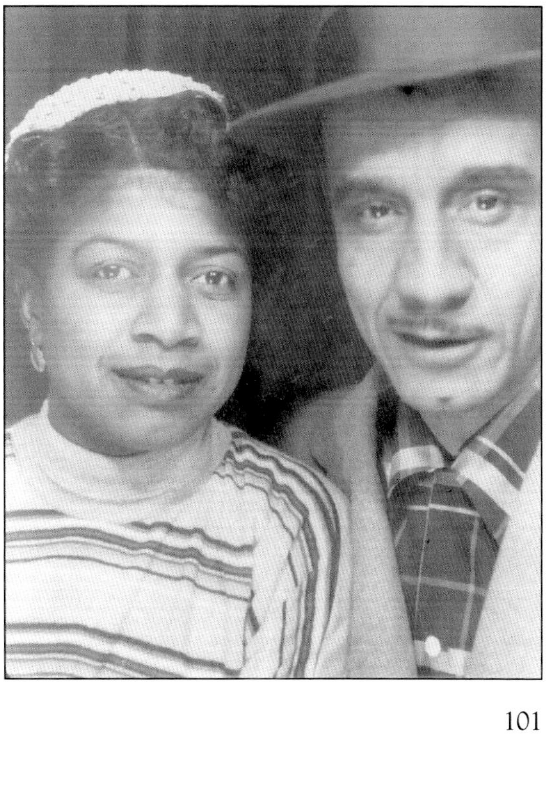

GEECHEE LOVERS, 1950. Edna is pictured with her partner, Ivan Ricardo La Roche (1910–1989), a native Charlestonian. The couple had a daughter, Ramona La Roche, and two grandsons, Ojas and Obsidian.

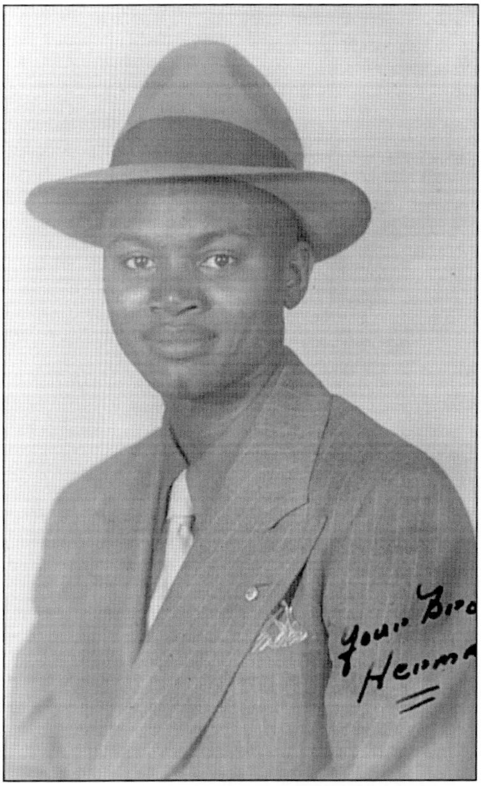

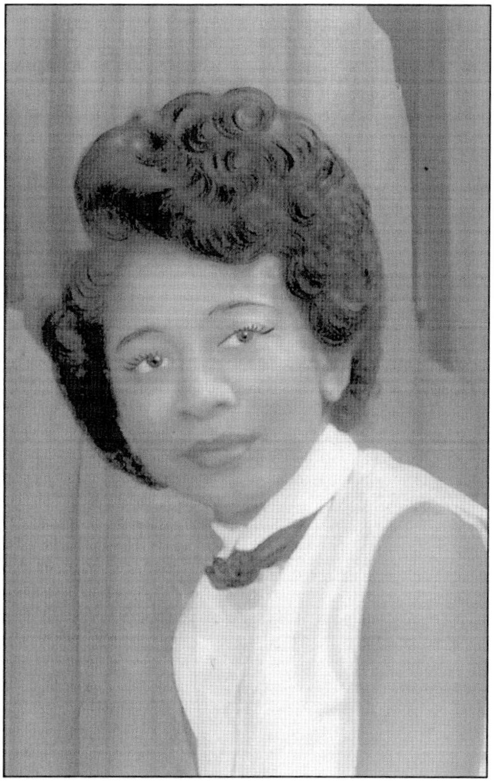

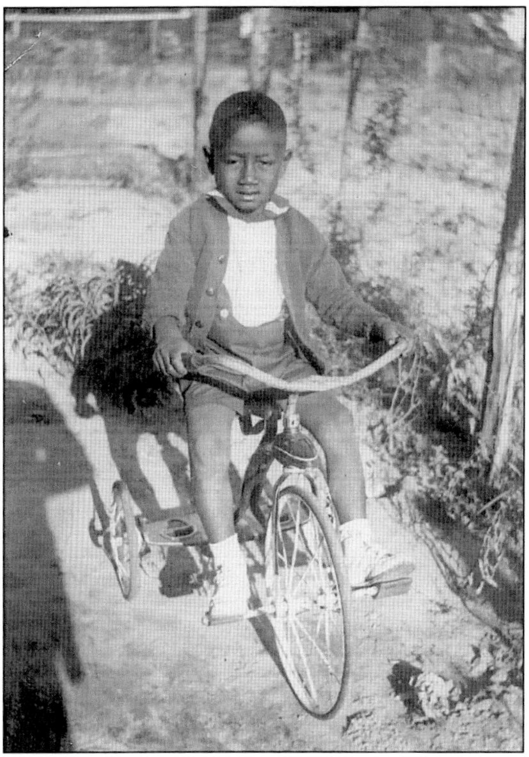

Top Left: **BROTHER TO SISTER.** This is a postcard photo from Herman King to his sister Edna. *Right*: **"QUEENIE."** Thelma King, the youngest daughter of Albert and Laura King, was a pianist. She played for Arnet A.M.E. Church until her migration to New York City. She is the former wife of Fredrick Douglas Dailey, deceased, and the mother of two children, Fredrika D. Richardson and Fredrick Jr.

BABY BOY. Ernest Jerome King (1935–1965) sits on his tricycle just outside of his homestead on Palm Street in Georgetown, 1938.

Four

SPIRITUALITY

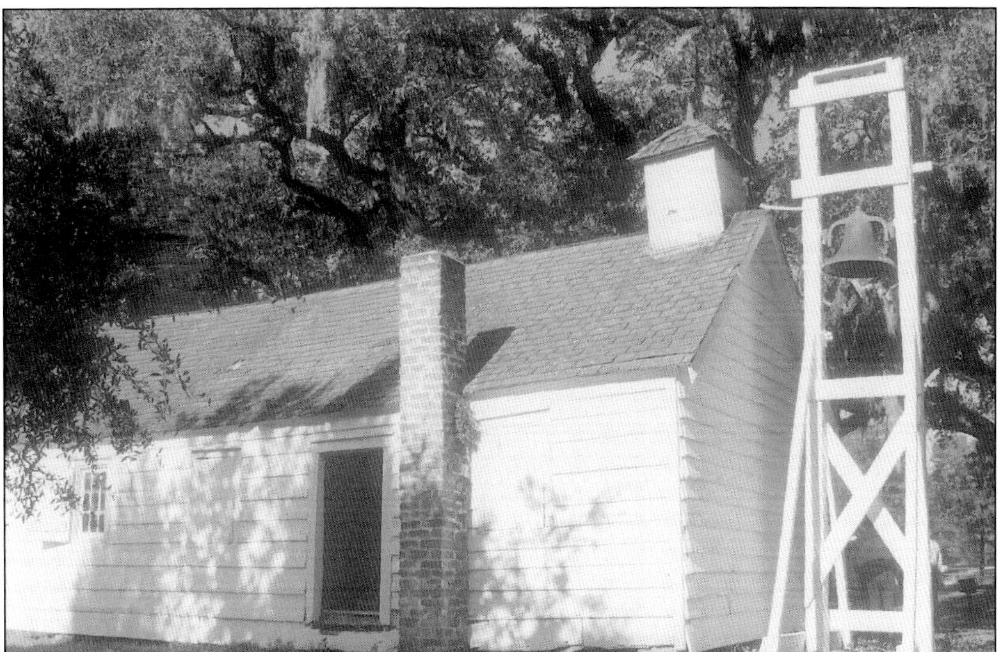

PRAISE HOUSE ON MANSFIELD PLANTATION.

"E stan jes like a man wa da build a house. E dig way down een de groun til e find de rock an lay de foundation on top ob dat rock. Wen de flood come, a whole heap ob wata hit dat house, bot de house ain't moobe. Nottin happen ta um, cause de man done build um on de rock. Bot anybody wa yeh me wod an ain't do wa A tell um fa do, stan jes like a man wa build e house on top ob de groun. E ain't dig down fa lay de foundation. Soon as de flood hit dat house, e fall down. Bam! E smash op!" Luke 6: 48-49.

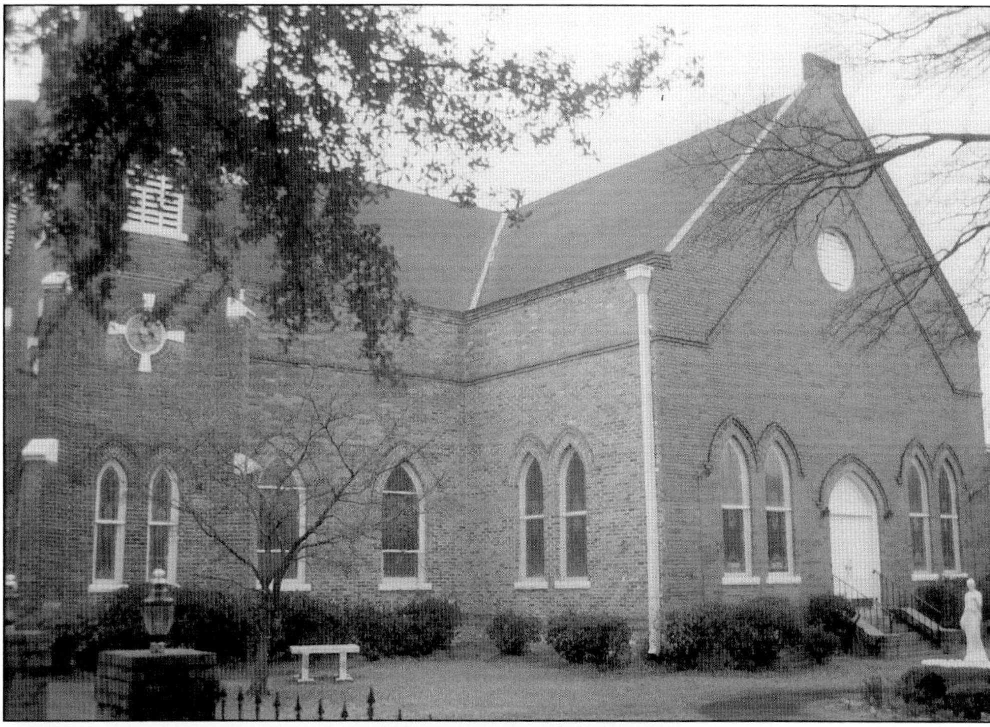

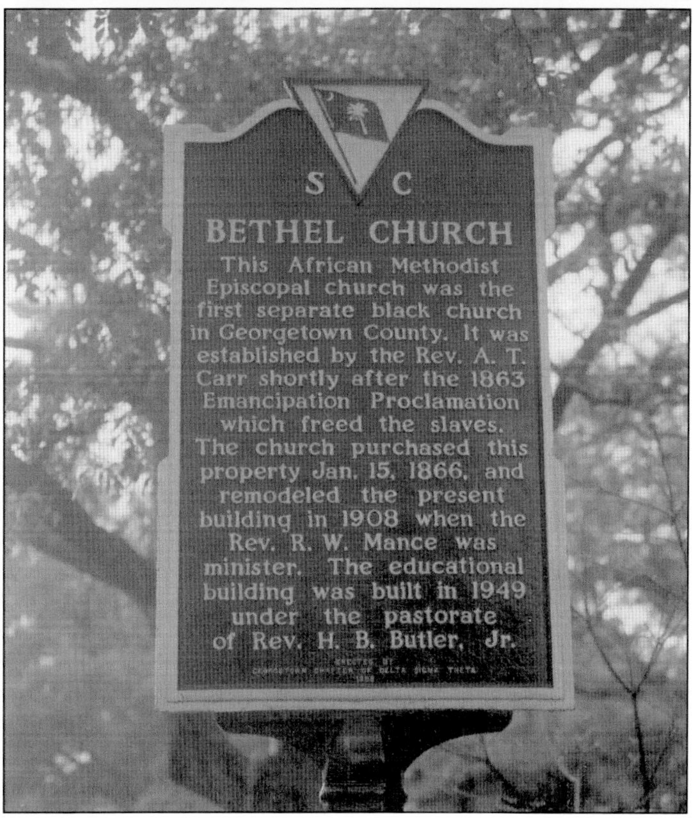

BETHEL AFRICAN METHODIST EPISCOPAL CHURCH. Bethel A.M.E. Church was organized by Reverend Augustus T. Carr in 1865. In 1866, the first small church was built where the old parsonage now stands. The present sanctuary was built as a wooden structure during the pastorate of Reverend Samuel Washington. The church was bricked over and remodeled in 1980.

An Emergent Leader. Reverend Augustus T. Carr, seen here c. 1910, organized and founded Bethel African Methodist Episcopal Church of Georgetown in 1865. Rev. Carr received his license to preach during his tenure at Duncan United Methodist Church. (Courtesy of the Committee on African-American History Observance.)

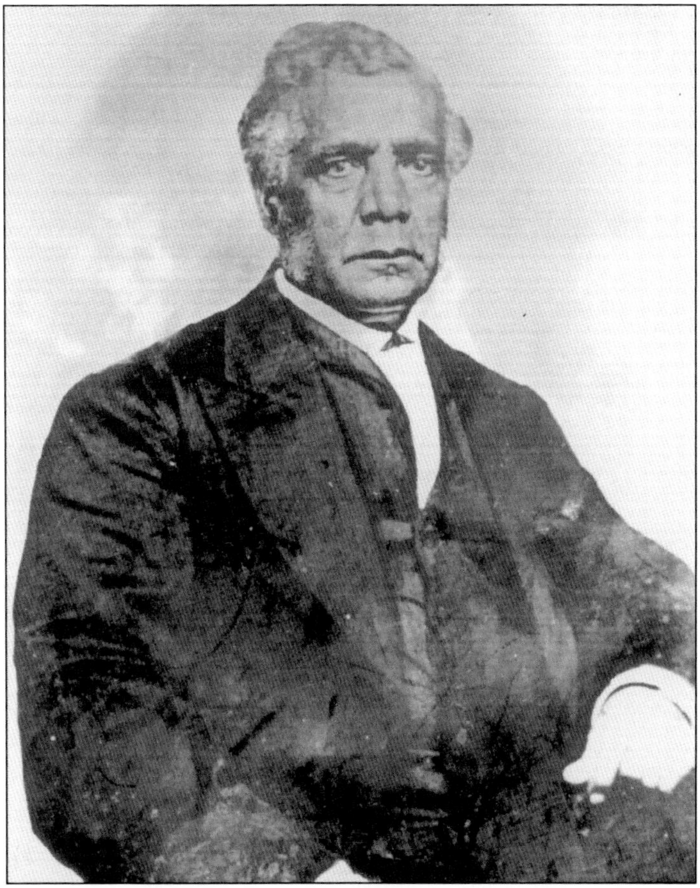

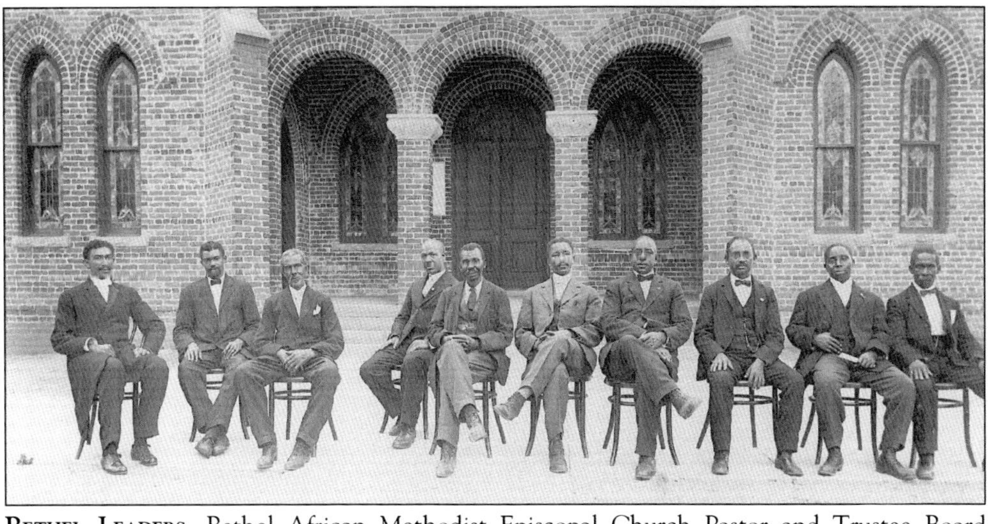

Bethel Leaders. Bethel African Methodist Episcopal Church Pastor and Trustee Board members are seated in front of the newly renovated building in 1908. From left to right are, J.E. Beard, Pastor, J.J. Burton, Adam Dunmore, J.B. Beck, R.B. Anderson, Dr. Brewington, unidentified, J. Prioleau, J.B. Brockingtron, and Tony Alston. (Courtesy of Georgetown County Library Morgan Collection.)

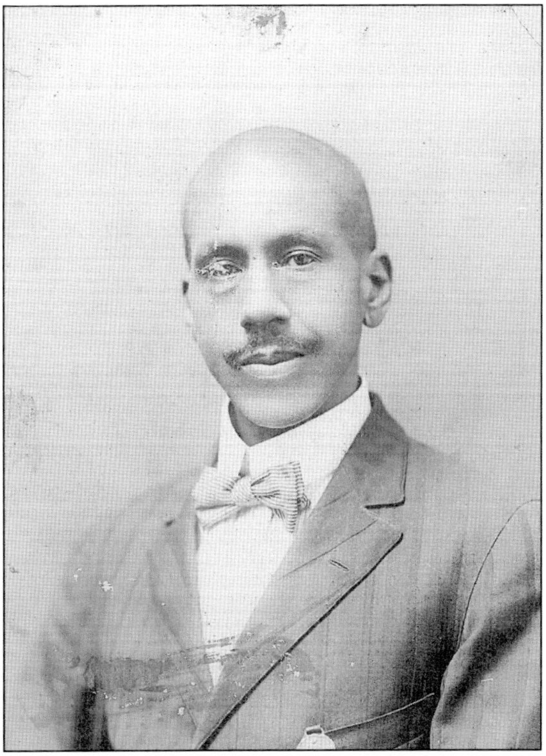

Sampson Dunmore, Contractor. Sampson Dunmore built the original parsonage for Bethel African Methodist Episcopal Church in Georgetown in 1905. He and his wife, Venus, had four children: Julian, James, Lawrence, and a daughter who died at birth. (Courtesy of Margretta Knox.)

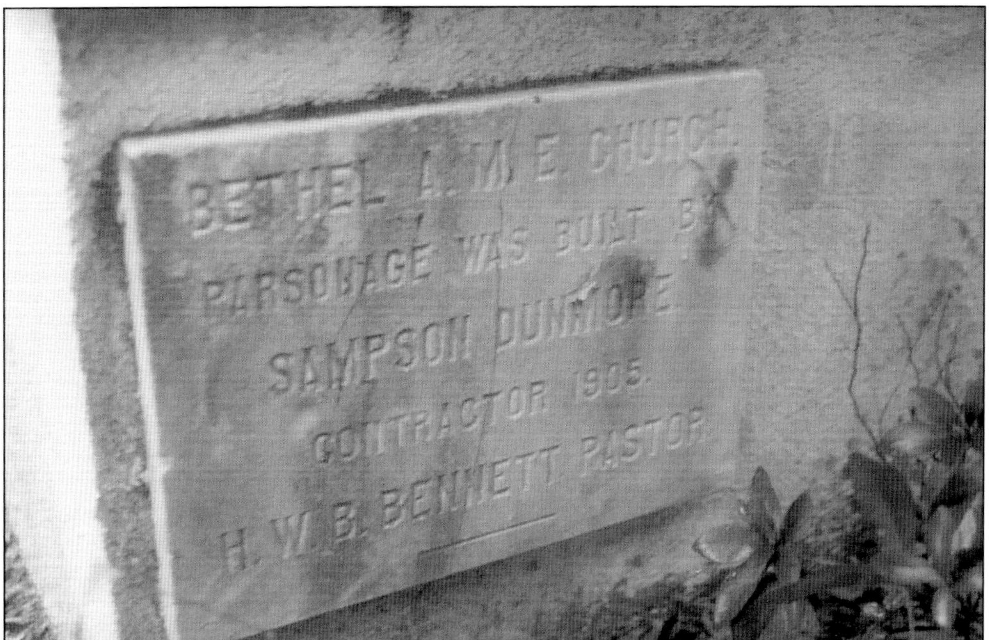

Bethel African Methodist Episcopal Original Parsonage Cornerstone. The parsonage was built in 1905, and H.W.B. Bennett was the pastor during that time. The building is located on Broad Street in the historic district of Georgetown.

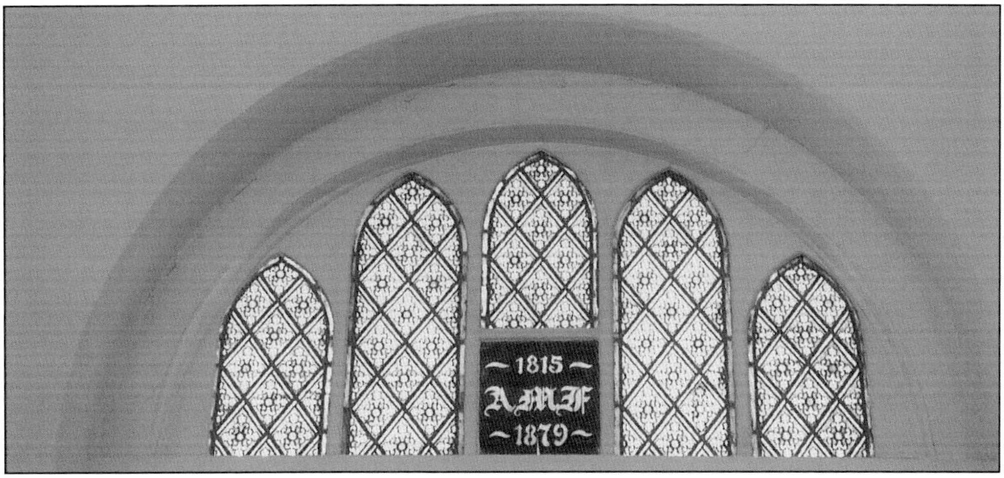

Prince George Winyah Episcopal Church. The only African Americans known to be buried in a white, Georgetown County cemetery are interred here. St. Mary's, an Episcopal chapel, was built for the enslaved African Americans of Hagley Plantation by Renty Tucker, an extraordinarily talented, enslaved carpenter in 1859. He worked closely with his owner, Plowden Weston. After the Civil War, in 1873, W. St. Julian Mazyck, heir to the Weston property, donated the English stained-glass windows, a gold communion chalice, and a bell for the church tower from St. Mary's Chapel to Prince George Church. The oak stalls and ornamental locks from the chapel went to Prince Frederick's Church on the Pee Dee. The stained-glass windows are above the altar and over the side doors. The center one depicts St. Mary, the mother of God, holding a lily, which is her symbol. The window on the right contains an Alpha and Omega, and the one on the left shows a lamb, Agnus Dei or "Lamb of God," with a banner. John, the Baptist, twice points out Jesus as "the Lamb of God, who takes away the sin of the world" (John 1:29 and 36). An unblemished lamb was used by the Hebrews to sacrifice

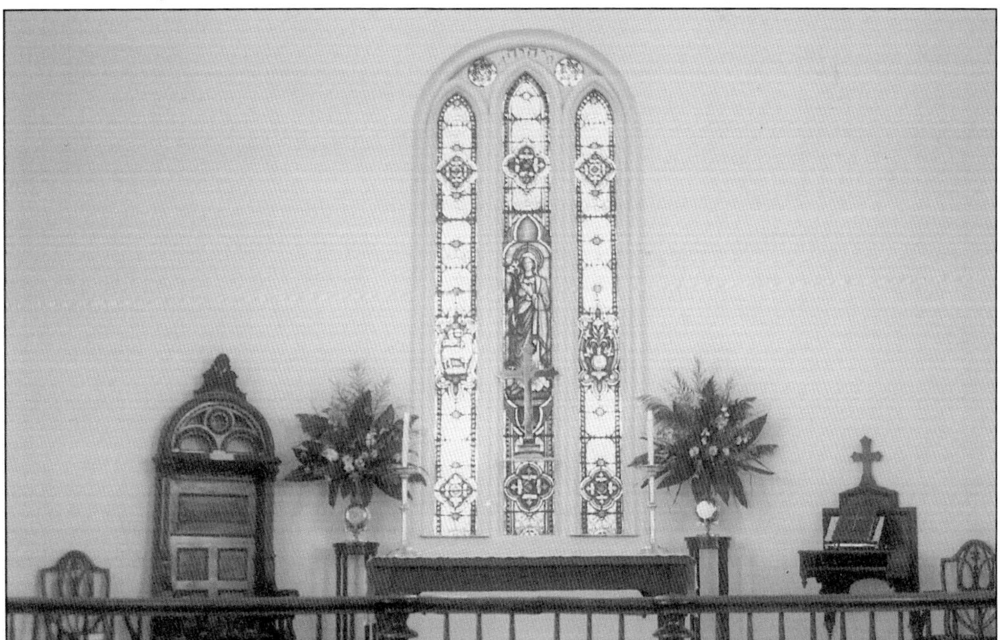

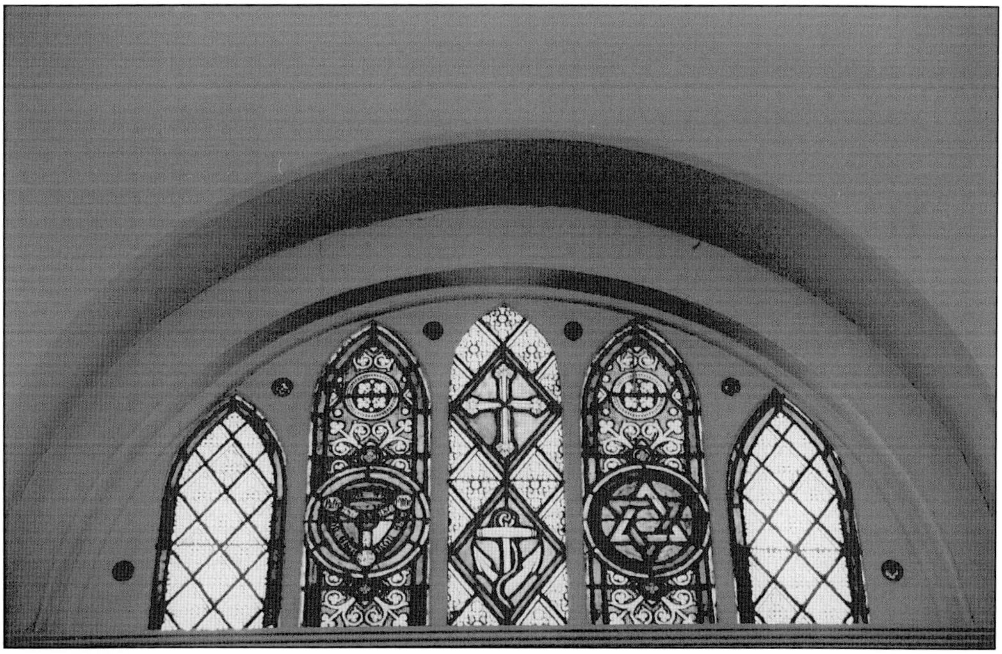

to God. The three rayed numbus, or halo, was used for God, saints, or the Holy Family, and the banner stands for victory. So this scene shows the sacrificial lamb victorious. In the "Shield of the Holy Trinity," the shield is a symbol of unwavering trust from St. Paul's description of a Christian's armor (Ephesians 6:16). This interesting design is used chiefly in stained glass of medieval churches. The works make two groups of sentences, one positive and one negative. The Father is God. The Son is God. The Holy Spirit is God. The Father is not the Son. The Son is not the Holy Spirit. The Holy Spirit is not the Father. In "The Six-Pointed Star," the Creator's star is an ancient emblem of God the Father, with the six points representative of the attributes of the Deity—power, wisdom, majesty, love, mercy, and justice. In six days, He created heaven and earth. That He is the Triune God is symbolized by this star being made of two triangles, emblems of the Holy Trinity. The "Anchor" dates back to the catacombs. It is a variation of the cross and signifies hope, based on the reference in the Epistle to the Hebrews of God's promise: "Which hope we have as an anchor of the soul." It is an emblem of St. Clement, a bishop of Rome, as tradition says he was bound to an anchor and cast into the sea during the persecutions in Italy. The "Cross Fleurie" depicts the resurrection of the crucified Christ. The window on the left has a Lily for purity, Mary, and the annunciation. The Crown of Life symbol denotes victory and sovereignty; it is also an emblem of the "king of Glory" (Psalm 24:7). Across the top of the window is the Alpha and Omega on each side, and the Hebrew word for Yahweh, or Jehovah, is between them. This word contains no vowels and was considered too sacred to be spoken.

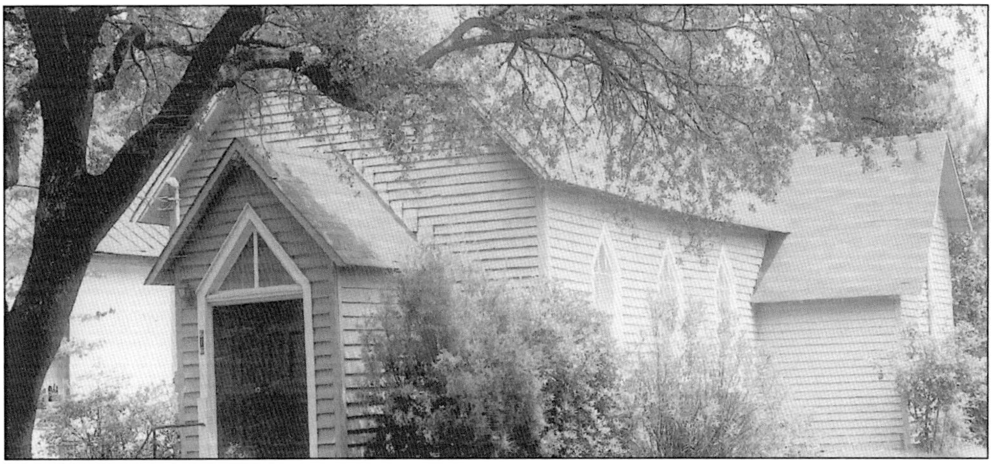

St. Cyprian's Episcopal Church. Renty Tucker was a master carpenter, builder, and a part-time house servant for the Westons at Hagley Plantation. He is said to have been trained in fine carpentry in England. For most of 1859, he was quite involved in the planning and constructing of a model of the plantation chapel for slaves. It would later be erected as St. Mary's Chapel. In 1860, Tucker was 28 years old, his wife, Josephine, a seamstress, was 26, and their son, Benjamin, was 6. Tucker built a summer home for the Westons on Pawleys Island. He was appointed sexton at Prince George Winyah Episcopal Church and was instrumental in founding St. Cyprian's Church. He approached the vestry of Prince George and requested help in building a church for African Americans who had previously been members of Prince George. The vestry decided to contribute personally rather than as a body. The cornerstone reads "Bought and remodelled 1924, Named St. Cyprians Church by Bp. Wm. A. Guerry, D.D. Rev. E.L. Baskervill." Due to financial restraints, the church was officially closed by the Episcopal Diocese in 1998. Many members of the small congregation transferred their membership to Prince George Winyah Episcopal or Bethel A.M.E. Church. The building remains standing at 616 Duke Street and has recently been purchased by a local children's day care agency.

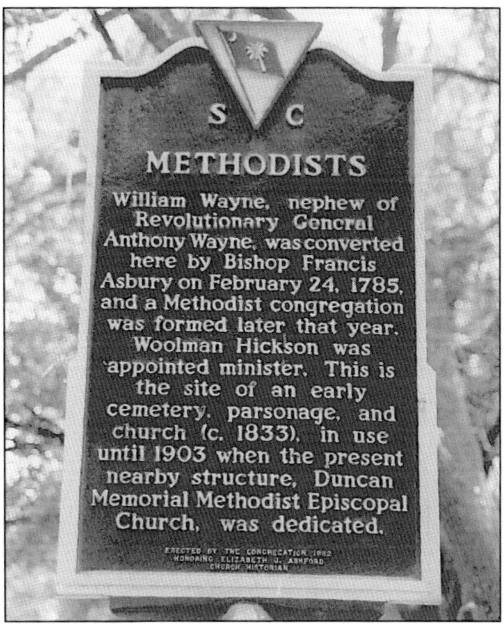

South Carolina Methodists—Duncan United Methodist Church Historic Marker. The marker was erected by the congregation, honoring Elizabeth J. Ashford, the church's historian, in 1982. Georgetown's first Methodist congregation was formed in 1785. An early site, with the church, parsonage, and cemetery, was located on High Market and Orange Streets, c. 1833.

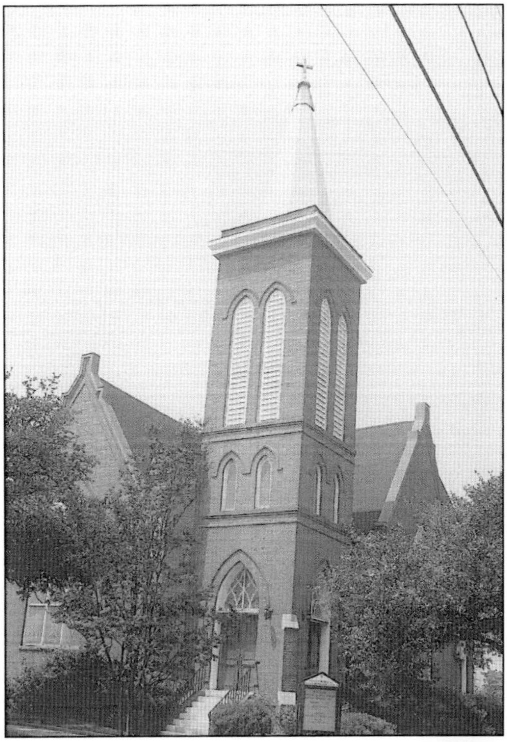

Duncan United Methodist Church. Erected in 1903, Duncan Church had a significantly large number of African Americans in its congregation from the late 1700s until the emancipation of slaves. In 1865, the majority of "coloreds" left and took membership with the African-American owned and administered Bethel African Methodist Episcopal Church in Georgetown. Leadership was provided by Augustus T. Carr, licensed preacher of Duncan. The last African American on the membership roll of Duncan Church, he served as Church Sexton until his death in May 1879.

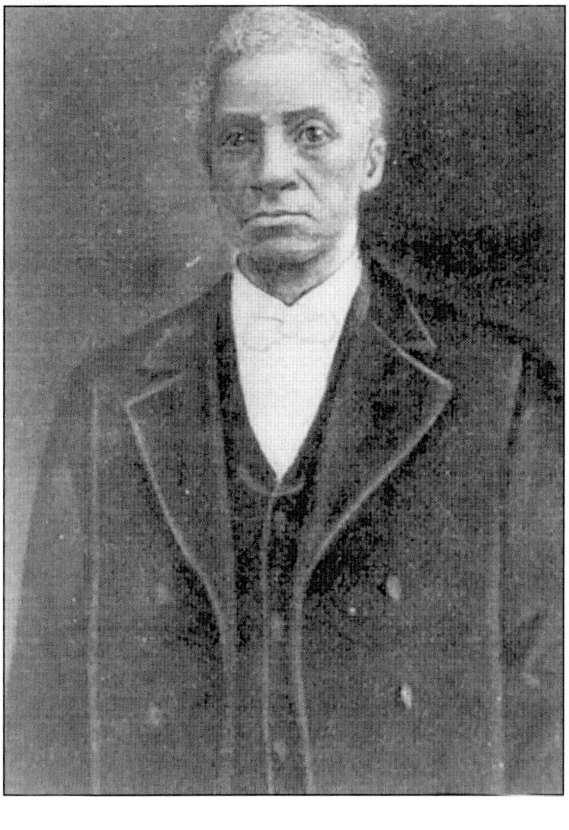

Reverend March Singleton.

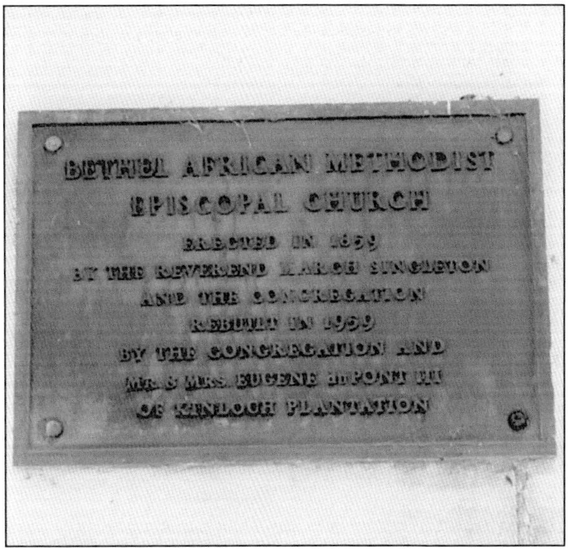

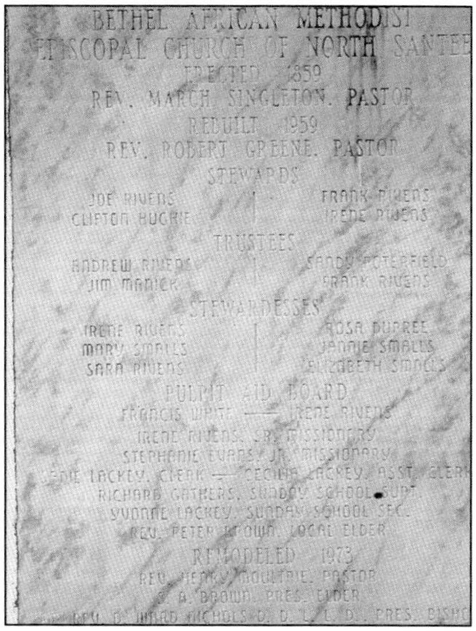

Bethel African Methodist Episcopal Church. The cornerstone on the left reads, "Erected in 1859 by the Reverend March Singleton and the congregation, rebuilt in 1959 by the congregation and Mr. & Mrs. Eugene du Pont III of Kinloch Plantation."

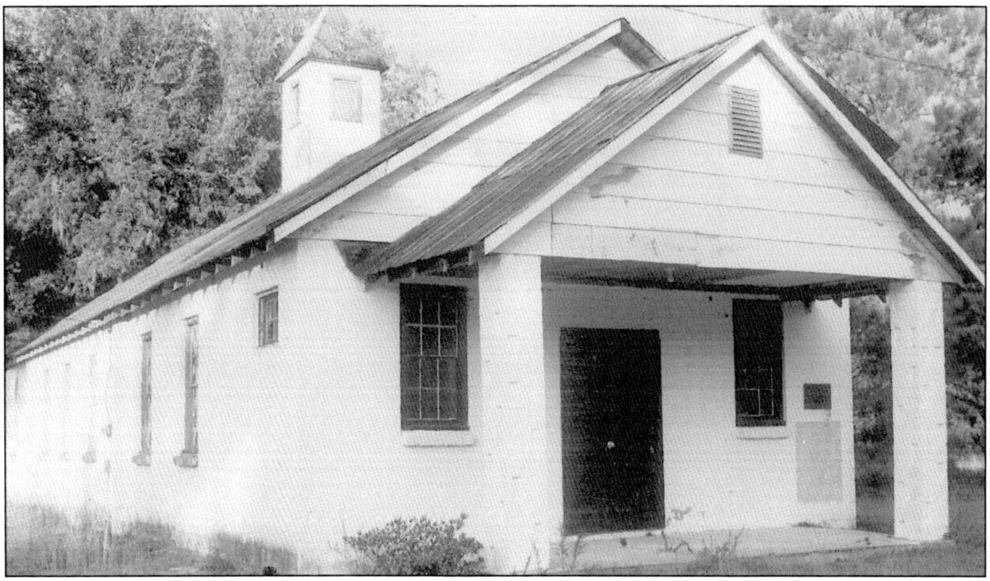

Bethel African Methodist Episcopal Church of North Santee. The church was erected 1859. The church's pastor Reverend March Singleton rebuilt the structure in 1959. Later members and leaders of the church are printed on the cornerstone at right: Reverend Robert Greene, (pastor); stewards Joe Rivens, Frank Rivens, Clifton Hughie, and Irene Rivens; trustees Andrew Rivens, Sand Poterfield, Jim Manick, and Frank Rivens; stewardesses Irene Rivens, Rosa Dupree, Mary Smalls, Jannie Smalls, Sara Rivens, and Elizabeth Smalls; the Pulpit Aid Board members Francis White and Irene Rivens, and senior missionary Irene Rivens; junior missionary Stephanie Evans; clerk Sadie Lackey; assistant clerk Cecilia Lackey; Sunday school superintendent Richard Gathers; Sunday school secretary Yvonne Lackey; local elder Reverend Peter Brown. Under the pastorship of Reverend Henry Moultrie and the leadership of S.A. Brown and Reverend D. Ward Nichols, D.D.L.L.D, the church was remodeled in 1973.

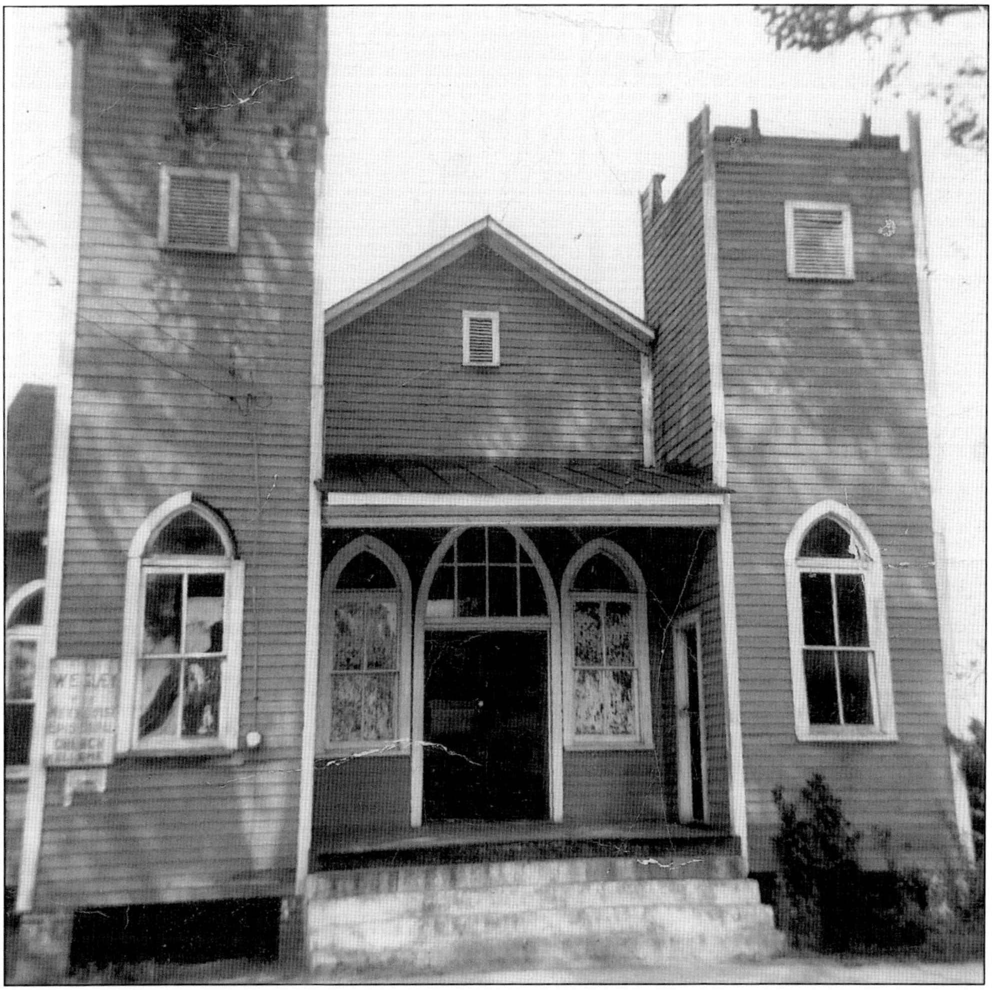

Wesley A.M.E. Church, 1955. The Wesley Church formally stood on the corner of Duke and Queen Streets. It officially closed several years ago. Most former members transferred to the Bethel A.M.E. Churches. (Courtesy of Minnie Kennedy.)

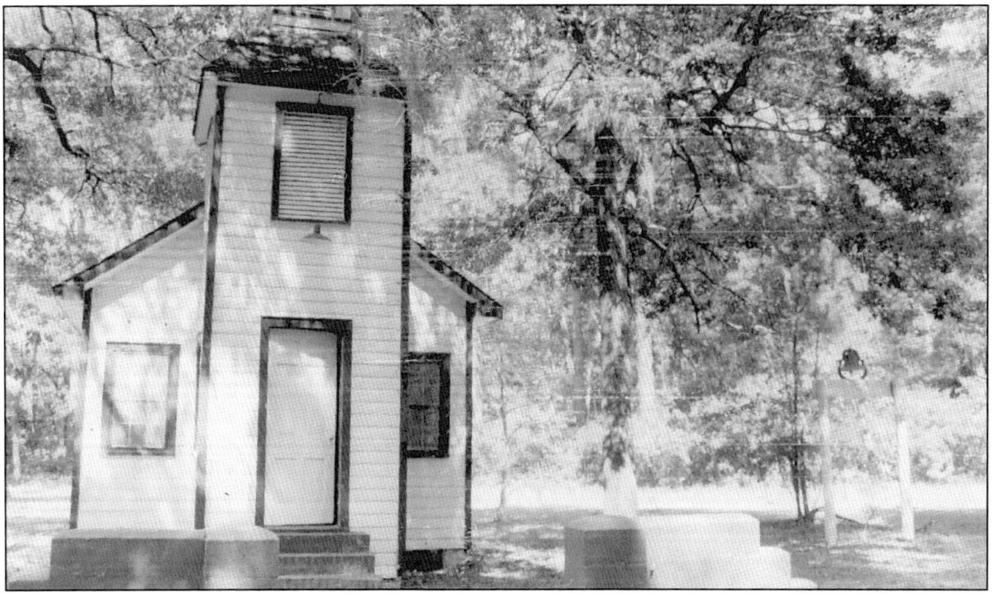

St. James A.M.E. Church. St. James Church is located on Cat Island and is only accessible by boat. The church is restricted to island residents, employees, and visitors of the Yawkey Plantation, also known as the Tom Yawkey Wildlife Center.

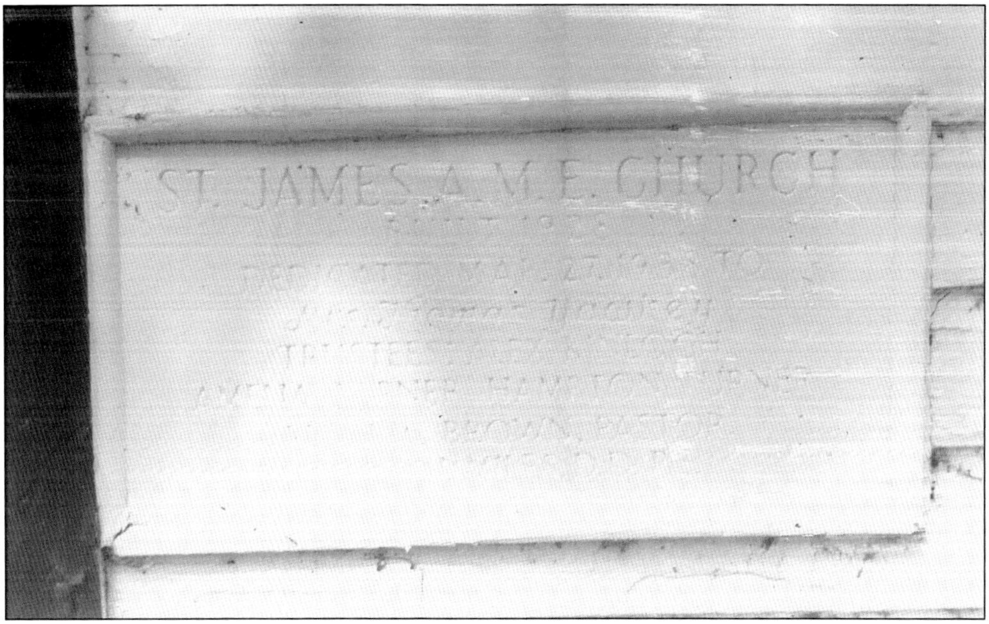

St. James A.M.E. A circuit church (services are held on the first and third Sundays of every month and a pastor is shared with Sandy Island Church of Maxwell Plantation) was built in 1928 and dedicated on March 27, 1938, by Mrs. Thomas Yawkey. Its trustees were Alex Kinloch, Amelia Turner, Hampton Turner, Reverend T.W. Brown (pastor), and Reverend T.L. Miles, D.D.PE (Yawkey Plantation: South, North, and Cat Islands). The church officially closed in 1979, when Martha Singleton, the "Church Mother," died. Past reverends included Alex Kinloch, James Canteen, Edward Marsh, Tisdale, Leroy Sabb, and Norman Vanderhorst (associate).

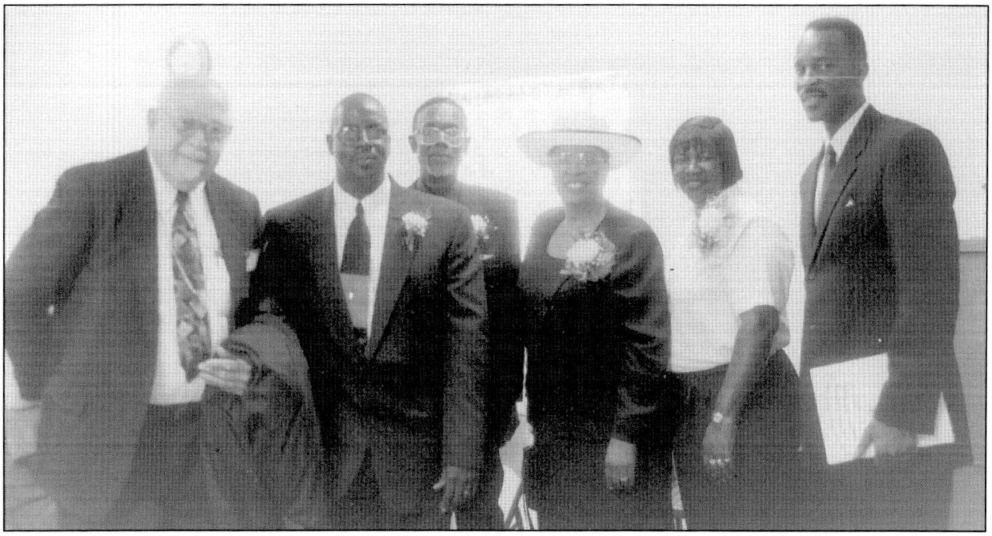

SINGLETON CHAPEL A.M.E. CHURCH REDEDICATION CEREMONY. From left to right are Right Reverend John Hurst Adams (presiding Bishop), Reverend Patrick Staggers (pastor of Singleton), Reverend Lee Seward (Presiding Elder Georgetown District), Mrs. Hurst Adams, Mrs. Michelle Staggers, Reverend Dr. William Swinton (pastor of Bethel A.M.E. in Georgetown, president, A.M.E. Ministerial Alliance) during the rededication ceremony for Singleton Chapel Church.

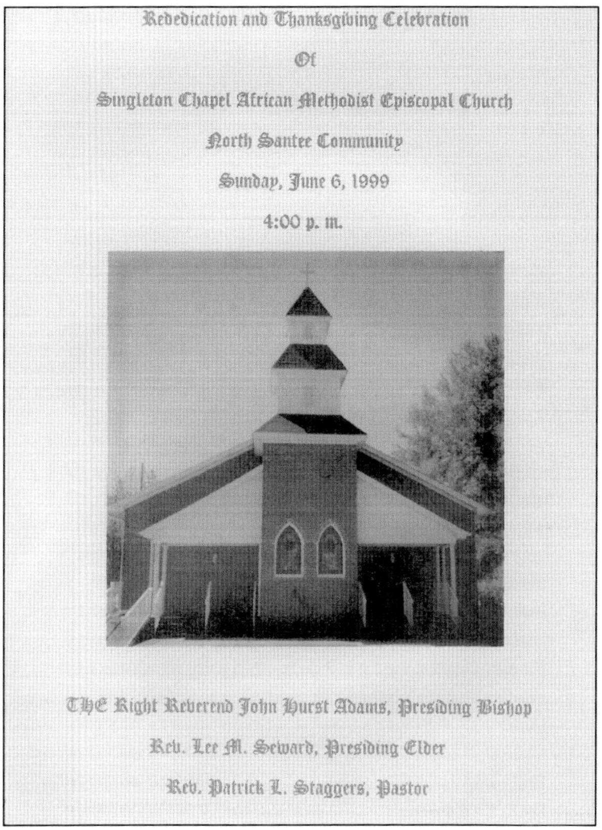

Rededication and Thanksgiving Celebration

Of

Singleton Chapel African Methodist Episcopal Church

North Santee Community

Sunday, June 6, 1999

4:00 p. m.

THE Right Reverend John Hurst Adams, Presiding Bishop

Rev. Lee M. Seward, Presiding Elder

Rev. Patrick L. Staggers, Pastor

SINGLETON CHAPEL A.M.E. CHURCH OF NORTH SANTEE REDEDICATION PROGRAM. The church held its rededication program in June 1999 to celebrate its spiritual renewal and most recent renovations.

Ruby's Garden. This is a memorial tribute to Mrs. Ruby "Miss Ruby" Forsythe.

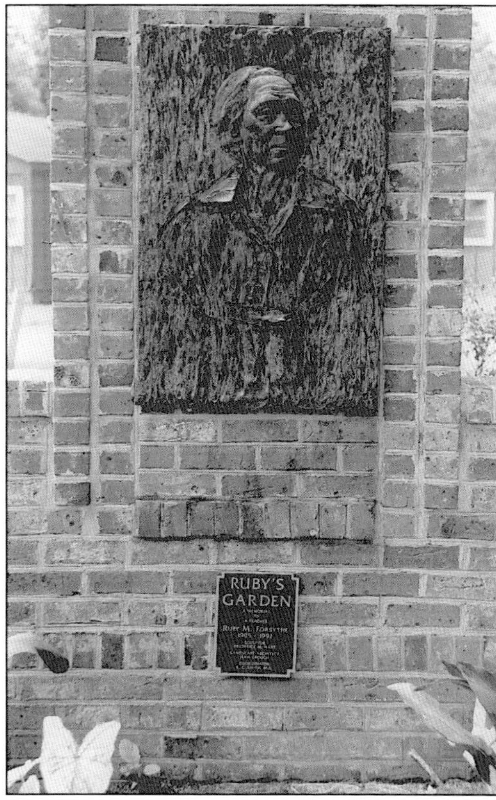

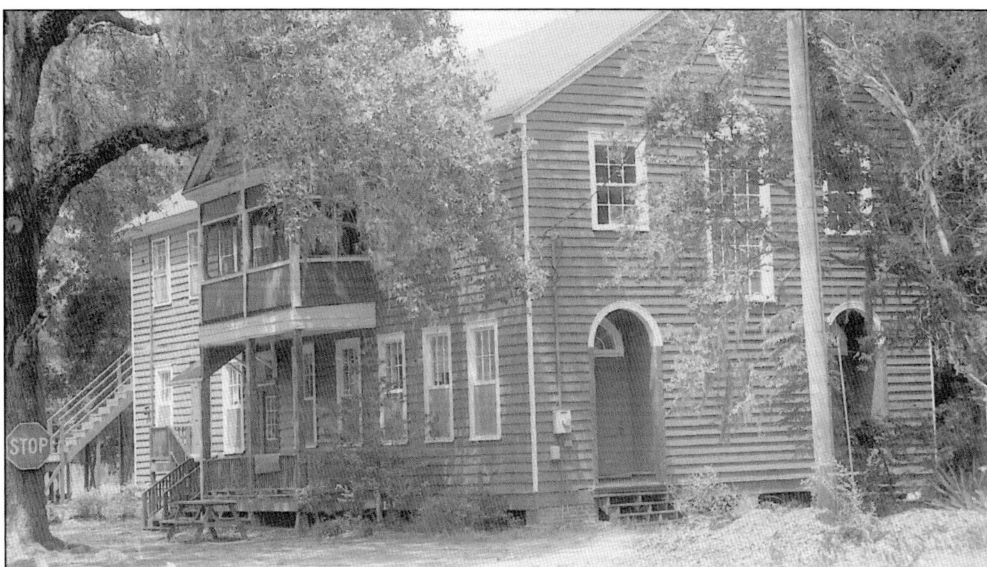

Holy Cross Faith Memorial School. This one-room school was established in 1903, and Father W.E. Forsythe was assigned to it by the Episcopal Church. During the 1930s, his wife, Ruby Forsythe (1905–1992), administered the school with four teachers. Upon Reverend Forsythe's death in 1974, Miss Ruby became the new director. A new school building was erected in 1933.

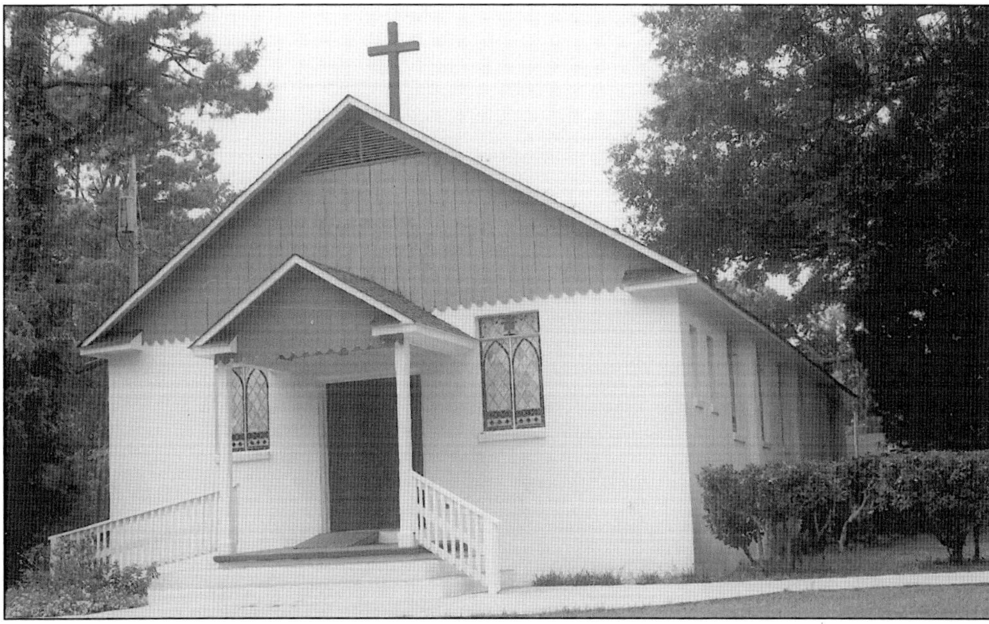

HOLY CROSS FAITH MEMORIAL CHURCH. The church shares a combined history with Holy Cross Church of Brookgreen, which consisted of four former plantations—Laurel Hill, The Oaks, Springfield, and Brookgreen—and with Faith Memorial Church of Waverly Mills. In 1953, Archer Huntington financed the building of a new church.

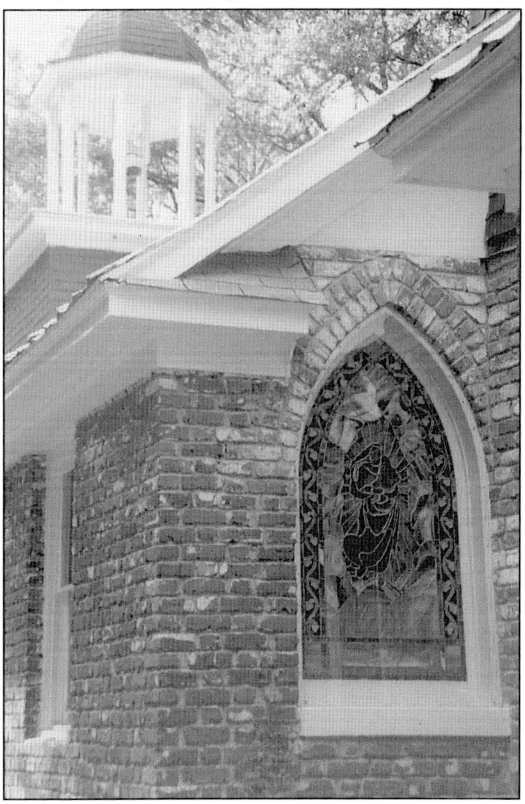

ARCADIA. Here is a detail of St. Anne's Church's stained-glass window and church bell on Arcadia, a former plantation site. The Arcadia estate was given its name by Dr. Isaac E. Emerson, when he bought the property in 1906. Arcadia includes the former plantations of Clifton, Rose Hill, Forlorn Hope, George Hill, Fairfield, Oak Hill and Bannockburn.

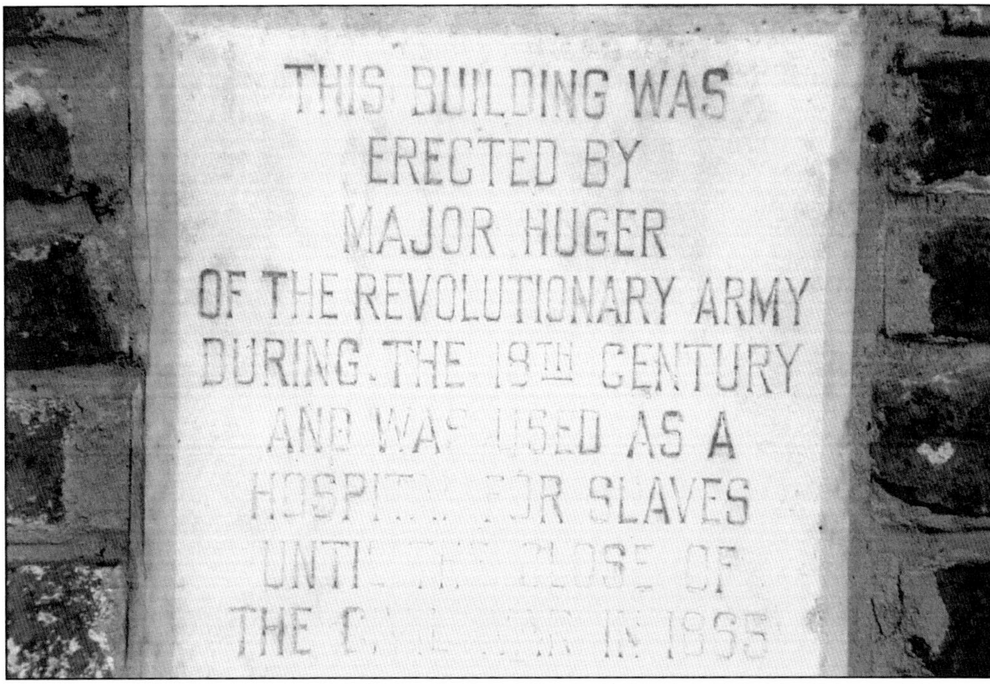

St. Anne's Church, Arcadia. The upper cornerstone of the church reads, "This building was erected by Major Huger of the Revolutionary Army during the 18th century and was used as a hospital for slaves until the close of the Civil War in 1865." The stone below reads, "Saint Anne's Church Rebuilt by Captain I.E. Emerson Owner of Arcadia Estate and dedicated to God 1927."

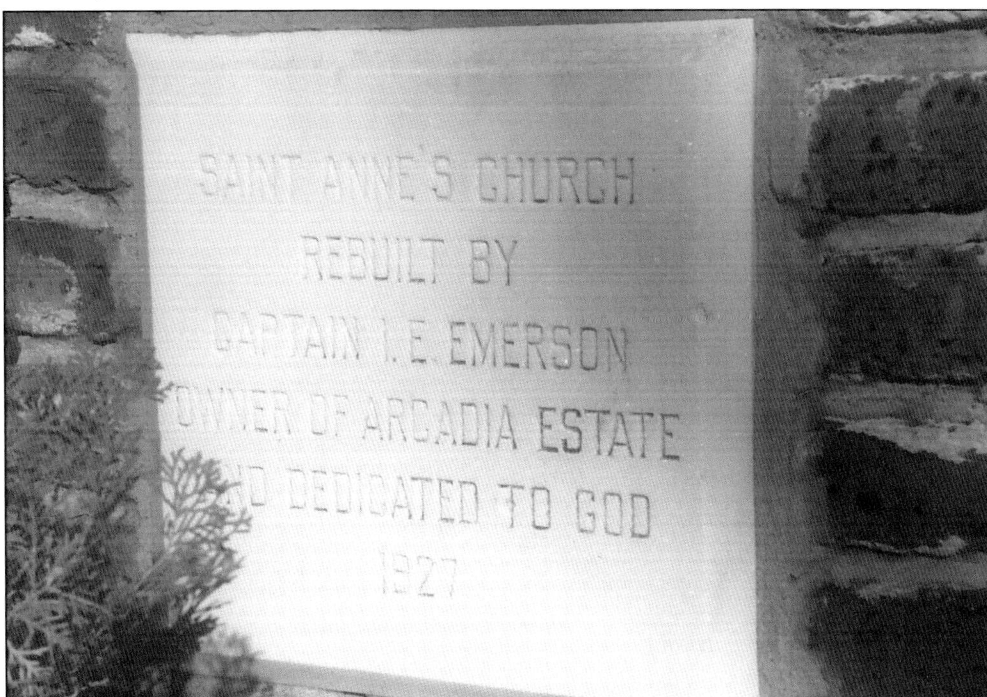

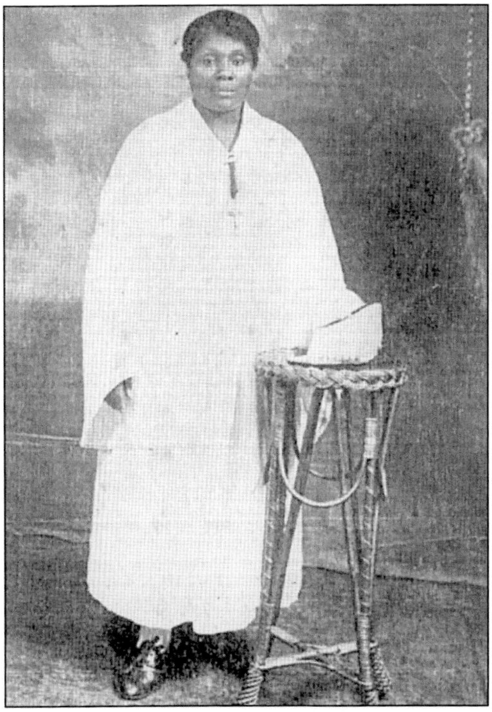

Sister E. Miles, Evangelist, Little Mt. Zion Baptist Church. Elsie Miles, originally from Pawleys Island, resided and served as evangelist for Little Mt. Zion in Brooklyn, New York. She returned home often and had soul-stirring revivals at various churches in Georgetown County during the late 1930s and early 1940s. She was the sister-in-law of Reverend George Bessellieu, who pastored at Mt. Zion (Parkersville), St. Anne's (Arcadia), and Brown Chapel (Bettsville) Baptist Churches on the island.

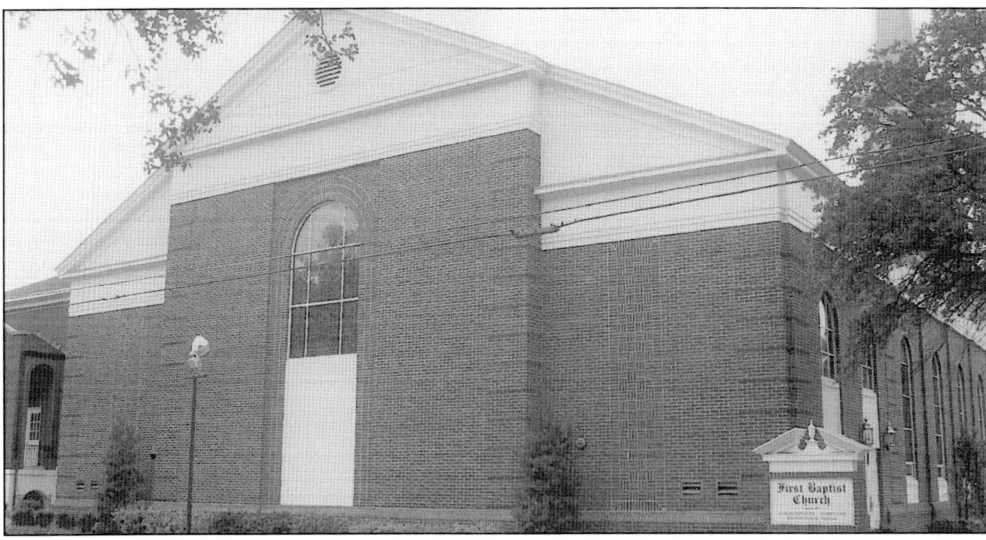

First Baptist Church. First Baptist Church provided its lecture room building to African Americans during the dark days of slavery. The pastor, "Maussa Glennie," preached each Wednesday. Bishop Philander Chase, a Midwest visitor, wrote the following in 1840 concerning his visit with Reverend Alexander Glennie (1804–1880): "The black children of a South Carolina planter know more of Christianity than thousands of white children in Illinois." For more than 30 years, Glennie gave religious instruction to both blacks and whites at All Saints and Prince George Winyah Episcopal Churches and 13 plantation chapels he founded around the Neck. In 1858, about 22,000 African Americans were formally enrolled members of Baptist churches in South Carolina. Today, the church is attended by whites and is located on Highmarket and Queen Streets.

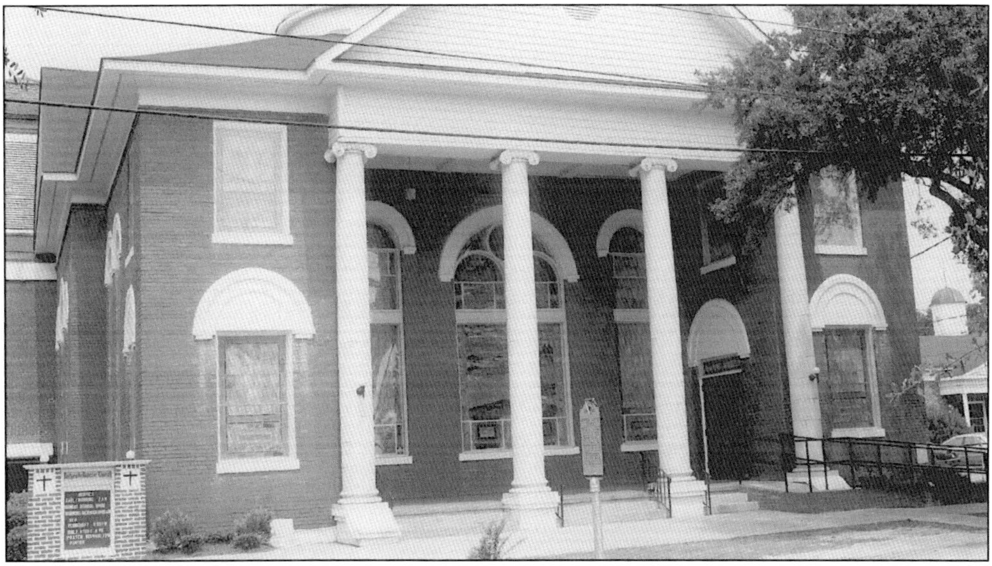

Bethesda Missionary Baptist Church. Bethesda was founded in 1865, under the leadership of Reverend Edward G. Rhue. Those first assembled at the meeting included Bennett Rowell, Primus Richard, Billy Green, Nathaniel Jenkins, Robert Spencer, Dabny Wyatt, Lucy Green, Julia Wyatt, Lindy Jenkins, Sara McCottrie, and others. Before the church was erected, the lecture hall of the First Baptist Church, with a seating capacity of 100, was rolled to the present location. The present site was purchased from Nicolos and Mary E. Conklin by Reverend Rhue and trustees Robert Spencer, Marcus Lucas, Cupid Rhue, Scipio Sumpter, Bennett Rowell, Murphy Thompson, and Hammond Smalls for $150 on May 14, 1867.

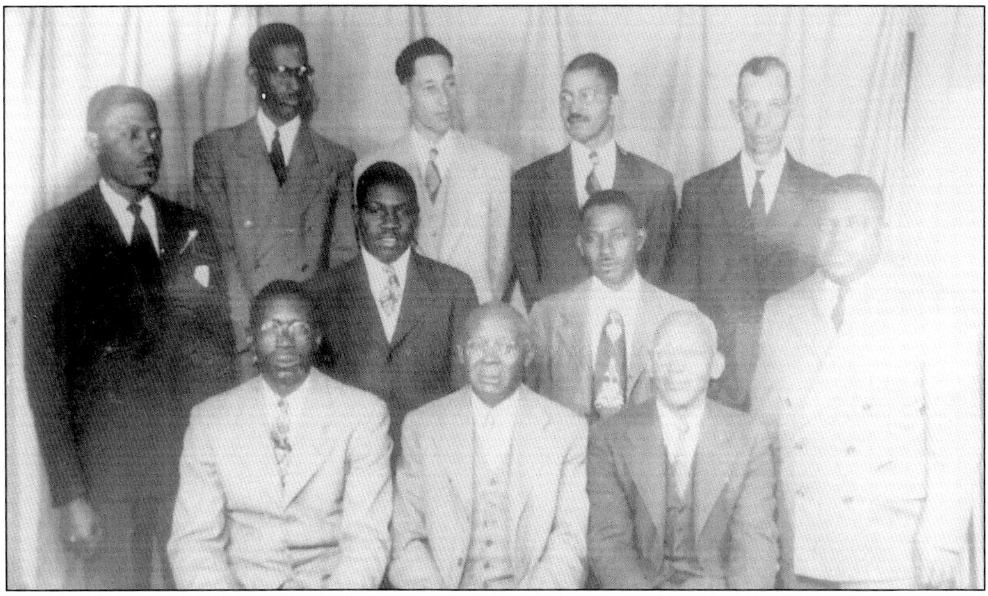

Bethesda Missionary Baptist Church Trustees. Bethesda Trustees pose for a group portrait. Pictured, from left to right, are the following: (front row) unidentified, Benjamin Wilds, Robert Jackson, and Letter Carrier; (middle row) Sam King, James Holmes, Samuel Grate, and Tom Fraser; (back row) Freddie Bessellieu, Thomas Moses, Raymond Jackson, and ? Bessellieu. (Courtesy of Barbara W. Huell.)

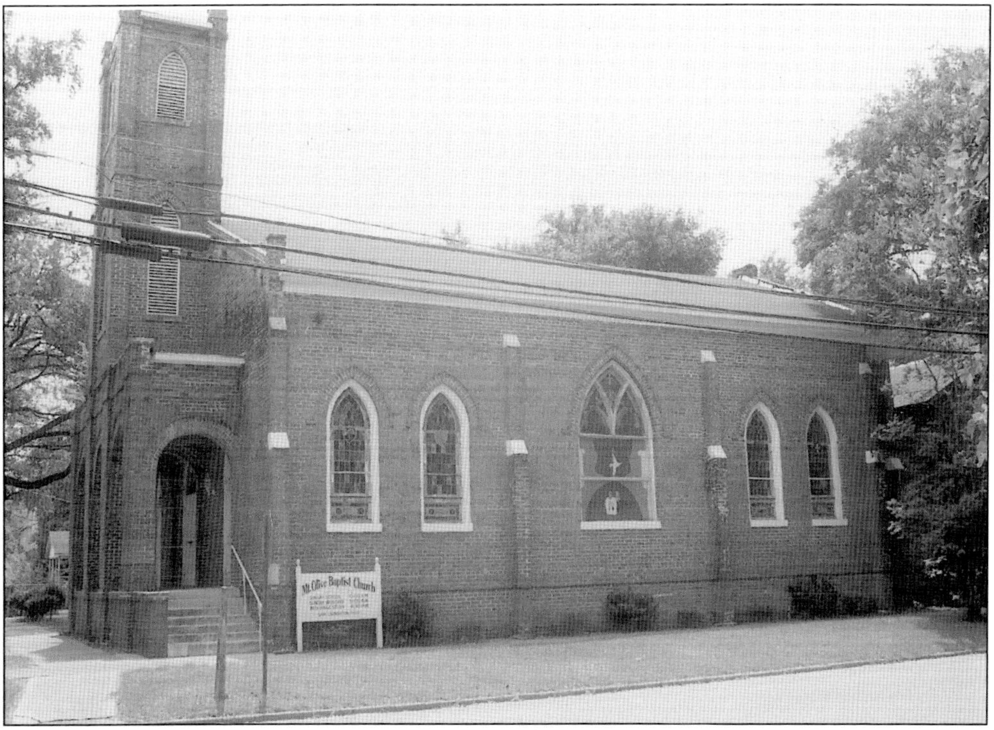

Mt. Olive Baptist Church. The Mt. Olive Baptist Church cornerstone reads, "founded 1866 by Rev. James Smalls, rebuilt 1920, Pastor in Charge, Rev. T.O. Mills, 1950." Rev. Sam Livingston is the present pastor, and the church has a membership of 50.

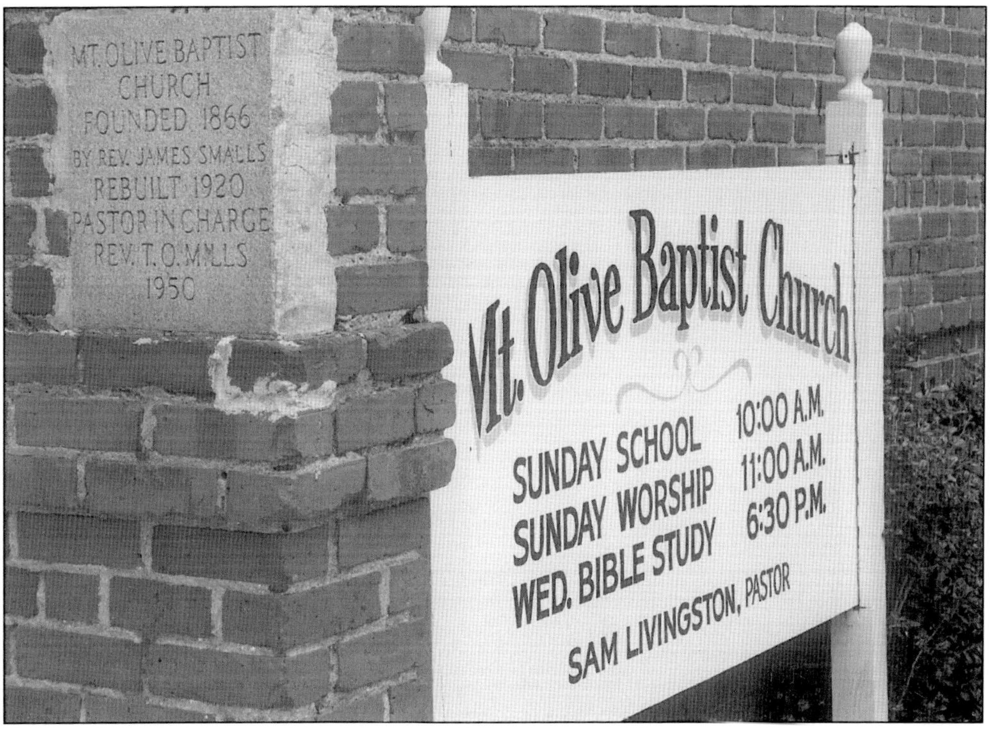

REVEREND DR. GEORGE GOINGS DANIELS SR. (1893–1961). Reverend Daniels pastored Bethesda Missionary Baptist Church from 1924 to 1941 and Piney Grove Baptist Church in Andrews. He went on to establish First Calvary Missionary Baptist in 1941. Active up until the time of his death, he also pastored Friendship Baptist in Conway, Bethlehem Baptist in Kingstree, and Mt. Carmel in Plantersville, in addition to First Calvary. He also served as a moderator for the Jerusalem Baptist Association for over 30 years, as president of the State Baptist Convention, and as secretary for the National Baptist Convention of South Carolina. Reverend Daniel was a graduate of Voorhees School in Denmark, Morris College in Sumter, and Gammon Theological Seminary in Atlanta, Georgia. Morris College and Benedict College conferred on him the degree of Doctor of Divinity.

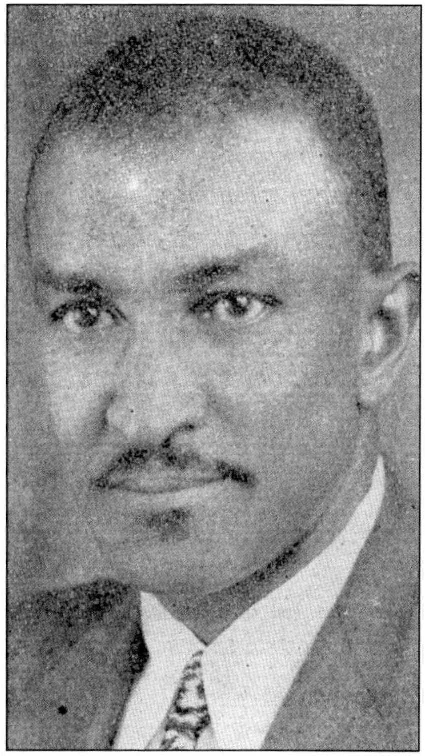

FIRST CALVARY CORNERSTONE. The cornerstone reads, "organized in 1941 by Rev. G. Goings Daniels, H.P. Shubrick, Chair of Deacons, Walter Ruffins, Chair of Trustees. Rebuilt in 1969. Rev. Frank Vereen, Pastor, Herbert King, Chair of Deacons, Houston Parson, Chair of Trustees."

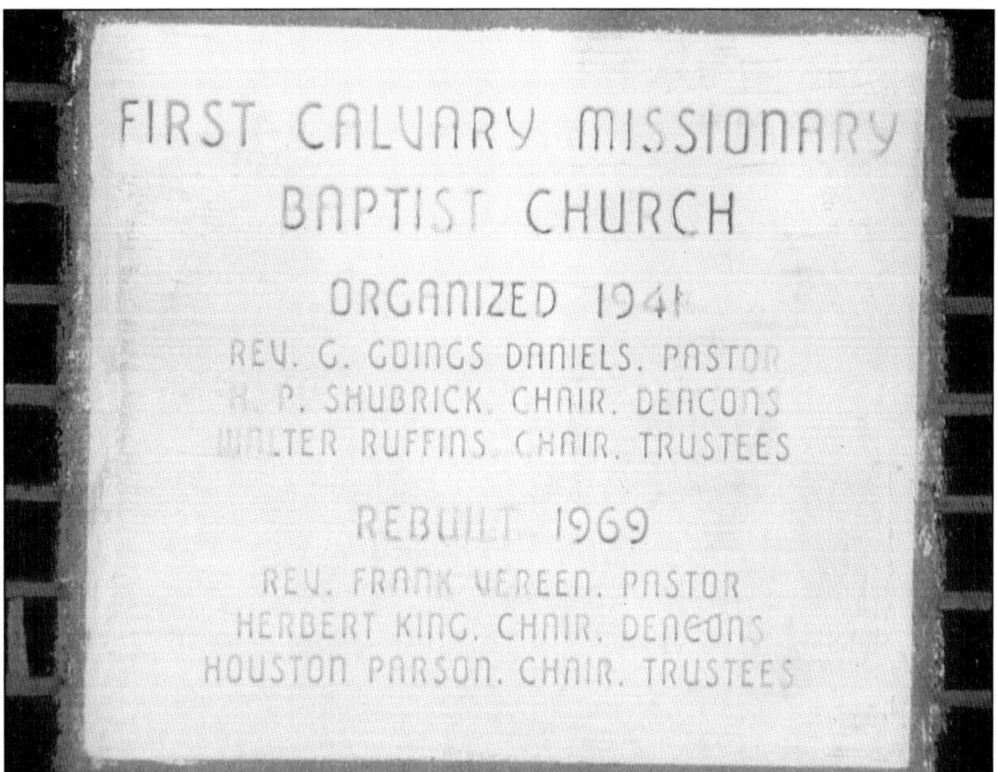

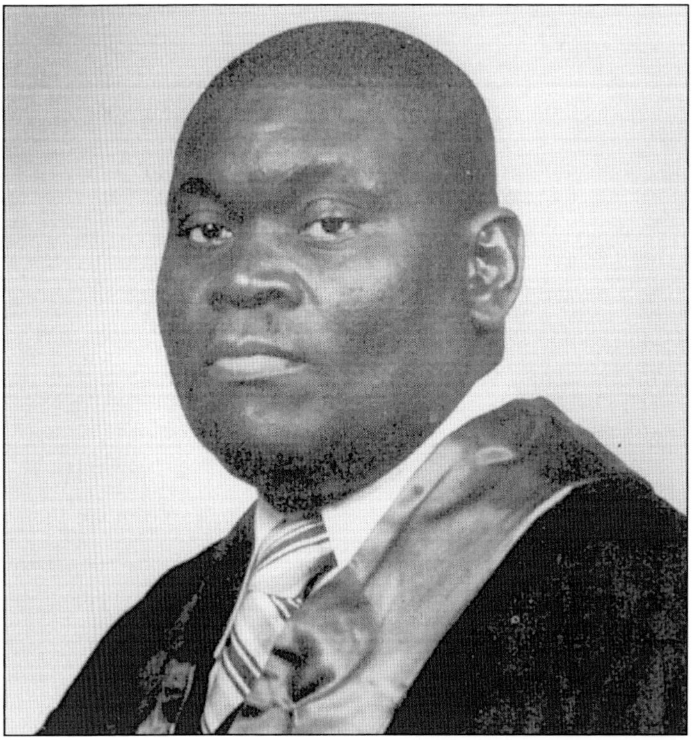

Rev. Frank Benjamin Vereen (1923–1994). Vereen pastored First Calvary Missionary Baptist Church from 1962 to 1994. Prior to that, he pastored Macedonia Baptist, a church he had been affiliated with for 30 years. Vereen was the vice-moderator of the Jerusalem Baptist Association, a member of Oak Grove Masonic Lodge No. 775, and a member of the National Association for the Advancement of Colored People. He attended Shaw University School of Religion.

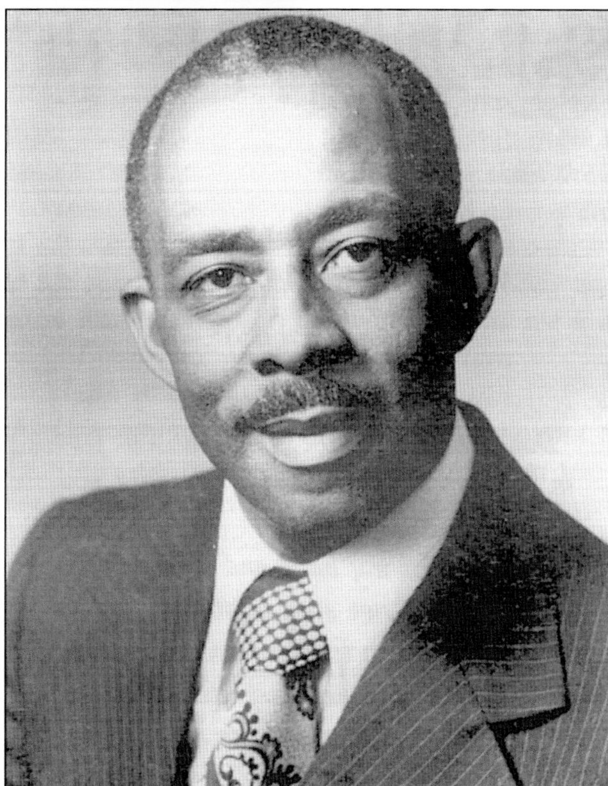

Reverend Dr. Westcott Allard Johnson (1928–1995). Reverend Johnson served as the pastor of Bethesda Missionary Baptist Church from 1956 to 1995. He attended Morris College and received degrees in Natural Science and Divinity, as well as an honorary Doctor of Divinity. An accomplished musician, he taught both music and science in Loris, South Carolina. He also studied hypnology and was a private pilot.

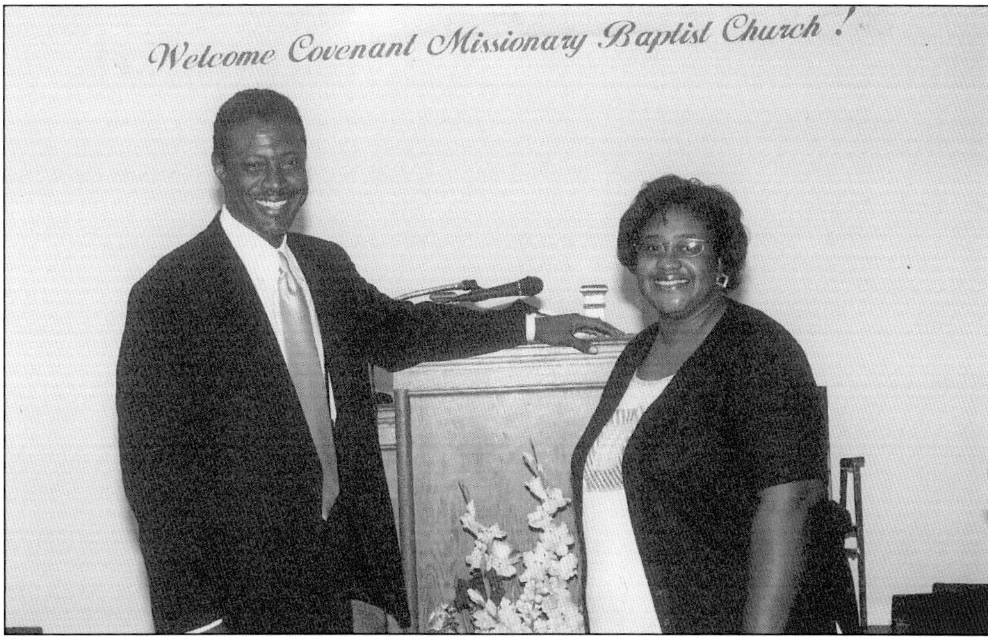

PASTOR AND FIRST LADY. Reverend James B. Lewis and Mrs. D'Jarlis Whipper-Lewis are with the recently established Covenant Missionary Baptist Church. The church grew out of a significant number of former members of Bethesda Missionary Baptist Church who were seeking change, the development of new leadership, and the empowerment of members.

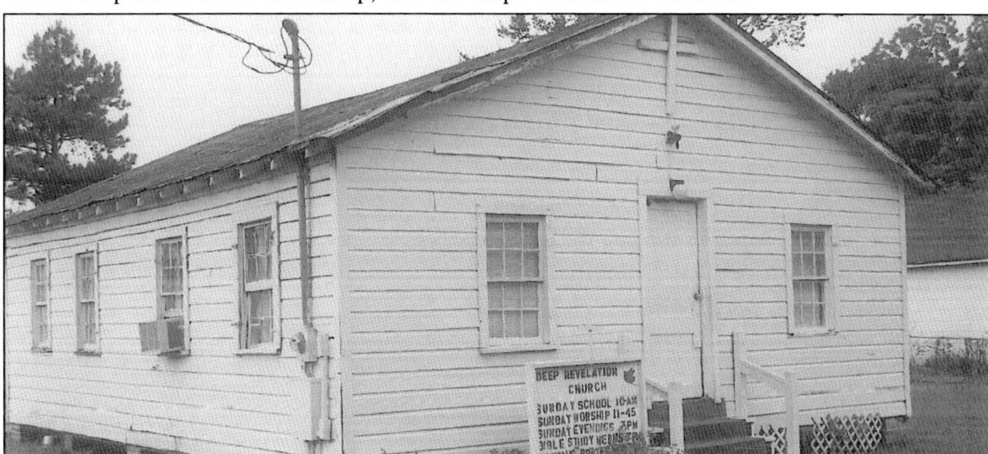

ROSEMONT HALL. This structure was relocated from Rosemont Plantation to Palm Street during the 1940s. It was built and continues to be managed by the Friendly Christian Aid Society. It initially served as a one-room county-supported school until the J.B. Beck school was built in 1954. A benevolent organization, it provided visits to the sick, frail, and elderly, delivering food, prayer, medicine, etc. The group was a precursor of insurance companies. In the event of the death of a community member, the family would be given assistance. "Sittin Ups" were all-night vigils provided during bereavement by society members. Founding community members included Joe and Thelma Weathers, Charlotte Young, Laura King, Viola Pringle, Reverend Joe Grant, and Jessie Green, who serves as the group's president. The society has always rented their building to religious organizations. The Deep Revelation Church has held services there for a few years.

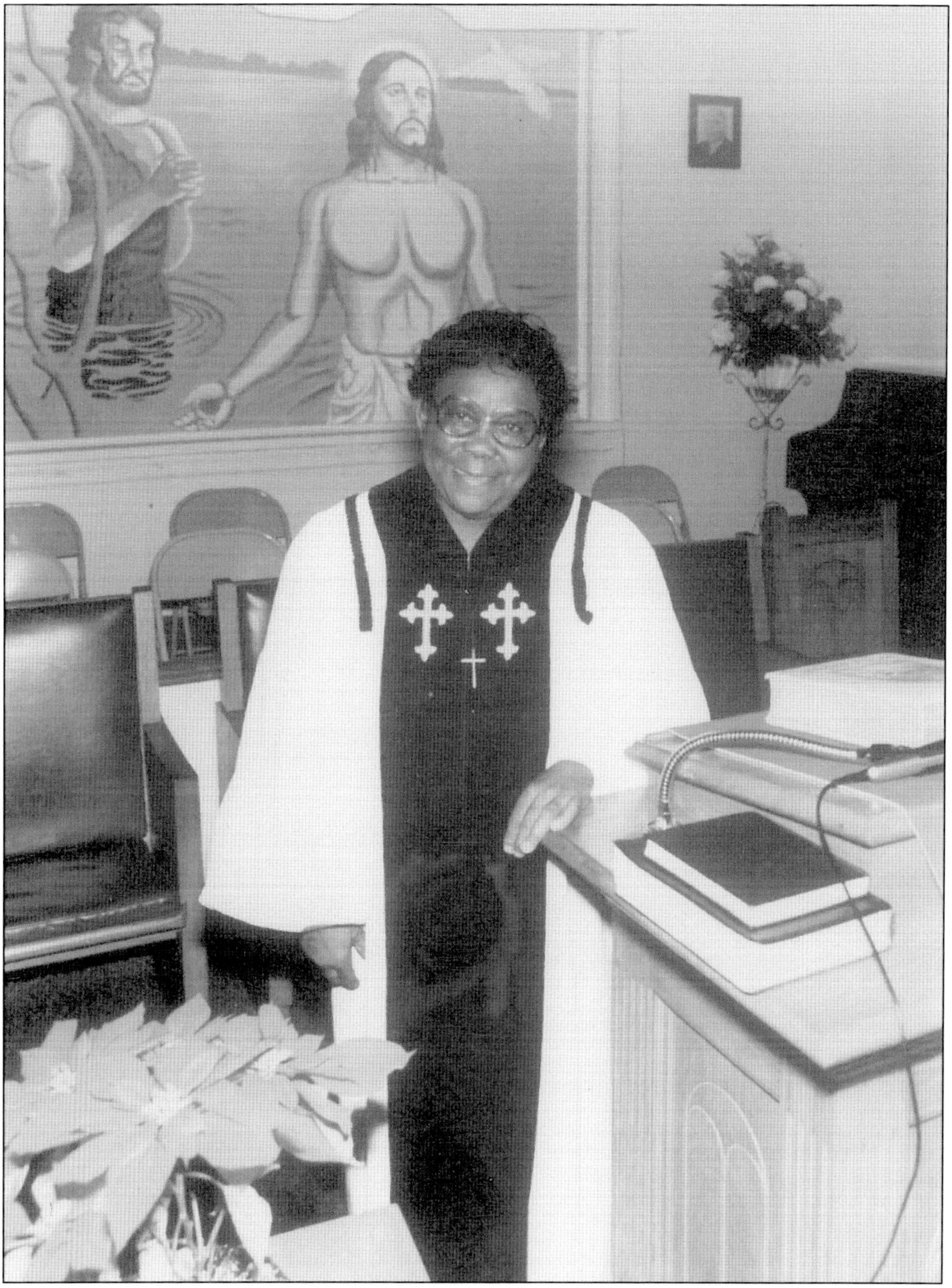

Helping Hand. Reverend Mattie Mae Dentley founded the "Helping Hand Club," which provides housekeeping assistance to individuals who are unable to clean their own homes and serves meals whenever necessary. An accomplished minister in the Fire Baptized Holiness Church (F.B.H.), Dentley is the founder of New Bethany F.B.H. Church in Andrews, South Carolina. (Courtesy of the African-American Committee on History Observances.)

Five

RECREATION

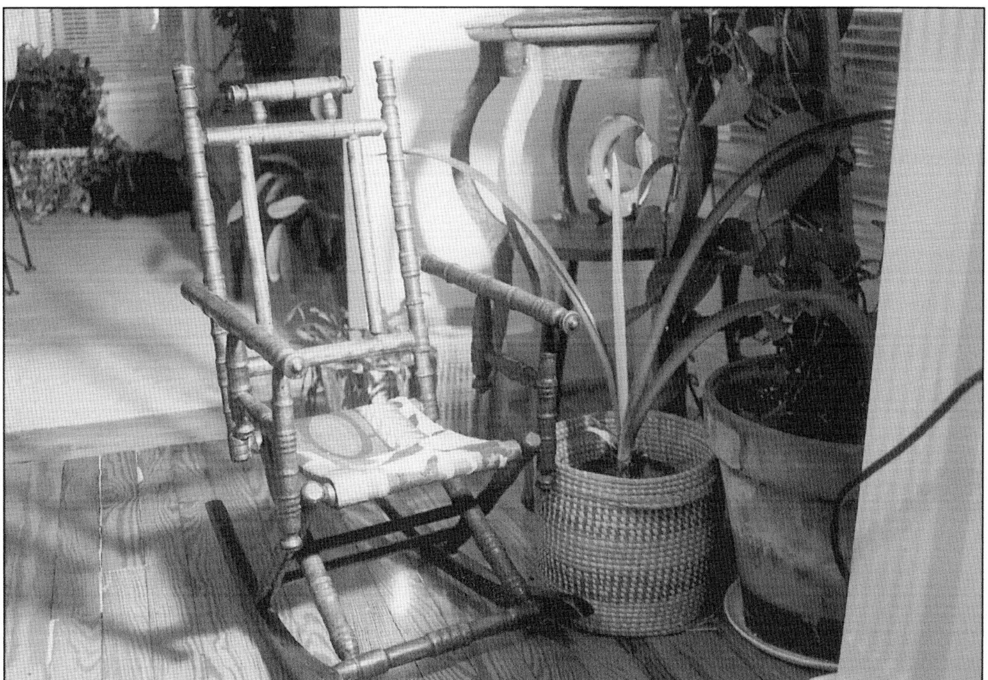

A CARPET ROCKER. The seat and back of the rocker were created from carpet remnants made by furniture companies during the late 1800s. This was W.J. Wilds Jr.'s childhood rocker. (Courtesy of Barbara Huell.)

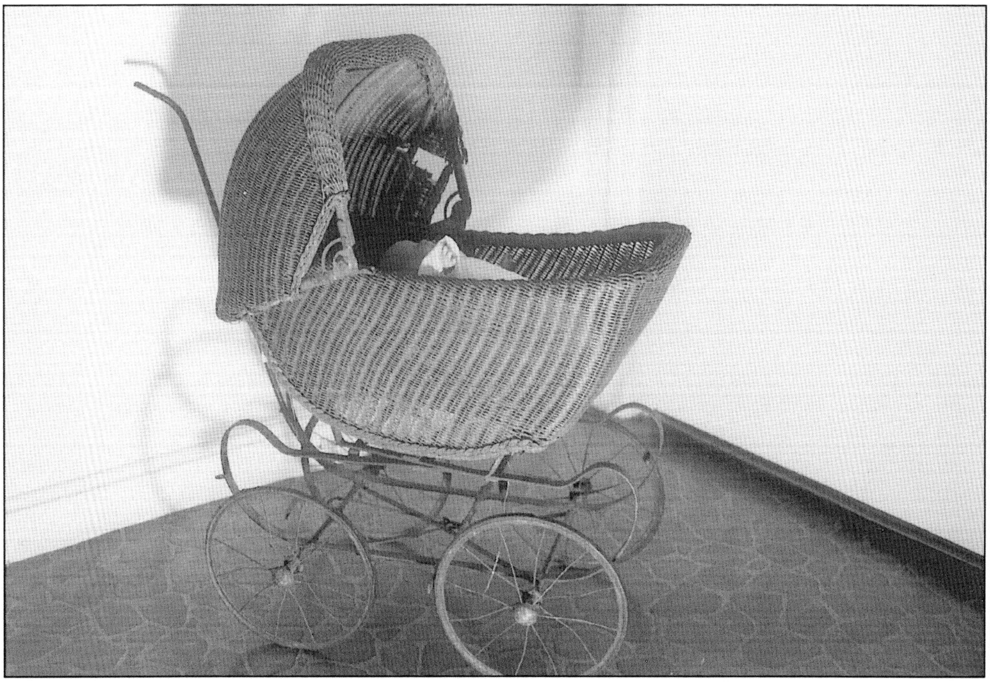

Wicker Buggy. This wicker buggy belongs to Clementine Atkinson Kelly; it was a gift from her father in 1927.

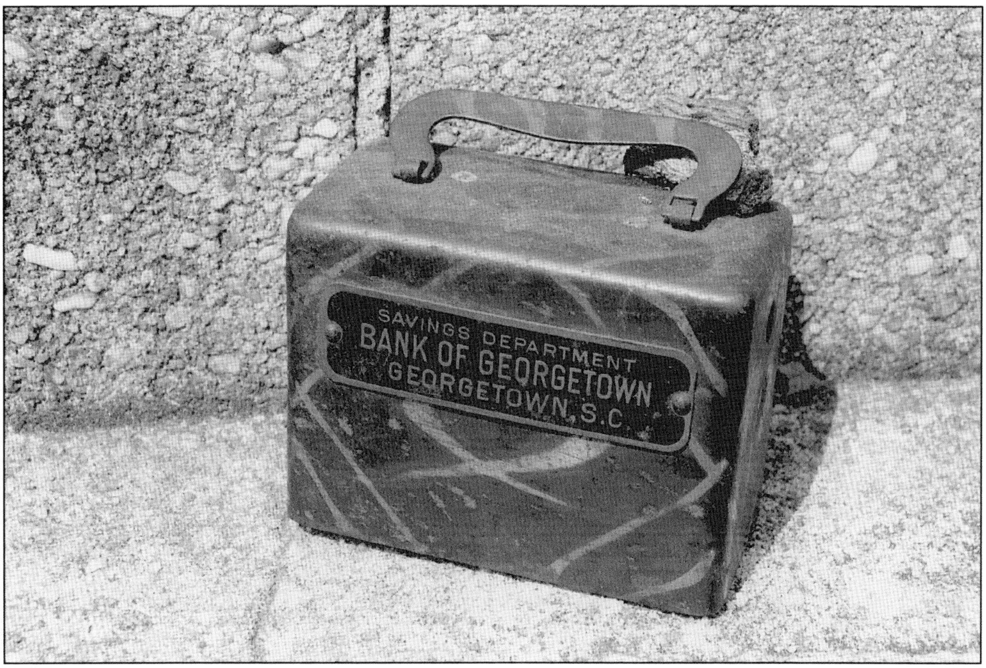

Bank of Georgetown Brass Bank. This bank, measuring 4 by 2 by 3 inches, belonged to Albert King Sr. (Courtesy of Ramona La Roche.)

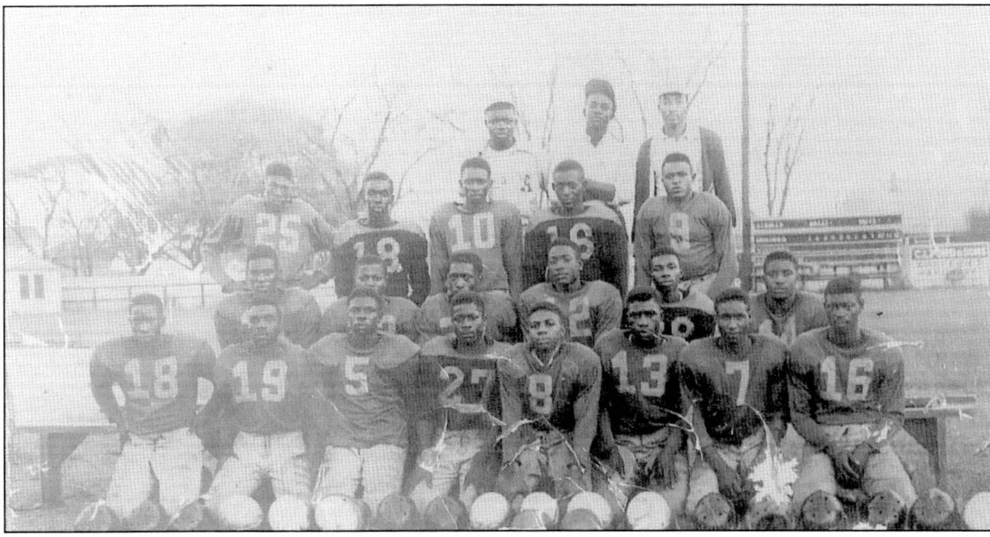

HOWARD HIGH SCHOOL FOOTBALL TEAM, 1949. From left to right are the following: (front row) Dan Blount, Andrew Pickney, Eugene Evans, Rudolph Thomas, unidentified, George Green, Thaddeus Smith, and Leroy Young; (second row) James Young, Roscoe Smith, Benjamin Jones, Edward Wright, Joe Brown, and Norman Myers; (third row) Walter Johnson, unidentified, Leon Burgess, Samuel Sumpter, and Willie Joe Maybank; (back row) Louis Simmons, George Sumpter, and Coach Dons. (Courtesy of Louis Simmons.)

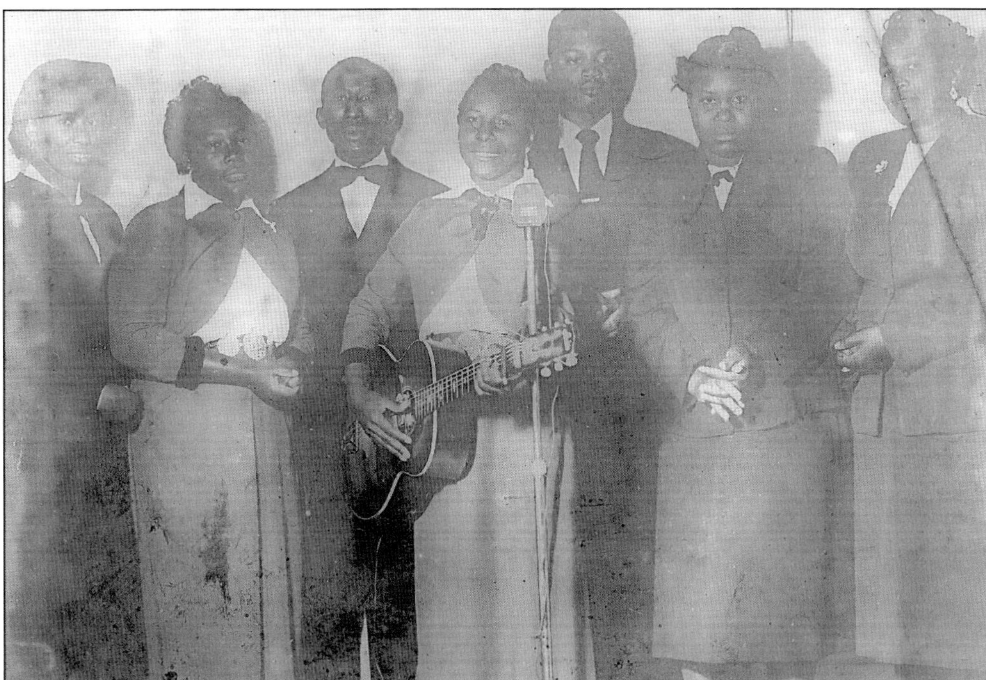

HALLELUJAH CHORUS OF FIRST CALVARY MISSIONARY BAPTIST CHURCH. The chorus members are, from left to right, as follows: Fannie Fields, Francis White, Deacon Gilliard, Annie Mae McCrae (on guitar), Herman King, Ernestine Gilliard, and unidentified. (Courtesy of the King family.)

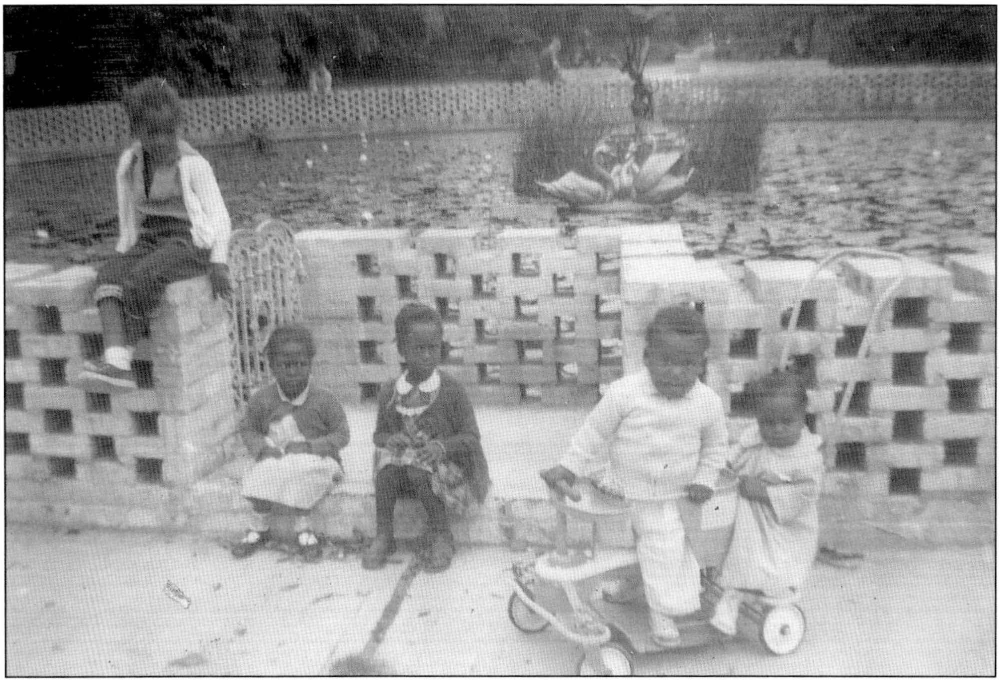

A Brookgreen Gardens Afternoon. Joan "Shorty" DeLorise, Catherine "Kitty" Weathers, and David and Toni Coley enjoy an outing to the gardens in the late 1950s.

Bibliography

Dusinberre, William. *Them Dark Days: Slavery in the American Rice Swamps*. Oxford University Press, 1996.

Gullah Bible, St. James, American Bible Society.

Hart, Lynne Taylor. *Bibles, Bullet's and Bushels of Oysters*. Duncan United Methodist Church, 1985.

Helsley, Alexia Jones. *South Carolina's African-American Confederate Pensioners 1923–1923*. South Carolina Department of Archives and History, 1998.

Joyner, Charles. *Down by the Riverside: A South Carolina Slave Community*. University of Illinois, 1984.

Lumpkin, Sarah Parker. *Heritage Passed On: History of Price George, Winyah, Parish*. R.L. Bryan Company, 1992.

Rogers, George C. *The History of Georgetown County, South Carolina*. University of South Carolina Press, 1970.

Rosengarten, Dale. *Row Upon Row: Sea Grass Baskets of the South Carolina Lowcountry*. The McKissick Museum, University of South Carolina, 1987.

Tindall, George Brown. *South Carolina Negroes, 1877–1900*, University of South Carolina Press, 1952.

Vlach, John Michael. *Back of the Big House: The Architecture of Plantation Slavery*. University of North Carolina Press, 1993.

Wood, Peter H. *Black Majority: Negroes in Colonial South Carolina from 1670 through the Stono Rebellion*. W.W. Norton & Company, 1974.